12.99

THE UNIVERSITY OF
WINCHESTER

D1141947

READING BY STARLIGHT

Science fiction's impact on popular culture has been striking. Yet sf's imaginative texts often baffle or dismay readers trained to enjoy only the literary or 'canonical'.

Reading by Starlight explores those characteristics in the writing, marketing and reception of science fiction which distinguish it as a mode. Damien Broderick analyses the postmodern self-referentiality of science fiction narrative, its intricate coded language and discursive 'encyclopaedia'. He shows how, for rich understanding, sf readers must learn the codes and vernacular of these imaginary worlds, while absorbing the 'lived-in futures' generated by the overlapping intertexts of many sf writers.

Reading by Starlight includes close readings of cyberpunk and other post-modern texts, and writings by such sf novelists and theorists as Brian Aldiss, Isaac Asimov, Christine Brooke-Rose, Arthur C. Clarke, Samuel R. Delany, William Gibson, Fredric Jameson, Kim Stanley Robinson, Vivian Sobchack, Darko Suvin, Michael Swanwick, Tzvetan Todorov and John Varley.

Damien Broderick, author of *The Architecture of Babel: Discourses of Literature and Science*, is an award-winning writer who sold his first collection of stories at 20, has published eight novels and holds a PhD in the semiotics of science, literature and science fiction.

POPULAR FICTIONS SERIES

Series editors:

Tony Bennett
Professor of Cultural Studies
School of Humanities
Griffith University

Graham Martin
Professor of English Literature
Open University

In the same series

Cover Stories:
Narrative and ideology in the British spy thriller
by Michael Denning

Lost Narratives:
Popular fictions, politics and recent history
by Roger Bromley

Popular Film and Television Comedy
by Steve Neale and Frank Krutnik

Popular Fiction:
Technology, ideology, production, reading
Edited by Tony Bennett

The Historical Romance 1890–1990
by Helen Hughes

The Monstrous-Feminine:
Film, feminism, psychoanalysis
by Barbara Creed

Reading the Vampire
by Ken Gelder

READING BY STARLIGHT

Postmodern science fiction

Damien Broderick

London and New York

First published 1995
by Routledge
11 New Fetter Lane, London EC4P 4EE

Simultaneously published in the USA and Canada
by Routledge
29 West 35th Street, New York, NY 10001

© 1995 Damien Broderick

Typeset in Times by
Ponting–Green Publishing Services, Chesham, Bucks
Printed in Great Britain by
T.J. Press (Padstow) Ltd, Padstow, Cornwall

Printed on acid free paper

British Library Cataloguing in Publication Data
A catalogue record for this book is available from
the British Library

Library of Congress Cataloging in Publication Data
Broderick, Damien.
Reading by starlight: postmodern science fiction/
Damien Broderick
p.   cm. – (Popular fiction series)
1. Science fiction, American–History and criticism.
2. Science fiction, English–History and criticism.
3. Discourse analysis, Literary.   4. Postmodernism
(Literature)   5. Semiotics and literature.   6. Narration
(Rhetoric)   7. Literary form.
I. Title.   II. Series.
PS374.S35B76   1995
813'.087620905–dc20   94–9505

ISBN 0–415–09788–6   0–415–09789–4 (pbk)

*For Jenny Blackford
and Russell Blackford*

CONTENTS

CONTENTS

ACKNOWLEDGEMENTS

Although portions of this book, somewhat modified, have appeared in the following journals, the global conception of the book preceded these several excerpts:

21C: 'Dangerous Dreams' (Autumn 1993).

Southern Review: 'SF as a Modular Calculus' (Vol. 24, No. 1, March 1991).

Science Fiction: A Review of Speculative Fiction: 'Reading by Starlight: Science Fiction as a Reading Protocol' (Vol. 11, No. 2, 1991).

New York Review of Science Fiction: 'SF and the Postmodern' (No. 30, February 1991); 'Reading SF as a Mega-Text' (No. 47, July 1992) and 'The Object of Science Fiction' (No. 58, July 1993).

Meridian: 'SF as a Mode' (Vol. 11, No. 2, October 1992).

Foundation: 'Allography and Allegory: Delany's SF' (No. 52, Summer 1991); 'The Multiplicity of Worlds, of Others' (No. 55, Summer 1992); and 'Sf as Generic Engineering' (No. 59, Autumn 1993).

Australian Science Fiction Review: 'Dreams of Reason' (No. 19, March 1989); and 'Dreams of Unreason' (No. 22, Summer 1989).

INTRODUCTION

At this pivot of the millennium, the high-energy, information-rich nations share a unique epistemic crisis. (I use the term *episteme* here as shorthand for a complex of discursive templates active within a given space and epoch.)[1] How could it be otherwise? Our social being is founded in rapid, virtually uncontrollable cognitive change, driven principally by science and technology. The map of myth is lost to us. Notoriously, the core of twentieth-century sensibility has been convulsed by a paradox of semiotics: an explicit and bitter conflict in those vast circulating discourses (often in covert mutual synergy), the humanities and the exact sciences: the so-called 'two cultures'.

Lofty though they are, such generalities can hardly be dodged when one tries to uncover the codes and strategies of science fiction. Whether it is viewed as a genre or a mode (even a fresh paraliterature entirely), its very name, for all its acquired taint of comical vulgarity, evokes that central paradox of mutual incomprehension. A theorised interest in sf endures precisely because of the unease with which science fiction poises its narrative modality (or perhaps several such modalities sharing a family resemblance) between *artistic* attention to the *subject* and *scientific* attention to the *object*.

Can such extravagant ambition pay off? In some measure, certainly; and by intriguing means. I shall show just how these narratives are generated and received (which implies considerably more than 'written' and 'read') within a specialised intertextual encyclopaedia of tropes and enabling devices, an armamentarium evolved within that specific history of discursive crisis.

Extraordinarily enough, given recent academic enthusiasm for popular culture, careful study of speculative fiction is still deemed a fairly dubious enterprise. True, both literary and scientific meta-theorists have come increasingly to view their objects of study as principally *textual*, as *narratives* which operate within social formations via processes of canonisation and negotiation. Somehow, though, sf largely remains excluded from the regard of specialists in both science and literature.

Why should this be so? Do its characteristic strategies guarantee that sf's products must be *bad art*? Must its early sources in wish-fulfilment oblige it to be *false science*? All too often, the answers to both questions have to be yes. Sf is a paraliterary form of narrative nearer in many respects to the mimetically estranged experience of dreaming than to the methodologically speculative or cognitive.

Several of these unwieldy but useful terms find their major sf-theoretic locus in the pioneering writings of Darko Suvin. In his *Metamorphoses of Science Fiction*,[2] Suvin proposed that sf is an ensemble of fiction tales marked by *cognition* and *estrangement* (Suvin, 1979, p. viii), a provocative definition to which I shall return. Suvin – followed in this by Samuel R. Delany and others – refers to sf as a

> paraliterature – the popular, 'low', or plebeian literary production of various times, particularly since the Industrial Revolution. . . . The noncanonic, repressed twin of Literature which, for want of another name, one calls Paraliterature is (for better or worse) the literature that is really read – as opposed to most literature taught in schools. Within it, SF is one of the largest genres, and to my mind the most interesting and cognitively most significant one.
>
> (ibid., p. vii)

Clearly, then, despite the bad art and worse science, much can be said in its favour.

If English-language sf of the last 60 or 70 years began pretty much as formulaic adventure fiction, it has developed (at its best) into a set of writing and reading protocols articulated about and foregrounding aspects of the *objective world* (as science tries to do), through the engaging invention of stories about imagined *subjects* – that is, aware, feeling, thinking persons (typical of literary fictions).

Why should that twofold process be important? The most ambitious answer is this: because its paraliterary texts, produced and read via their distinctive narrative strategies and tactics, constitute a singular window on our vexed episteme.

What's more, its current development is often explicitly and recursively theorised by its practitioners: Samuel R. Delany, Ursula Le Guin, Joanna Russ, Brian Aldiss, Stanislaw Lem, George Turner and others are highly articulate about their positions as writers and readers. In particular, Delany is a striking example of an sf writer advancing both fictive and theoretical narratives side by side, in his case from an explicitly poststructuralist position. I shall trace both these trajectories of Delany's, and position them against those of other exemplary sf practitioners.

The real plausibility of such an exploration in semiotics arose with the major revival of literary theory (specifically that variety of meta-theory which meant to think about thinking about literature) during the last two decades. It became feasible once more to dig deep into the processes of writing and reading, rather than simply ('simply') reading and evaluating or situating examples of pre-defined and valorised literature.

This shift offers an opening for the investigation of science fiction, which on most other grounds has been ruled out of court in advance. Privileged exceptions like Orwell's *Nineteen Eighty-Four* had proved far from central, interestingly enough, to the emerging folk canon established by sf enthusiasts – by, that is to say, readers and writers with specialised training in the codes of construction and reception of sf.

As a science fiction writer myself, I was intrigued by certain questions: What makes an item of sf a good example of its kind? Why is sf relished by practised readers or viewers, while others loathe it?

One crucial factor is that sf is written in a kind of code (on top of – and sometimes displacing – all the other codes of writing) which must be learned by apprenticeship. This necessity, of course, merely intensifies the sceptic's bewilderment at the trouble taken by those who learn it in the first place. No doubt this is true to some extent of all genres, but the coding of each individual sf text depends importantly on access to an unusually concentrated 'encyclopaedia'[3] – a mega-text of imaginary worlds, tropes, tools, lexicons, even grammatical innovations borrowed from other textualities. The enormously ramified intertextuality of sf makes it a specialised mode. For a story to be sf, it is insufficient for a writer to invoke, say, futuristic or extra-terrestrial locales. The narrative-technical constraints of what has been done before by acknowledged sf writers are crucially important (so that Paul Theroux's *O-Zone*, say, reads to the knowing eye more as a clumsy parody of an unfamiliar genre than an example of it).[4]

What's more, a lively interest in diverse kinds of information seems to feed heavily into an enjoyment of sf. Some technological and scientific awareness, at least of a popularised kind, seems essential. Hence the notable monthly presence of just such articles, for 30-odd years, by the late Isaac Asimov in the *Magazine of Fantasy & Science Fiction*, otherwise the most literary of the American sf magazines. Hence the regular pieces by scientists and mathematicians in *Analog* on research topics such as Many-Worlds cosmologies, Kaluza-Klein 10-dimensional spacetime, superstrings, and so forth. Hence, indeed, its playful re-evaluations by physicists of the possibility of actualising certain sf tropes, such as time travel, usually considered theoretically absurd.[5]

All these issues point to a semiotics and stylistics of sf – an investigation of the textual strategies which constitute the writing and reading of sf. What are its generic components? How are they put together? How concretised by readers? How, in turn, do they construct their potential readers?

In theoretical terms, the rise of popular culture studies, discourse theory and deconstruction de-privilege in various ways the literary canon which excluded sf from serious critical attention. These fresh, transgressive modes seem to valorise the sportive qualities which sf embodies in a marked degree.[6]

If certain current meta-scientific analyses find science to be primarily yet another form of discursive negotiation and construction, to be textuality without referent, and nothing more,[7] does this shed any light on sf's inventions and plays? Or vice versa?

I should confess immediately to two possible hazards in my approach here. First: if, as I argue, rich responses to sf texts require a sort of apprenticeship by the reader, it is scarcely feasible to approach sf theory and criticism without a certain familiarity with many sf texts. Just as a brilliantly articulate English user with rudimentary cafe Italian cannot simply pick up Dante or Eco and begin a nuanced enjoyment of *The Divine Comedy* or *The Name of the Rose*, the sf neophyte must work her way into the specialised narrative structures and vocabulary of sf. I do not insist that readers of this book know by heart the work of Theodore Sturgeon, Isaac Asimov, Robert Heinlein, Alfred Bester, Joanna Russ, Samuel R. Delany, Ursula Le Guin, William Gibson and a dozen or a hundred of their peers. Still, unless you've read one or two of the most celebrated fictions of each of the authors named you will see only the shadow of my discussion.

Is this stipulation cruel and unusual? Not at all. Science fiction is a suitable site for complex theorised reading, but only for those who share some preliminary familiarity with at least a sampling of its best-regarded texts. New studies of Shakespeare or Dickens, after all, rarely go in for detailed plot summaries. Nor should a theorised study of a popular form such as sf proceed out of an assumption of *terra nullius*, the legal fiction that traditional inhabitants of some newly discovered piece of real estate can be ignored (even exterminated) by doughty and well-armed colonists.

That is my first confession. The second is perhaps less pardonable. It is this: I believe that at a time of paradox and crisis in both literary and scientific theory and criticism – when meta-theory continually challenges and erodes canonised methods and their traditional objects of scrutiny – traditional formal methods of exposition and argument ought not to remain protected by a hermetic (that is, a high-priestly) seal.

Indeed, once the central critiques of poststructuralism have been taken into account – no matter that one might quibble about the details or the political implications of any given practice associated with this epistemic innovation[8] – it becomes self-defeating, even absurd, to cling to the very methods which have been so strenuously debunked. So I've adopted a technique based in part on montage or collage, the postmodern device *par excellence*. In doing so, I explicitly acknowledge those powerful presentations which assert that traditional notions of reason and argument are egregiously partial and deceitfully 'transparent': which declare, in fact, that while conventional academic discourse tends to proceed with an appearance of the highest rigour, it is usually to ends ('discoveries', 'findings') established well in advance.[9]

Kim Stanley Robinson, one of today's finest sf writers and critics, makes a similar point rather drolly in his novel of spatial, psychological and sociological exploration, *Red Mars*:

> 'The only part of an argument that really matters is what we think of the people arguing. X claims *a*, Y claims *b*. They make arguments to support their claims, with any number of points. But when their listeners remember the discussion, what matters is simply that X believes *a* and Y believes *b*. People then form their judgement on what they think of X and Y.'
> 'But we're scientists! We're trained to weight the evidence!'
> John nodded. 'True. In fact, since I like you, I concede the point.'[10]

In an effort to break free of both self-validating and self-defeating mechanisms of discourse, I have drawn inspiration from a fertile speculation advanced by the philosopher Elizabeth Grosz, who lists the likely outcomes of the confrontation between traditional phallocognitive philosophy and feminist critique and construction of an alternative procedure.[11] Confrontations of this kind are by no means purely iconoclastic. As Genevieve Lloyd observes: 'Such criticisms of ideals of Reason can in fact be seen as continuous with a very old strand in the western philosophical tradition; it has been centrally concerned with bringing to reflective awareness the deeper structures of inherited ideals of Reason.'[12]

While Grosz writes specifically of a new feminist philosophy, I take her observations to have a certain general validity. The new critical philosophy diverges in several important ways from previously canonised approaches. Hardly monolithic, or orchestrated around a 'transcendental signified', it is neither relativist or pluralist[13] but *perspectivist*: 'acknowledg[ing] other points of view but den[ying] them equal value'.[14] That is, it asserts commitment without falling into coercive univocity or undecidable agnosticism. This approach, born under the sign of poststructuralism but hardly identical with it, deviates from the Western tradition in a crucial break: '[I]t can openly accept its own status (and that of all discourses) as context-specific.' Perspectivism can openly avow its own political position: 'all texts speak from or represent particular positions within power relations. . . . Instead of aspiring to the status of truth,' such a philosophy 'prefers to see itself as a form of strategy'. But these strategies are not abstractions. 'Instead of dividing theory from practice [among many other dichotomous impositions] philosophy may regard theory *as* a form of practice.' Far from either valorising or condemning traditional ways of arguing logically from hegemonically ordained premises, it 'expands the concept of reason' (Grosz, 1990, pp. 167–9).

There are serious difficulties in abandoning boring old forms of logic. What's more, I am by no means convinced that the programme of an expanded literary, philosophical or scientific discourse can or ought to take the step into the abyss which Grosz proposes (a step which is implicit, admittedly, in many texts by such poststructuralists as Lacan, Foucault, Derrida and Baudrillard).[15] The newly dimensioned space required to replenish writing and thinking, Grosz speculates, 'may be capable of sustaining several types of discourse, many perspectives and interests (even contradictory ones). No one form dominates the others' (ibid.).

These are large claims, but their intent is generous, more insistent on a declaration of a speaker's position, and those of a speaker's opponents, than to any certified truth; open to a measure of passion and rhetoric usually regarded within the academy as indecorous at best.

The analytic technique I'm trying to employ in this book is grounded also in the view that to a much larger extent than is usually understood the reader constructs her own argument as well as her own text. This is why I frequently urge my case by means of collage, sometimes scathingly rather than coolly framed, displaying exemplary citations alongside each other in a rhetorically heightened context which presses to a conclusion without feigning to 'prove' it.

Even so, there *is* an architecture to the book, a course of argument. Sf's texts, and their special strategies and tactics, have emerged in a number of stages which can be correlated, to some extent, with its historical, economic and ideological contexts. This development – beginning definitively with 'Modern science fiction' in the 1930s and 1940s – is explored in detail from a variety of alternative starting-points. Chapter 1 examines sf's literary lineage, definitions of sf in terms of themes, scientific and mock-scientific content, and its role as a formula for consolation. Examples of effective sf are displayed against bad or routine material. In Chapter 2, sf's formal specificities and historical vectors are traced in the light of semiotic analysis of *genre*. Chapter 3 develops the view that sf is better seen as a *mode* of writing, and scrutinises some of its academic theorists (Eric Rabkin, Tzvetan Todorov, Darko Suvin). We see that sf is marked by its use of new words put together in new ways. By Chapter 4, we begin to understand that even this does not account for the way a vast number of sf texts support and contest each other through a collective 'mega-text'. Chapter 5 finds these threads of 'Modern sf' drawn together in the early semiotic theories of Samuel R. Delany. The analysis in Part I concludes in Chapters 6 and 7 with close readings of the cyberpunk texts of William Gibson and the *Helliconia* trilogy of Brian W. Aldiss.

The field's most recent development is explicitly theorised by certain of its practitioners, especially Delany, who now forwards both fictive and theoretical narratives from an explicitly poststructuralist position. Part II traces both trajectories, positioning them in Chapter 8 against exemplary theorists of the postmodern (especially Fredric Jameson and his followers). From Chapter 9, my emphasis is on Delany's texts, which are examined critically and combined with results from the earlier semiotic analyses to yield a new model of sf textuality in Chapter 10.

Testing (and contributing to) this modular development, two important moments in Delany's fiction are given close analytical readings. The first is *The Einstein Intersection*, a complex modernist novel marking the high-point of his early work in 1967. Chapter 9 shows that this novel is itself an allegory of writing and reading sf, and constitutes an essay in 'writing the other' (which I dub 'allography'). The second is *Stars in My Pocket Like Grains of Sand*, from 1984, an extravagantly rich and impeccably theorised postmodern sf text, which we consider in detail in Chapter 11. The final chapter of Part II closes with an elaborate, annotated definition of science fiction that attempts to summarise the most important elements we have surveyed.

Part I

MODERN SCIENCE FICTION

1

NEW WORLD, NEW TEXTS

A very secret revolution, which bears no name: objective knowledge, supposed, has taken the place of the subject. This transformation gives rise to a new world, to new texts, to another kind of thought.

(Michel Serres)[1]

Abstract thoughts in a blue room: Nominative, genitive, elative, accusative one, accusative two, ablative, partitive, illative, instructive, abessive, adessive, inessive, essive, allative, translative, comitative. Sixteen cases of the Finnish noun. Odd, some languages get by with only singular and plural. The American Indian languages even failed to distinguish number. Except Sioux, in which there was a plural only for animate objects. The blue room was round and warm and smooth. No way to say *warm* in French. There was only *hot* and *tepid*. If there's no word for it, how do you think about it?

(Samuel R. Delany)[2]

Sf? Already we are in trouble, because these initials are the accepted abbreviation of a whole sheaf of classificatory terms applied to texts produced and received in ways marked only (as we shall see) by certain generic, modal or strategic family resemblances. Sf, or sometimes SF, can stand for 'scientifiction', 'science fiction', 'space fiction', 'science fantasy', 'speculative fiction', 'structural fabulation' (just possibly including 'surfiction'), perhaps 'specular feminism' and, in sardonic homage to right-wing sf at its most florid, 'speculative fascism'.

A mass media version is the odious 'sci fi', a journalistic term[3] taken over with bleak wit by some practitioners to denote junk sf – which is to say, crudely wrought or ill-conceptualised entertainments constructed around a few poorly understood narrative devices ripped rootless from any but the most meagre 'sf mega-text'[4] or shared universe established by generations of earlier sf-canonical writers. Those exhausted tropes are all too familiar: mad scientists, galumphing robots, thundering spaceships, ray-gun battles, cosy holocausts.

In the first part of this book I restrict my attention largely to what has come to be called 'Modern science fiction',[5] which hasn't got much in common with literary modernism. In the second half, we turn to writing that is better dubbed 'postmodern', this time in both senses of the word. Taken together, these comprise the corpus of commercial, usually American, post-World War II sf writing readily available in English.[6]

THE LINEAGE OF SF

Like parvenus attempting to purchase respectability by the adoption of extinct arms, some sf enthusiasts have sought to establish a direct lineage springing from, for example, the ancient Mesopotamian Epic of Gilgamesh, and passing through the non-realistic chapters of various sacred scriptures to Lucian of Samosata's *True History* (c. 150), More's *Utopia* (1516), Bacon's *New Atlantis* (1627), Kepler's *Somnium* (1634), and scores of other texts, not excluding myths, legends, folklore and fables.[7] None of this, finally, is persuasive. Sf, which is often crucially concerned with the strictly unforeseeable social consequences of scientific and technological innovation, is principally a *diachronic* medium – that is, a medium of historical, cumulative change, in which each step is unlike the last.[8] Myth, by contrast, operates typically and primarily in a synchronic or 'timeless' dimension, while fairytale, and often legend and archaic 'history', tracks the 'cyclical' time of individual psychic and social development.[9]

In *Billion Year Spree*[10] Brian Aldiss argued for Mary Shelley's *Frankenstein* (1818) as the Ur-sf novel, a view which has prevailed widely without much acknowledgement, to Aldiss's public annoyance, that his was the case which established it. Subsequently he remarked that

> perhaps the quest for the First SF Novel, like the first flower of spring, is chimerical. But the period where we should expect to look for such a blossoming is during the Industrial Revolution, and perhaps just after the Napoleonic Wars, when changes accelerated by industry and war have begun to bite, with the resultant sense of isolation of the individual from and in society.[11]

The late Dr Isaac Asimov, sf practitioner and interested observer, summed up this case for a recent emergence of sf as a distinctive kind of writing:

> True science fiction deals with human science, with the continuing advance of knowledge, with the continuing ability of human beings to make themselves better understand the universe and even to alter some parts of it for their own comfort and security by the ingenuity of their ideas. If that is so, then science fiction becomes quite a modern phenomenon and cannot claim the respectability of age.[12]

Leaving aside the remarkable complacency of this passage, surely humans have employed systematised knowledge prior to the present blessed epoch?

4

Well, explains Asimov, it is the rate and scale of the thing which is crucial. Until recently, 'such advances were made so slowly . . . that individual human beings were not particularly aware of change in the course of their own lifetimes. . . . It is characteristic of technology, however, that it is cumulative. The further it advances the faster it advances.' Eventually, the pace hotted up to the point where individuals could appreciate from the testimony of their own lives that 'the world was changing and that it was human thought and human ingenuity that was the agent of the change':

> We can then define science fiction as that branch of literature that deals with the human response to changes in the level of science and technology – it being understood that the changes involved would be rational ones in keeping with what was known about science, technology and people.
>
> True science fiction . . . could not have been written prior to the nineteenth century then, because it was only with the coming of the Industrial Revolution in the last few decades of the eighteenth century that the rate of technological change became great enough to notice in a single lifetime.
>
> (Asimov *et al.*, 1983, pp. 10–11)

More than a generic description, this is a fervent valorisation of sf as, quite explicitly and with no indication of the problematics involved in the claim, '*today's* literature; and, more than that, *tomorrow's*' (ibid., p. 12).

Asimov's account unblushingly echoes a clarion call raised thirty years earlier by John W. Campbell, Jr, usually regarded as the prime shaper of Modern science fiction. Introducing his landmark volume *The Astounding Science Fiction Anthology*,[13] drawn from the magazine he edited, Campbell announced a stunningly hubristic agenda:

> Science fiction is the literature of the Technological Era. It, unlike other literatures, assumes that change is the natural order of things, that there are goals ahead larger than those we know. That the motto of the technological civilization is true: 'There must be a better way of doing this!'
>
> Basically, of course, the science fictioneer is simply the citizen of the Technological Era, whose concern is, say, the political effect of a United States base on the Moon.
>
> (Campbell, 1952, pp. xiii, xv)

In all truth, Campbell's innovative stable of writers produced work far more various and provocative than such a one-dimensional, gung-ho programme would seem to encourage or even permit. Still, as writer, editor and bullying folk-theoretician, Campbell was so saliently placed during the rise of Modern sf that his manifesto is worth citing at some length. Like the stories it prefaced, it was 'representative of the moods and forces at work in the development of the new literature of the Technological Era':

It is essential in the nature of things that there is, at such a period of change-over, two different literatures. One, the old, will at this period be bitter, confused, disillusioned, and angry. Those novelists dealing with broad themes will have stories of neurotic, confused and essentially homeless-ghost people: people who are trying to live by conventions that have been shattered and haven't been able to build new ones, who have seen every effort to build a new stable society wrecked by new forces.

The new literature will tend to be filled with a touch of unreality, but will tell of goals and directions and solid hopes. Naturally it has a touch of unreality; the old goals are gone, the new ones not yet here. Therein is the implicit unreality of any hopeful, optimistic literature of such a period; it asserts that the goal is real, but not yet achieved. Most people want goals that *someone* has already achieved and reported on fully.[14]

(ibid., p. xiv; italics in original)

Does this make sf the peak of literature to date? Given the textual surface of some of the effective but strikingly primitive stories he included in his anthology – 'The creature crept. It whimpered from fear and pain, a thing, slobbering sound horrible to hear. Shapeless, formless thing yet changing shape and form with every jerky movement'[15] – Campbell wisely failed to go so far in his claims. 'Science fiction isn't as yet the mature literature it should be, and will be,' he confessed. Still, its prospects were firm. It 'has a place that never existed before – but will exist forevermore' (ibid., p. xv).

DEFINITIONS

There has been no lack of attempts to reach a satisfactory definition of this 'new literature'. The first edition of the authoritative *Encyclopedia of Science Fiction*, edited by Peter Nicholls *et al.*,[16] cited no less than 22 such definitions plus several additional caveats, before summarising (rather feebly): 'A survey of the accounts of the genre quoted above reveals two main expectations: that a work of sf should be concerned with the extension of scientific knowledge and all manner of consequences thereof; and that it should be imaginatively and intellectually adventurous; and even the former is not universally accepted' (Nicholls *et al.*, 1979, p. 161).

Sf historian Brian Stableford asserts that the earliest use of the expression is found in one William Wilson's *A Little Earnest Book Upon a Great Old Subject* (1851), in which, discussing 'the Poetry of Science', he defined Science Fiction as a kind of literature 'in which the revealed truths of science may be given, interwoven with a pleasing story which may itself be poetical and *true* – thus circulating a knowledge of the Poetry of Science, clothed in a garb of the Poetry of Life'.[17]

This can be seen, though, as merely an elaboration of the project glimpsed prophetically half a century earlier by Wordsworth in his Preface to the second edition of *Lyrical Ballads*: 'The remotest discoveries of the Chemist, the Botanist, or the Mineralogist, will be as proper objects of the Poet's art as any upon which it can be employed, if the time should ever come when these things shall be familiar to us . . . as enjoying and suffering beings.'[18] In short: nothing human is alien to the poet, and if the human practice of science should ever receive general currency its subject matter will perforce enter the discourse of letters. An example of just this is Don DeLillo's *White Noise*,[19] a novel dealing with industrial and intellectual pollution – hardly sf by contemporary standards. The fifties retro image many people have today of sf, pulp magazine tales of brass-bra'd space kittens struggling in the ghastly clutches of bug-eyed monsters, was not quite what either Wilson or Wordsworth had in mind.

The nineteenth century was thick with rudimentary sf of one kind or another. Darko Suvin's bibliography of sf books published between 1848 and 1900 in the UK comprises 72 pages.[20] The two innovative giants are usually held to be Jules Verne and H. G. Wells, the first preceding the second by some 30 years.[21] The definitions immanent in their works have proved fecund: Verne playing with the known, to the best of his ability, mining newspapers for plausible details, Wells inventing from first principles. An important shared characteristic of the 'scientific romances' and 'extraordinary voyages' of Wells and Verne was their work's accessibility to a wide general readership. Sf had not yet become stigmatised as a genre for undersexed male adolescent swots and underachieving white-collar wageslaves – partly because it had not yet largely been restructured to that purpose, as it was shortly to be, by commercial interests.

Generic sf was given its definition in the first issue (April 1926) of the bedsheet-sized pulp *Amazing Stories* magazine. Hugo Gernsback editorialised:

> By 'scientifiction'[22] I mean the Jules Verne, H. G. Wells and Edgar Allan Poe type of story – a charming romance intermingled with scientific fact and prophetic vision. . . . Not only do these amazing tales make tremendously interesting reading – they are always instructive. They supply knowledge . . . in a very palatable form. . . . New inventions pictured for us in the scientifiction of today are not at all impossible of realisation tomorrow.[23]

Campbell, as noted earlier, presented sf as the optimistic literature of the future. Moreover, he proposed what has been termed in a borrowing from physics the *Gedankenexperiment* – or 'thought-experiment' – paradigm:

> Scientific methodology involves the proposition that a well-constructed theory will not only explain away known phenomena, but will also predict new and undiscovered phenomena. Science fiction tries to do

7

much the same[24] – and write up, in story form, what the results look like when applied not only to machines but to human society as well.[25]

A MYTHOLOGY OF TOMORROW

At an extreme remove from Campbell's positivist prospectus, sf is often claimed as the myth-form of the industrial age. Whether or not sf is best identified as myth, it clearly has this much in common with myths and dreams as we have come to understand them in an era shaped by structuralism and psychoanalysis: science fiction stories make little sense in isolation from others of their kind. Without its unorthodox vocabulary and grammar, its generic intertextuality, science fiction is next to meaningless. Once acquired, it becomes a tongue muscular in the expression of cognitive excitement, wonder, awe, astonishment: states and emotions repressed in a workaday world. More, these sentiments are linked, in sf, to the century's motor: to knowledge sought and gained by science.

The couple is not direct. If dreams often express wishes and fears we would rather disown (like the 'black arts' of magic), science fiction is an outlet for what might be called 'black science'. Dreams of omnipotence through abstract knowledge, hunger for gods out of the machine. These are dangerous desires. They lead too easily to goose-stepping, to napalm nightmares: all the monsters bred, as Goya foresaw, of the dreams of reason. They are, in short, a regression to the pleasures of infancy, the endlessly accepted temptation to which commercial sf all too often delivers itself.

Indeed, more than two decades ago, the fine sf writer and poet Thomas M. Disch advanced this insight as his key to accounting for 'most of what was radically wrong with SF, as well as a good part of what was right. . . . [S]cience fiction is a branch of children's literature'.[26]

Is this an outright condemnation? No, said Disch. It is, however, a limitation, 'intellectually, emotionally, and morally' (Disch, 1978, p. 143).

> [T]here are, here and there, children bright enough to cope with the *Scientific American* or even the *Times Literary Supplement*, but crucial aspects of adult experience remain boring even to these prodigies [such as] sex and love . . . the nature of the class system and the real exercise of power within that system. . . .
>
> Genre fiction may be distinguished from other kinds of writing in being shaped by the (presumed) demands of its audience rather than by the creative will of its writers [who] accommodate their talents to the genre's established formulae [which] exist in order to guarantee readers the repetition of pleasures fondly remembered. . . . It follows that we may learn more about any genre by examining its readership than by studying its writers.
>
> (ibid., pp. 143–5)

While Disch is here neither exactly proclaiming the death of the author nor reinventing reception aesthetics,[27] his sardonic and perhaps self-punishing appraisal of science fiction correctly deems most sf to be stimuli tailored to the evocation of soothing daydreams, a species of craft writing directed to the satisfaction of lower middle-class and working-class hungers for solace and consolation in their presumed misery. Brian Aldiss, whose sf has never catered to the kind of fandom which congeals around Anne McCaffrey's Dragon tales, for example, or Julian May's paraphysical galactic-cum-time-travel fantasies, despite his regular attendance at conventions, lambastes this element of the devoted sf readership:

> [M]en and women, or rather, boys and girls, weighty around stomach and hips, protuberant of buttock and breast, most having achieved, if not maturity, avoirdupois, all be-badged if not actually in fancy costume, all addicts of Green Mouth's pre-pubertal planet.[28]

Disch also is explicit: 'By far the greatest part of all pulp science fiction from the time of Wells till now was written to provide a semi-literate audience with compensatory fantasies' (Disch, 1978, p. 149). Not that this is to be condemned, in Disch's view, on narrowly moralistic grounds: such fantasies can sometimes be a rehearsal for practical achievement (p. 151). But for the sophisticate who retains from adolescence a taste for sf, it constitutes an embarrassment.

Suave city mice, Disch surmises, are hardly likely to 'erect wonder, novelty, and the massive suspension of disbelief into first principles of their aesthetics' (p. 150). Yet these gaucheries can be merely poignant to the 'mainstream' literary critic, exemplified for Disch by Leslie Fiedler who, slumming, hoped that sf might not lose 'its slapdash quality, its sloppiness, or its vulgarity' (cited p. 141). Less beguiling, for Disch is sf's working-class resentment which, 'because it has its source in repressed anger, is usually expressed in indirect forms. Thus, the chief advantage of the ruling classes, their wealth and the power it provides, is dealt with in most science fiction by simply denying its importance' (p. 150).

A curiously parallel perspective is Fredric Jameson's trawling for 'authentic *ressentiment*' to capture the ideologemes (or chunks of narrative which figure the transactions of entire social classes) with which he stocks the political unconscious. '[T]he narratives of ideology – even . . . daydreaming or wish-fulfilling text – are . . . necessarily collective in their materials and form.'[29] Authorised ideologemes all too readily colonise the machinery of literary naturalism, the absence of which Disch is deploring in sf. In high realism, Jameson observes,

> alternative narrative registers begin to disappear and a massively homogeneous narrative apparatus – a kind of obligatory 'indicative' register – to take their place. Beneath the stifling and definitive weight

9

of empirical being, even alternative social worlds, such as they are, must find representational expression, and the result is the Utopian or science-fiction novel.

(Jameson, 1981, p. 193)

Disch's meditations presuppose that the chief embarrassment of science fiction is that which the sophisticates suffer at the sight of the common run of sf readers imbibing what is seen as their pitiful and slightly disgusting piped dreams.[30] Of course the real embarrassment for Disch, Delany, Le Guin, Lem and other theorists of sf who are also practitioners, and for the majority of useful critics of sf who have not merely dutifully 'done their homework' but themselves passed through the dementia of sf intoxication, is the embarrassment of the complicit.

Those who missed out on this teenage drunkenness might imagine 'dementia' rather too strong a word. After all, this is just trash entertainment we're discussing, isn't it? Well, no, not for the child who has become imprinted, as it were, on science fiction, rather in the way ethologist Konrad Lorenz's baby chicks locked onto his moving figure in preference to its true parent. The intellectually gifted Robert Silverberg discovered sf pulp magazines at the age of 11 or 12, in the late 1940s, and his account of the result is typical, even in its overwrought character:

> Their impact on me was overwhelming. I can still taste and feel the extraordinary sensations they awakened in me: it was a physiological thing, a distinct excitement, a certain metabolic quickening at the mere thought of handling them, let alone reading them. It must be like that for every new reader – apocalyptic thunderbolts and eerie unfamiliar music accompanying you as you lurch and stagger, awed and shaken, into a bewildering new world of images and ideas, which is exactly the place you've been hoping to find all your life.[31]

Not all victims of this exotic virus and others like it are so pleased to recall the fever of their infection. Grown old enough to understand how thoroughly their chosen path to transcendence is disparaged in the wider world, they can come to feel profound shame in its enjoyment. So even as popular-culture semiotics is invoked to justify vampires in terms of the oral tradition, a peevish note of censorious reproof often drones in the background. Kingsley Amis's chief defence of sf is as a sociological sideshow. Fans of the action novel do likewise, so that hard-boiled thrillers are approved above all for the light they shed on the underbelly of society, for the stink of evil they sniff out in politics and high society – rather than for the fun of getting lost in them.

RUNNING THE UNIVERSE

Such manoeuvres are not always a sign of bad faith. One's taste matures, after all, and even the most faithful cultural pluralist or practitioner of *différance* has to confess the frailty of generic writing. To save face and self-respect, the sophisticated advocate of non-canonical forms is regularly prodded into contortions of indictment and self-justification. Consider Tom Disch's recursively ironic but cruel poem, 'On science fiction' which begins

> We are all cripples.

and ends

> You are welcome, therefore, Stranger, to join
> Our confraternity. But please observe the rules.
> Always display a cheerful disposition. Do not refer
> To our infirmities. Help us to conquer the galaxy.[32]

It is worth asking if deconstruction's logic of supplementarity might not provide a useful key to any discourse whose principal intellectual coloration is embarrassment.[33] A Derridean reading of onanism, notoriously, reprieves its supplementarity, making it an account of desire's source in absence; this logic lies at the heart of Samuel R. Delany's aesthetic, the most provocative formal system yet advanced for the criticism of sf, and one to which we shall return.[34]

Reading science fiction was until recently very much a solitary vice. Power fantasies set in the near or remote future – although to some extent commonplace via mass media such as radio, film and television serials, newspaper comic strips, and sf elements in universal favourites like *Superman* comics – are intrinsically 'far-fetched'. Non-realist codes of storytelling have been, since at least the nineteenth century, broadly restricted to childhood storytelling.[35] To carry them into adolescence and adulthood is easily regarded as a sign of immaturity, of failure to take responsibility for one's complicity and obligations in the empirical world. Given the crassness and vulgarity of sf's usual packaging – titles, covers, blurbs, and, latterly, advertising – it is little wonder that the sensitive felt ashamed of reading the contents, or at any rate of being caught doing so.

THE CATLIKE MREM

To capture the flavour of this infantilisation of much mass-market science fiction (and there is very little else available), it is sufficient to cite a random selection of publishers' announcements of titles released in US mass-paperback format:

CYBERSTEALTH, S. N. Lewitt – The Cyberstealth pilots are the best of the breed. But Cargo, the best of the best, needs more than expert flying to seek and destroy a traitor.
THE LILLIPUT LEGION, Simon Hawke – The time commandos journey to *Gulliver's Travels.*

REVENGE OF THE VALKYRIE, Thorarinn Gunnarsson – Here is the blazing epic sequel to *Song of the Dwarves*.

This hilariously awful prose captures with some precision the market realities of today's sf: often pseudonymous authors, painful bathos. Blazing sequel to dwarves, indeed! These three titles are from Ace; other publishers share similar tastes. Consider these blurbs from Bantam/Spectra, Leisure, and Pocket/Baen:

> GUARDIANS OF THE THREE VOL. II: KEEPER OF THE CITY, Bill Fawcett – This is a magnificent epic of adventure, romance, and wizardry set in the unique world of the catlike mrem.
>
> BROTHER TO DEMONS, BROTHER TO GODS, Jack Williamson – From the test tubes of a dying humanity comes the first of a race of gods.
>
> LIMBO SYSTEM, Rick Cook – Demonic aliens had been trapped in a single planetless system for a million years. Now the Earthmen have uncorked the bottle . . . [36]

One of the comforts of this list, for habituated readers, is that the catlike mrem live in a world which is precisely *not* unique. Reading page after page of these advertisements, it is easy to see why the Earthmen uncorked the bottle. Of course, while scorn comes easily, it is not always entirely appropriate. Professor Williamson's book might conceivably prove, after all, to be a masterpiece homogenised by a publicist's reflex and the demands of trade. *Cyberstealth*'s author could be a worthy peer of 'cyberpunk' innovators William Gibson and Bruce Sterling.

Yet the poverty of most mass-market sf is visible even in the new work of attested and once-fresh writers from the 1950s, perhaps the genre's finest hour. Asimov's was the most deplorable of these falls, but he never made claim to artistic standing. Consider, though, the following flagrant example of a narrative defect pilloried in sf writing workshops under the apt name 'expository lump'. It is drawn almost at random from *The Shield of Time*, a 1990 addition by Poul Anderson to his genuinely innovative 'Time Patrol' tales of the 1950s. Shalten, an operative from the far future, briefs Midwestern Patrolman Manse Everard on events Everard (though not the reader of this sequel) has recently suffered through:

> Shalten nodded and went on, maddeningly deliberate: 'Let me spell out my reasoning, although given this hint, you can doubtless reconstruct it unaided. You will recall that, when their attempt to commandeer Atahuallpa's ransom failed, the Exaltationists bore off as captives the two men whose presence had – momentarily, they hoped – frustrated them, Don Luis Castelar and our disguised Specialist Stephen Tamberly. They identified the latter as a Patrolman and, in their hiding place, interrogated him at great length under kyradex. When Castelar broke

free and escaped on a timecycle, bearing Tamberly with him, the Exaltationists had gained considerable detailed information about our man and his background. Your team struck at them immediately afterward, and killed or captured most.'

Of course I recall, God damn it! Everard snarled in his head.[37]

The reader might be forgiven for snarling as well. Perhaps, though, it is the sort of thing (even Homer nods) that can happen to anyone working long and hard for 40 or more years in a species of writing shaped by the consumer demands of an audience with no great critical skills or discernment.[38] I draw attention to this particular failing precisely because it is *uncharacteristic* of competent sf, by which I mean science fiction texts that blend exposition of unfamiliar backgrounds with a seamless diegesis: the 'lived-in future' perfected by Robert A. Heinlein. Yet to the unapprenticed reader, even the finest sf seems unnecessarily cluttered with stray or forced items of information. At its worst, it resembles the shovelled-in 'authenticity' of, say, an airport blockbuster, only wrought with less artistry – as in this indigestible fragment from Philip Jose Farmer's careless *Inside Outside* (1964):

He stepped through the portal and into a hallway a hundred feet wide and three hundred feet high, however, the corridor was no more than three hundred yards long, then, through a hundred-foot high but ten-foot wide entrance into the Exchange itself.[39]

In marked contrast, there is no doubt that some contemporary sf is at least as well wrought as its high-toned mainstream cousins, and better than any sf from the past. The following paragraphs from recent novels confirm it. Each of these has an expository character, like the Poul Anderson passage, yet neither could be termed 'lumpish'. Quite the reverse: they sing, and beautifully. The first is from John Crowley's *Aegypt*, perhaps closer to magical fantasy (but not magical realism) than to science fiction:

There were angels in the glass, two four six many of them, each one shuffling into his place like an alderman at the Lord Mayor's show. None was dressed in white; some wore fillets or wreaths of flowers and green leaves in their loose hair; all their eyes were strangely gay. They kept pressing in by one and two, always room for more, they linked arms or clasped their hands behind them, they looked out smiling at the two mortals who looked in at them. All their names began with A.[40]

And here is the rapturous reworking of Dante that closes Geoff Ryman's novel of genetic engineering, *The Child Garden*:

All her separate selves were freed: the infant and the child, the orphan in the Child Garden, the actress and the director, the wife and the People's Artist, Milena the Angel, Milena the oncogene, Milena who carried the mind of Heather, and the Milena who remembered Rolfa.

They rose up like the white pages of a written speech thrown to the winds. The pages blew like leaves, were scattered to their individual and eternal Nows. The Nows were no longer linked by time or by a self. They went beyond time, to where the whole truth can be told. It takes forever to tell the truth, and it is bound into one volume by love. That is the third book, beyond words or low imagining.[41]

The Child Garden posits a future Britain governed by the worst excesses of reductive science and idealist ideology masquerading as materialism. Like most fashionable postmodern novels it is also a text about the creative process of reading. Its sustained inventions are often metaphors that seem drawn directly from current high literary theory, as Umberto Eco's are, and like Eco's are, happily, steeped as well in traditional learning and storytelling. For it is above all an impressive reconstruction of Dante Alighieri's journey, 700 years ago, from the Inferno through Purgatory to a transcendental and beatific vision. Quite literally, it proposes (and embodies) *The Divine Comedy* as a twenty-first-century Wagner might conceive it in a Bayreuth as large and inescapable as the polluted sky.

Milena, amnesiac refugee to British purgatory from Czechoslovakian hell, halfway through her truncated life, is a prim, sour Tenniel Alice who commits Dante's own sin – she forgets her (lesbian) Beatrice, a wild woman composer named Rolfa Patel, genetically engineered for life in the Antarctic to the form of a great polar bear.[42] By the standards of the ruling party, Milena's sin and crime is to love Rolfa in the first place. 'This was a semiological product of late period capitalism. Milena suffered, apparently, from Bad Grammar' (p. 2). Her story is a *Bildungsroman*, taking Milena from cramped repression to insight, redemption, indeed sainthood. It is funny while genuinely moving, teemingly fecund, baroque yet cleanly and beautifully written.

Subtitled 'A Low Comedy', it is that and much more. Ideas tumble about the page like performing animals, like humans infected by diseases of information. Most of its characters are educated/indoctrinated by designer viruses, and get their sustenance straight from sunlight through their rich, mutated purple skin. What is more, nearly everyone dies by 35, a side-effect of the contagious cure for cancer. Retarded children, preternaturally learned via their viruses, drolly debate Derrida. '"Now what is Derrida really talking about in his article on Plato?" "Writing!" chorused the Lumps. Then, washed by the same viruses, they remembered other answers' (p. 178). If Rolfa is Milena's Beatrice, the viruses (especially one that encodes the persona of dead Heather, who reads all Marx's works to the child and cannot be shut off) are her collective Virgil. Ryman's book comes very close to being the long-awaited work that successfully bonds the force and aspirations of both literature and sf.

14

AT PLAY IN THE FIELDS OF THE WORD

To read fiction of any kind is to help create a world, built out of words and memories and the fruitfulness of imagination. Usually we miss the complexity of this process. Like poetry and postmodern fiction, all sf tests the textual transparency we take for granted, contorting habits of grammar and lexicon with unexpected words strung together in strange ways.

Words, memories and imagination might be the common bricks and blueprint of all fiction, but how can they construct the future? By offering us new words to name objects and practices that do not yet exist. Near-future dystopias, the closest most literary readers (and writers) ever get to sf, sharply rein in their lexical inventiveness, reflecting the impoverished worlds they guardedly deploy. More buoyant futures put out luxuriantly flowered tendrils, and so prove alarming. Beyond the odd vocabulary, altogether necessary as well as extremely pleasurable once a taste is developed (akin to the delight an art connoisseur finds in Roger Bacon's Screaming Popes), these images unfold according to the syntax of a non-existent culture.

We ordinarily approach such perplexing density only in, for example, a baffling pastiche like Jean-Luc Godard's 1982 film *Passion*. As Fredric Jameson notes, it is by no means certain that 'the heavily charged and monitory juxtapositions in a Godard film – an advertising image, a printed slogan, newreels, an interview with a philosopher, and the *gestus* of this or that fictive character – will be put back together in the form of a message, let alone the right message.'[43]

Sf can use a similar method. In Terry Dowling's future Australia, for example, deployed in several collections of linked short stories, a metaphysical transformation is underway.[44] It finds its parallels in the very shape of the landscape, the cultures that have evolved to its new form, and the lilting folktale format Dowling devises (with borrowings from sf masters Cordwainer Smith, Jack Vance and J. G. Ballard) to tell of it. Virtually nothing is explained explicitly. In this Australia, for a start, there is an artificial inland sea, presumably thousands of years old. Only because an adjacent university town is called Inlansay do we have a lexical hint of the elapsed time involved.

As now, a blend of European and Pacific Rim peoples, the Nationals, live in many cities and towns along the periphery of the continent. In its mysterious interior, a wholly new culture has emerged, blending genetic engineering, artificial intelligence and space technologies with ancient tribal Dreaming mythologies – indeed, the accumulated myths of all humankind. Nuclear energy and powered domestic flight, though not space travel, seem forgotten or forbidden. Across these bleak, ancient deserts move the few permitted dirigibles and wind- and solar-powered charvolants, or sandships. Captain of one such, the *Rynosseros*, is Blue Tom Tyson – a sort of incarnation of Tom O'Bedlam, the visionary, pathetic Shakespearian madman.

Capturing these imagined landscapes and populations calls for a richly inventive tongue. Dowling has it (though it falters painfully in several crucial places). By these strange namings, he builds up with cumulative intensity an Australis Incognita. Despite a sense of brooding development, the books resemble a Thousand and One Nights of the future, a medieval display of epiphanies locked into a certain timelessness.

Dowling's words and images are lavish: belltrees (thousands of ancient carved roadposts whose artificial minds are slowly dying as this enigmatic culture changes), biotects, the brinraga wind, totemic artefacts halfway between machine and plant:

> The cauchemars sweated resin, the orreries clicked and shifted like bone carousels, the trochars pumped away, the rorschachs lifted symmetrical platelets to the burning sun. Many of the big columnar bioforms – the sergeant-majors, the sandwives, xoanons and coralline dexters, even the spinnerets, looked dead and functionless, but we knew the unlocked ones turned imperceptively like the hour-hands of antique clocks, angling slowly to follow the course of the sun.
>
> (*Blue Tyson*, p. 230)

Such terminological play is not without its hazards. The rulers of this future Australia, with their Clever Men and Princes, their patriarchal defloration rituals and incessant intertribal wars, prove to be DNA-altered descendants of today's dispossessed Kooris. Dowling dubs them, alas, Ab'Os, recalling the Australian shorthand term 'Abo', a usage now regarded as belittling and racist. Perhaps the coinage has its own curious logic; many African-Americans derisively call each other 'nigger', young Australians of Italian or Greek descent have adopted 'wog' . . . and Tyson's world is millennia in the future. Still, we are reading about it *now*.

Captain Tyson's emblematic adventures make it clear that he is a mediator and bearer of transcendental insight to this stressed society with its own authenticated 'haldane Dreamtime', a collective unconscious stocked with the mythic detritus of human prehistory – dinosaur dragons, trance-induced identification with powerful Heroes, effective death songs.

But can such fancies have any salience to our own time? No less, perhaps, than those resonant icons which art reprieves from expired faiths. In one tale, the plot is less important than Dowling's images: a ziggurat in the secret places of the desert watched from space by a lethal satellite. Surely this is the truncated pyramid (familiar from US dollar bills) with its hermetic Eye gazing in judgment and power. Dowling's borrowing is hardly without art:

> Usually the house sang. It was built to make music out of the seven winds that found it on its desert rise. Vents in the walls, cunning terraces, cleverly angled embrasures in the canted terrazzo facings drew them in; three spiral core-shafts tuned them into vortices and descants, threw them across galleries, flung them around precise cornices and

carefully filigreed escarpments so that more than anything the house resembled the ancient breathing caves of the Nullarbor.

(ibid., p. 167)

SF AFTER 19?

Splendid as these exceptions are, however, the awful blurbs by and large reflect the reality of what is for sale. A fan critic, John Foyster, has drawn attention to this publishing trend, one which has reversed the minor current which in the 1960s encouraged publication of stylistically and cognitively challenging adult work (I mean work ranging from Cordwainer Smith's memorable if reactionary fables to Ursula Le Guin's confrontations of gender and politics). Today's increasingly adolescent tendency extends beyond sf to airport fiction and encroaches on bestselling Gothic realists like John Irving. 'Bluntly put, the question is "is there, or should there be, science fiction after nineteen?"'[45] Foyster's implicitly negative answer poses in contrast Philip Larkin's lament, two decades ago, at the early failure of publishers to show interest in Barbara Pym's writing. Perhaps no writer could be further from the concerns and techniques of sf. Pym's subject matter was the most ordinary of upper- or middle-class English lives, all chronicled in a barbed, incisive style. Larkin wrote:

> I like to read about people who have done nothing spectacular, who aren't beautiful or lucky, who try to behave well in the limited field of activity they command, but who can see, in the autumnal moments of vision, that the so-called 'big' experiences of life are going to miss them.[46]

Even the most heralded of recent 'cyberpunk' science fiction, it seems, patently failed such a comparison. Gibson's *Neuromancer*, to which I shall return with my own approbatory stylistic analysis, is for Foyster just the sort of 'rubbish' which Larkin deplored:

> built around a latter-day equivalent of psi and the rocket-ship combined: the mind powers released by humans linked into computer networks. Psi and the rocket-ship were the glamour icons of lonely teenagers in the 1940s and 1950s whereas in the 1980s the computer, and especially the computer in a network, has a similar iconic function. Indeed, of the major icons of male teenagers of the 1980s only the rock guitarist is missing.

(Foyster, 1989, p. 13)

This is a telling critique to the extent that, among pulp genres at least from the time of Hugo Gernsback, editor of *Amazing Stories* (1926), the signal feature of sf has been its express claim to a status well beyond the supplementary. It was said emphatically to be not consolation but preparation. In Brian M. Stableford's words, 'It was to look forward – in both senses of the phrase – to the wonderful future made possible by technology, advertising its wonder and inspiring the imagination of the young, whose destiny it was to live in and participate in the Age of Power-Freedom.'[47] On the evidence, as we have seen, that agenda, itself an embarrassment to our grim hindsight, did not stay long on the table. 'By the time Campbell took over *Astounding*, however,' Stableford observes, 'this prospectus no longer seemed convincing – *Astounding* itself had been founded not to perpetuate this mythology but simply to take advantage of a new *milieu* for . . . costume melodrama set in gaudy futuristic scenarios' (Stableford, 1979, p. 3).

For all but a very small proportion of science fiction texts, that is what it has remained. Still, the very strategies called upon in the practice of writing or reading sf offer benefits which might not be visible in scrutinising individual texts, rather as the stagecraft of drama can extend our sensibilities and challenge our limitations even when it is instantiated in faulty scripts, inadequate sets or clumsy acting.

For the notable New York sf editor David Hartwell, besotted wonderment and a subsequent nostalgia for its impossible re-evocation is at the heart of science fiction, a heart that starts beating in early adolescence. 'The Golden Age of Science Fiction Is Twelve', candidly declares the first chapter heading of Hartwell's wryly titled *Age of Wonders*: 'Immersed in science fiction. Bathing in it, drowning in it; for the adolescent who leans this way it can be better than sex.'[48] Perhaps the most romantic and besotted history of the genre, and one altogether convincing to an inducted sf reader of a certain age, is Alexei and Cory Panshin's *The World Beyond the Hill*. This richly detailed if rather gushily New Age volume bears the revealing subtitle *Science Fiction and the Quest for Transcendence*.[49] Nor is a rush of delight in cosmic spectacle, and the sense of transcendent significance evoked by it, indicative only during initiation. Hartwell argues that out of it comes everything central to the genre. Fandom – the company of other initiates – is its social embodiment. I believe Hartwell is correct in finding here a key to sf's singularity among genres:

> The fans and professionals eat together, drink together, play together (sleep together, exclude one another, criticize one another), act in some ways as an enormous extended family.
>
> What fandom has done on a social and cultural level for or to the writers in the SF field is to provide them with a paradigm of the life of the writer quite different from the two major paradigms available to all other writers outside SF: the life of the artist (working in isolation from the marketplace to achieve art; supported by the academy, by grants, by awards, perhaps by the admiration of peers) and the life of the commercial writer (after an apprenticeship, writing books and stories or articles primarily for money by big publishers according to the dictates of the marketplace . . .).

The life of the SF writer is a life of continual socializing and communication with a rather large audience of loyal and vocal readers together with the majority of other writers working in the field. The response of these people to a writer's work is always in the forefront of his consciousness and may even be the controlling factor in his writing. . . .

Fandom, then, is at the center of a discussion of SF, without which all else falls apart.

(Hartwell, 1985, pp. 174–5)

All this is true, and quite beyond the intuition of even trained critical readers familiar only with other modes of writing. Still, there are limits to its generality and salience: Hartwell writes as an American, when fandom is strongest and major conventions occur every weekend. A more sardonic and less engulfed reaction is typical of writers in the UK, exemplified in the amused disgust of Aldiss's narrator for the swarming fans 'protuberant of buttock and breast'.

In geographically or culturally isolated markets such as Australia,[50] local fandom has a considerably more restricted capacity to conscript and shape the consciousness of the few writers able to compete on the world stage. No doubt this accounts in part for the maverick character of non-American sf, and for its general failure to achieve the large success which brought the US-fan-endorsed writers fame, wealth and devoted readership during the last decade or so.

CHANGING PARADIGMS

The corollary of this fannish rapture and the subculture built upon its memory is a fear of any paradigm challenge to its canonical form. On the one hand, new readers are drawn increasingly to sf's imagery through 'dumbed-down' mass media varieties. Of late, Hartwell notes with dismay, 'the younger writers and the younger fans got their initial imprint of SF from sci-fi, from media'. On the other hand, ambitious young writers well schooled in literary devices and standards are turning to sf simply because it is the best available fiction market. Hartwell's anxiety is revealing:

And while they may produce works of some merit to people of taste, they are becoming dangerous to the SF field just because there are so many of them, and they write so well, and they get published and praised by peers – but they aren't really contributing to the SF field. Rather, they are often taking something from it by creating a major distraction, a confusion of goals.

(ibid., p. 188)

It is possible to have some sympathy with Hartwell's qualms, while

19

concluding that if sf is to retain any claim to the lofty status sometimes sought for it – a bridge between the two cultures – it must do so largely on credit extended to the as-yet-unwritten. Perhaps science fiction's best hopes are discernible as the virtual shadow of an absent bridge: formal schemata tentatively to be glimpsed through the inartistic and immature trappings of a genre funded by bored or harried readers in search of opiates or displaced unconscious wish-satisfactions, dreams of some ultimate 'scientific' quick fix for a reality irredeemably disappointing.[51]

Yet in an age of simulations and hyper-reality, even virtual realities are not without their powerful impact. In the next chapter, we examine the historical development of sf as a genre, a kind of paraliterary writing with the peculiar ability to encode the deep experience of the epoch of information, computation, mass education and, above all, an unappeasable thirst for anticipation: for the imaginative creation, out of the already-known, of its own fecund futures and alternatives.

2

GENERIC ENGINEERING

For their audiences, generic productions can be perceived as mnemonic plays upon an anaesthetized matrix; this matrix – this associative net of expectations or trammels – comprises plot segments, character icons, Production Code opacities, visual syntax, sexual skews, segmented tropes, channelled tropes, blocked tropes, and everything perceived of as typically existing *prior to* the work watched, in the vast affinity of previous works defined as making up or contributing to the particular genre or subgenre in question. . . . [A]ny dissonant notes the audience can register . . . tend to fog the plate, so that film tends to become indecipherable, untrue to the network of precedents, and begins to threaten the reader, just as life does, outside the play dark. Generic works are devices for casting back, not neologisms to greet the world afresh.

(John Clute)[1]

Sf is usually regarded as a distinct 'genre', a kind of writing with singular rhetorical moves and a common intertext of related fictions. Anglo-Canadian critic John Clute, the most exhilarating and vexing of sf commentators, here links generic readings to the articulation of systems of tropes and intertextual givens. Clute's inevitable conclusion to this line of argument, a *reductio ad absurdum* of any wish that art be 'transparent' to the pre-intentional world, is that any authentically unique text would be literally unreadable. With patently generic texts, 'even while you're pretending to be hallucinated you can *remember* what's going to happen' (Clute, 1975, p. 116).

But how did readers and writers first become inducted into Clute's ramified systems of tropes, and how in turn did those systems arise and settle into comparative stability? As with all forms of discursive practice, the evolution of both individual and collective competences in an emergent genre occurs by mutation within what one might term, by analogy with developmental biology, an 'epigeneric landscape' – the surround which nourishes and channels the growing form, curtailing certain options in its defining 'recipe', encouraging others to achieve expression.

In sf's case, the principal habitats which the struggling new species colonised were the mass-market magazines and comic-strips, and, later, movies and television plays or series. These former were the outcome of a process of mass literacy and urban experience then fairly recent. Richard Ohmann remarks:

> A vigorous penny press developed in New York after 1835. There was a paperback revolution of sorts in book publishing in the 1840s. But despite these and other events . . . a national mass culture was not firmly established in [the USA] until the 1880s and 1890s. . . . Only in the eighties and nineties did book publishing become a business with regular methods of hype, with many dependable outlets across the nation. . . . The establishment of a best-seller list in 1895 can serve as an indication that the book industry took something like its modern form at about the same time as newspaper publishing and the business of sports.[2]

Specifically, then, sf's first effective niche was the American pulps, the twentieth-century Depression offspring of this publishing heritage. Despised as they might well be by critics of canonised art, the pulps as a general entertainment medium manifested extraordinary demographics. As Frank Cioffi observes,

> An approximate figure for pulp magazine circulation of the mid-thirties is ten million – and since most magazines were read by at least three people, it can be fairly guessed that the pulps were read by thirty to forty percent of the literate American public. . . .
> While most other pulps disappeared by the 1940s, the science fiction magazines survived. Indeed, the genre seemed to continue its late thirties momentum. . . . The science fiction pulps offered something that could not be found in other formats: the metaphor for experience they provided was so unprecedented and immediate that the genre could survive even in an outmoded format.[3]

These pulps specialised out of generalist magazines which, while perhaps constituting a genre of their own, contained fiction, non-fiction, and 'non'-fiction in a variety of sub-genres, all of them paraliterary rather than literary. While sf was not without such dedicated or high-culture forebears as Verne and Wells, its transformation into 'Modern science fiction', at least in its important American form, clearly occurred inside these formulaic pulps. Significantly, Cioffi's study of the rise and early typical structures of the genre is entitled *Formula Fiction?* – at once granting sf's algorithmic character and simultaneously putting that despised feature into question. His starting point is unarguable:

> The emergence of a genre is a more important phenomenon than the

appearance of an isolated writer whose works fail to fit established forms, [requiring] not only the existence of a group of writers who concurrently want to escape set patterns of literary expression, but the formation of an audience as well.

(Cioffi, 1982, p. 3)

In physics, a mathematical space 'whose coordinates are given by the set of independent variables characterising the state of a dynamical system', able to map onto infinitely many dimensions, is called a *phase space*.[4] I propose that genre is a negotiated territory in narrative phase space.

OUT OF THE PULPS

The possibilities in generic phase space which became actualised in the discourses we name as sf were shaped in the audience needs of the pulps. This historical, contingent fact ensured that the form was popular, 'programmed', brash and vigorous. Its readers were rarely highly educated members of the executive or leisure classes. Hence, among other consequences, sf's invocation of the tropes of science and technology were inevitably closer to the incantatory than to the learned formulations of textbook or lab report. Cioffi is right to admit that

'Mainstream,' or 'serious,' literature generally resists imitation and replication; the subtle tones, moods, nuances, and multifaceted characters it employs are difficult to describe and define, and even more difficult to imitate. . . . Whereas serious literature emerges without easily recognizable antecedents, popular literature seems to feed upon itself.

(ibid., p. 8)

And not only upon itself: paradoxically, Cioffi asserts that sf is centrally referential. It is 'analogical or mimetic [following] oft-repeated patterns that suggest an overlap with experiential reality [which] respond to the concerns of the historical period in which they were created. They embody a shared social consciousness – one, in fact, that readers of the 1980s no longer share' (p. 9). We might say that its readers and writers constituted a semiotic community, sharing class-based sociocodes as well as generic protocols.

While Cioffi's case seems to me oversimplified, his anatomy offers an interesting first approach to a narratology of early Modern science fiction. Certainly his insistence on incorporating the historical dimension within which these formulae emerged is persuasive, when set against other attempts to understand sf in terms of more generalised and timeless themata (such as, at its best, Gary K. Wolfe's icons, to be discussed in Chapter 4).[5] It is also of paramount importance not to scamp the artistic dimension. Wolfe himself notes:

23

I am not, of course, suggesting that we abandon the study of the artistry that goes into science-fiction narrative in favor of some broad-based social anthropology of the genre. . . . Like other popular genres, science fiction has its formulae, but I doubt that these formulae can be expressed quite as simply and elegantly as scholars such as John Cawelti have expressed the formula of detective stories and Westerns. . . our work has barely begun.[6]

(Wolfe, 1979, p. 229)

A useful comparison may be drawn with the occasional remarks of a specialist in high culture, Harry Levin, addressing the issue of 'Science and Fiction'. Levin begins with Lord Snow's 'Two Cultures'; he ends with the Russian formalist Vladimir Propp and his followers, categorising folktales by their elementary rules of construction:

[T]he ultimate cosmos of science is not far removed from the artificial microcosms of literature. . . . And within the domain of fiction . . . the fabrications of science are not so far removed from the fantasies of the literary – or, beyond the self-consciously literary, the traditional and popular – imagination. . . . Since [Stith Thompson, in his *Motif-Index of Folk-Literature*] has ordered his vast range of materials by a thematic scheme of classification, it is revealing to observe the principal themes: cosmogony, the creation of life, arcane knowledge, magical trans-actions, otherworldly journeys, ogres and ordeals, raising the dead, foreseeing and controlling the future. What are these folkloristic categories but the standard situations of science-fiction?[7]

One must note, as so often in visitors from high culture, the almost inevitable fatal slurring into haughtiness: 'Personally, I remain enough of a sceptical rationalist to feel somewhat uneasy over the cultural currents that have been remystifying and remythologizing our precarious century. Our technorevolutions seem to foster, not so much a rule of reason, as an efflorescence of credulity. Perhaps the last word should be left to P. T. Barnum' (Levin, 1980, p. 21). Cioffi's approach is quite different. Rather than search for invariants continuous with all literature, or at least with all paraliterature, he identifies five terms of a formula, and three principal patterns in which these are deployed.

SCIENCE FICTION'S FORMULAE

The terms are

mimesis (the portion of the narrative in which the experiential, realistic, quotidian world of the writer is evoked); *anomaly* (the unprecedented

24

but logical changes introduced into this world – the element that makes a story SF); *conflict*; *resolution*; and *authorial stance*.

(Cioffi, 1982, p. 11; my italics)

On the face of it, then, the sole novel element is the anomaly – what Darko Suvin has dubbed the 'novum'.[8] Yet in Cioffi's deployment, each of the other more conventional elements is transformed in practice by the need to confront this drastic discontinuity while retaining imaginative and empathic links with the procedures of assessment we routinely apply to waking life in a real, resistant world.

His three basic patterns are the *status quo*, the *subversive*, and the *other world* varieties of sf tale. These are idealised abstractions, of course, though certain of the Ur-stories he invents to encapsulate them ring rather uncomfortably familiar to the sf aficionado. In the first pattern, while everyday reality is affronted by a major anomaly, convention is at last recuperated. In the second pattern, the anomaly is not expelled; like the barbarians at the gates of Rome, it either puts the empire to the torch or changes it utterly from within.

In the third and most sophisticated variety, from which the bulk of latter-day sf derives, the baseline social order is already drastically different from our own empirical reality. Anomaly enters as a second-order estrangement effect. A classic instance is Asimov's 'Nightfall' (1941), often voted favourite sf story of all time, in which the natives of a planet with many suns are driven mad by its rare but cyclical plunge into darkness. More recent examples are Brian Aldiss's Helliconia trilogy (to be discussed in Chapter 7), where something similar happens, and Gregory Benford's *Great Sky River* and *Tides of Light*.[9] In each, the events occur on distant worlds, and to 'humans' radically other than ourselves.

If horror tales simultaneously domesticate our most dreadful terrors and leave us relieved that the world, however awful, is at least better than *that*, status quo sf is seen by Cioffi as reassuring readers embedded in the Depression sociocode (and reality) that 'old-fashioned values' might prevail even in the face of unprecedented upheaval.

[B]y using a science fictional story type, in which the reader's attention is displaced from the naturalistic, such values [as courage, loyalty and love] can be faced with impunity. They are operative, indeed, on an implicit level because, were they not so cast, they would be rejected as precisely the kinds of values that seemed no longer to be of any importance, whose applicability to modern life had been as much as usurped by the large-scale social and economic collapse of the thirties.

(Cioffi, 1982, p. 55)

This curious argument seeks to redeem precisely those hackneyed and offensively stereotyped features of early sf which offend literary and fan readers alike. Instead of a Toffleresque embrace of the anomaly which emblematises the future shock of daily life, our attention is directed to the soothing benefits of a reasserted background order, a kind of proleptic nostalgia. (*Prolepsis* is a term from rhetoric useful in discussing sf; it means 'taking forward' or 'anticipatory'.) Interestingly, this is precisely the dynamic which governs the narrative choices of British global-doom fiction of the 1950s, the John Wyndham 'cosy catastrophe' formula. It is quite absent, though, from the bleak, detached versions of this recurrent trope patented in the 1960s by J. G. Ballard, and from the exuberant embrace of urban entropy typical of cyberpunk texts.[10]

In all three kinds, narratives plot briskly through phases of conflict and resolution. The factor which Cioffi terms 'authorial stance' is more accurately seen as axiological: an implied narratorial evaluation of the anomaly. The 'transplanted status quo' begins in a world already alienated from the reader's reality: aboard a spaceship, on another world, cast into the future. Within this frame, a further anomaly intrudes. A. E. van Vogt made his name with a series in this modality, revised and collected in the 'fix-up' volume *The Voyage of the Space Beagle*.[11] Even today, most derivative science fiction series on the order of *Star Trek* use the device.

In the 'inverted status quo' sf story, the novum proves attractive, even beneficial. Almost inevitably this format blurs into Cioffi's second category, the *subversive* formula. Now reality cannot contain the threat, and telling the tale fails to affirm traditional stereotyped values. Doubtless this formula marks the transition to most of the characteristics highly prized in subsequent sf. Certainly it is the basis for that strong current of satirical and taboo-challenging sf embraced but overemphasised by Kingsley Amis. In the 1950s, it provided many *Galaxy* stories which were patent allegories of McCarthy-era depredations against American democratic folk-wisdom. In later decades it has in turn subverted much of that wisdom, most notably in the development of techno-military and feminist idioms and narratives.

For Cioffi, two major strands of subversive sf are the 'destructive' and the 'incorporative'. In the first, perhaps heralded by Wells's Time Traveller woefully regarding a world emptied of human consciousness, anomaly destroys everything we hold dear. In the second, when the trumpet sounds we are all made new. Recent examples of these tendencies can be found in novels by Greg Bear. *The Forge of God*[12] shows human life exterminated by aliens, while *Blood Music*[13] sees it transcended into nanobiological form, literally incorporated into the seething intelligent artificial viruses which swallow up flesh while retaining spirit.

The final formula, perhaps best seen as a development of the transplanted status quo version, is the *other world*. Now no element of our own reality can be counted upon automatically to remain as a given, although ideological analysis may readily locate, precisely here, representations of those features rendered invisible by power and usage even as they dictate our lives. In its grandest form, the other world is an entire cosmos, a universe with a history almost discontinuous with our own. The crass sagas of E. E. Smith embodied this trope for early sf. By the 1960s, it had been renewed by Cordwainer Smith's extraordinary fragments from the remote future of the Instrumentality of Mankind, with its immortal Lords, its underpeople, its robots with the laminated brains of mice, its poets and redeemers.

Today it can be taken for granted that many of the most interesting sf locales are other worldly in this sense, from Le Guin's Ekumen to Varley's 'Eight Worlds' and Gaea, to David Zindell's *Neverness*,[14] a first novel of remarkable accomplishment which manages to blend into the vast intertext generated by all these other works while expanding and enriching it with fresh figurative images and idioms from higher mathematics. These fictions are versions of what Cioffi dubs the 'ascendent [*sic*] other world': 'All of these stories ask . . . how contemporary reality will be viewed against the larger backdrop of future history, or against the wider context that alien cultures can provide' (Cioffi, 1982, p. 133).

It is crucial to recognise that in none of these variants is the *soi-disant* 'scientific' content meant to be taken seriously or centrally *as science*. It functions, Cioffi asserts, as a 'verification device', though this does not prevent its being already a kind of crude bridge between the 'two cultures', or, better, between classes separated by education, power and income:

> Its . . . usual ignorance of the facts and complexities that real science deals with allows the story to be a corridor into what often seems an inaccess-ible, hermetically sealed discipline, but one that has – for better or for worse – great impact on large numbers of people. SF offers this apparent entry into a given field, and demystifies its concepts and ambiguities. That these demystifications are often scientifically naive or wrong is finally of little moment: for the value of the story, in the methodology I have proposed, inheres in the way it speculates about social adaptations to anomalous circumstances, not in its scientific accuracy.
>
> (ibid., p. 145)

Certainly the sf of the 1930s through to the 'Golden Age' of the 1940s seems well captured in Cioffi's formulae, and as I have indicated much of today's sf can be illuminated in this focus as well. It might be objected that under the auspices of John W. Campbell the Golden Age writers and their heirs provided more authenticity to their scientific 'speculations'. While this is true to an extent, it is undeniable that the majority of sf's enabling devices – even those in common use by trained scientists such as Asimov – are mock-scientific at best.[15]

HOW MUCH CHANGE?

To stress anomaly and the variety of logically possible responses to its irruption – which in essence is what Cioffi's schemata are doing – is to concentrate again on sf as a literature or paraliterature of change. Yet to propose such a generic anatomy in the first place is to argue a certain paradoxical rigidity in sf's capacity to deal with change.

Some of that rigidity is doubtless due to the sociolects or distinctive class dialects within which the fiction, of whatever era, is being written and read. It is in discerning both the formulaic character of what is foregrounded, and the ideological stamp of what is placed in the text unconsciously, that the most artistically deleterious consequences of 'generic' patterning become evident. Even in what appear to be subversive or discontinuous inventions, the routine or algorithmic aspects of the texts predominate (that is, the components that seem to be generated by a pre-set programme). To those who wish to harness sf's freedom of perspective to radical ends, as Joanna Russ and Samuel R. Delany, for example, have done, Cioffi's conclusion offers little hope:

> The picture that this fiction suggests is of marionette-like people, less interested in who controls the strings. . . . The focus is not on the instilling, say, of knowledge, or on the development of social/personal/ political possibility. Instead, SF depicts individuals adapting to sudden, drastic, media-transmissible change – which is, in a society in which information has become more important than knowledge, a well-known form of change. . . . Science fiction is an understandable expression of a society in which world views can change as rapidly as technology.
>
> (ibid., p. 148)

This disturbing portrait of humans at the mercy of their physical and cultural environment, shared in certain respects by poststructuralist analyses of the posthumanist condition, is thus located within the traditional codes of sf construction. If the standard surface of sf is a curious blend of eighteenth-century mercantile liberalism and militarist conservatism, made up often of tales of brilliant individualists eager to die for the flag, the subtext is as often one of the bleakest mechanical determinism and obliteration of the volitional subject.

Perhaps the most explicit instance of this tendency, and one of the best-loved by sf readers over the past 40 years, is Isaac Asimov's Foundation sequence. Always a sociological nightmare presenting humankind as a statistically predictable and manipulable hive, within which individual subjectivity is an obstacle to be removed by discursive control and paranormal coercion, the original trilogy was expanded in the 1980s to show that this entire galactic epoch was shaped by a single rule-deontological (and therefore, for Asimov, 'ethical') machine. The best that can be said is that Asimov bequeaths this robot a certain measure of moral choice and subjective responsibility.

How different all this is from the established literary canon has been stressed by Professor Robert Scholes in his series introduction to the short-lived Oxford University Press volumes on science fiction writers:

For the first eight decades of this century critics of fiction have reserved their highest praises for novels and stories that emphasize individual psychology in characterization, unique stylistic nuances in language, and plausibility in the events presented. It is an interesting feature of literary history that during this same period of time a body of fiction has flourished which privileges the type over the individual, the idea over the word, and the unexpected over the plausible event.[16]

This is a portrait of sf clearly akin to Joanna Russ's provocative prolegomenon, regrettably never followed up in detail, 'Towards an Aesthetic of Science Fiction', where Russ found that sf,

> like medieval painting, addresses itself to the mind, not the eye. We are not presented with a representation of what we know to be true through direct experience; rather we are given what we know to be true through other means – or in the case of science fiction, what we know to be at least possible.[17]

Scholes was, of course, one of the first American scholars to recover sf from the trash can and announce a place for it in the academy. His *Structural Fabulation*[18] is representative of early attempts to situate sf in the company of metafictions typified by the non- or magic-realist writings of Coover, Pynchon, Barth, Hawkes and others. Scholarship had stumbled on sf in the late 1950s, but science fiction did not gain even a marginal institutional niche until the late 1960s.[19]

UNCANNY AND MARVELLOUS

Tzvetan Todorov is no doubt the most distinguished of the structural theoreticians to develop a complex generic schema for 'the fantastic', a category which he quite explicitly restricted to certain nineteenth-century texts. It is incapable of dealing with Kafka, for example, let alone postmodern or sophisticated sf texts. Still, it has been invoked in the analysis of many contemporary non-mimetic or ambiguous narratives.[20] Best seen as psychoanalytic in genesis and impulse, Todorov's reading of the fantastic places its effectivity, under the direction of the artful text, within the reader, and not least within the reader's unconscious.

Key events in narratives of this kind are perforce construed by the reader, according to Todorov, as neither clearly natural nor supernatural, which precipitates a kind of epistemological and even ontological oscillation, with consequent creepy or ghastly affect. Because this undecidability is structured into the text, it cannot be dissipated by a poetic or allegorical reading, or ought not to be. A poetic reading treats the words as sculpture in language. For an allegorical reading, they are staged as a homology of a deeper or 'referential' level of discourse.

As a result of these encoded constraints, bizarre diegetical incidents hang as aporias, undecidable between one explanatory regime (the *uncanny*, a borrowing from Freud), and its alternative (the *marvellous*). On this view, the fantastic is not so much a genre proper as the interface between categories of work arrayed along Todorov's schema:

UNCANNY | FANTASTIC UNCANNY | FANTASTIC MARVELLOUS | MARVELLOUS

The uncanny is the return of the repressed. It is therefore like the past, the actual. The marvellous, invoking the unknown beyond the grave, is like the future, the metaphorical. The utility of this schematisation for casting light on sf is immediately put in question. For Todorov, the stuff of science fiction's narrative has to be 'natural', susceptible of scientific or quasi-scientific explanation. Yet one feels certain that his categories would be at least as well served by identifying sf with the marvellous – not supernatural, but the natural not yet understood within the current paradigms of an always fallible and evolving scientific knowledge.

The failure of his theoretical model to meet minimal generalised demands is patent in Todorov's weak declaration that Kafka's tales are 'the coincidence of two apparently incompatible genres'.[21] That is, they are marvellous, but unambiguously so to the point of naturalisation. Brooke-Rose attempts to redeem this failure with the suggestion that 'in effect . . . the pure fantastic is not so much an evanescent *genre* as an evanescent *element*' (1981, p. 63). Encoded into the text, it is an additional dimension or parameter called upon in the reader's internal performance of generic narratives which in other respects might well be comedies, epics or tragedies.

DIAGRAMMING THE FANTASTIC

This suggestion is alien to Todorov's own structural ambition, but it fits well with an alternative model, that of Eric S. Rabkin, sometime co-author with Scholes, who proposes an intriguing Venn diagram of the fantastic, including sf.[22] For Rabkin, the fantastic is something like a coloration on other genres, which can be arrayed in any number of frames in a linear order from the less to more fantastic. Detective fiction 'occupies not a point but a range along the continuum of the fantastic', from Conan Doyle's modestly fantastic 'The Speckled Band' to, 'at the extreme Fantasy end', Cortázar's thriller 'Continuity of Parks' (Rabkin, 1976, p. 136). Science fiction is a work whose

> narrative world is at least somewhat different from our own, and if that difference is apparent against the background of an organized body of knowledge. [. . . This] notion of difference . . . must be defined in terms of the world outside the text as that text recreates it.

(ibid., pp. 119–20)

30

Constituted by 'the grapholect of the text' (its individual dialect, as it were), this pseudo-empirical world establishes the *given* which the fantastic violates: 'The fantastic depends on reversal of the ground rules of the *narrative* world' (ibid., p. 120). Science fiction's staging of such transgression is, for Rabkin, well captured in its name, understood on a Kuhnian model of science as a cycle between stability and revolution:

> What is important in the definition of science fiction is not the appurtenances of ray guns and lab coats, but the 'scientific' habits of mind: the idea that paradigms do control our view of all phenomena, that within these paradigms all normal problems can be solved, and that abnormal occurrences must either be explained or initiate the search for a better (usually more inclusive) paradigm.[23]
>
> (ibid., p. 121)

In Rabkin's most ambitious move, a super-genre is proposed, graphed as a Venn diagram of three intersecting sets: Science Fiction, Satire, and Utopias, including Dystopias. Sharing aspects of all three genres are the utopian *Looking Backward* (1888) and the dystopian *We* (1924). Linking satire and sf is *The Space Merchants* (1953), while Asimov's *I, Robot* (1950) is seen as pure sf, *Childhood's End* (1953) as conjoint sf and utopia, and *The Time Machine* (1895) as dystopic sf. David Karp's *One* (1953) is pure dystopia. *Animal Farm* (1945) is dystopic satire while *News from Nowhere* (1890) is utopian satire, and *Candide* (1759) is the paradigmatic pure satire. Empirically, Rabkin notes, texts marked by the utopian dimension seem to valorise the power of community while satire prioritises the individual. Generic hybrids blend these values. The quotient of the fantastic shifts down the diagram, so that the satirical sf *Stranger in a Strange Land* (1961) is more fantastic than the utopian sf *Childhood's End*, and so forth.

That so simple a categorisation scheme can tidy up such an array of diverse texts is not unimpressive. It is far from clear, however, that Rabkin's analysis carries us much closer to an understanding of the precise signification processes which identify and delimit science fiction. Reversal within a paradigmatically ordered implied world is exactly the mark of satire also, as his super-genre presupposes. Surely the reversal must be occasioned within a framework which is reflexively paradigm-making and paradigm-challenging: that is, it must be cognitive as well as estranging.

COGNITIVE AND ESTRANGED

Perhaps the most influential theorist of sf, Darko Suvin, placed its poetics in precisely such a structural theoretic context, founded in a 'genological [*sic*] system' schematised on 'the two parameters or binary oppositions of naturalistic/ estranged, and cognitive/noncognitive':[24]

The concept of SF cannot be extracted intuitively or empirically from the work called thus. Positivistic critics often attempt to do so; unfortunately, the concept at which they arrive is then primitive, subjective, and unstable.... *SF is distinguished by the narrative dominance or hegemony of a fictional 'novum' (novelty, innovation) validated by cognitive logic.*

(Suvin, 1979, p. 63; italics in the original)

In Suvin's term, sf is a literature of *cognitive estrangement*, its 'two main species or models, the extrapolative and the analogical' (p. 27),[25]

a literary genre whose necessary and sufficient conditions are the presence and interaction of estrangement and cognition, and whose main formal device is an imaginative framework alternative to the author's empirical environment....

Once the elastic criteria of literary structuring have been met, *a cognitive – in most cases strictly scientific – element becomes a measure of aesthetic quality, of the specific pleasure to be sought in SF.*

(ibid., pp. 8–9, 15; italics in the original)

Oddly enough, Romantic pastoral shares this classification with sf in Suvin's grid, while 'realistic' literature is *cognitive naturalistic*. 'Realist subliterature', 'from Renaissance street-ballads to contemporary *kitsch*' (p. 20) is *noncognitive naturalistic*. Myth, folktale and fantasy are *noncognitive estranged*. This grid can be made isomorphic with another which employs parameters of temporal dimensionality and history rather than cognition and 'realism': again, sf and 'realist' fiction have the richer textual spaces available to them. Brooke-Rose usefully contrasts the schemata of Todorov and Suvin:

In Todorov's theory, science fiction is a development of the marvellous. . . . In Suvin's theory, science fiction is opposed, horizontally to realist fiction on the distancing criterion, and, vertically, to the marvellous, the fantastic, and myth, on the cognition and pluritemporality criteria, which *unite* it to realist fiction.[26]

In very large degree, Suvin is the implicit Newton or Lévi-Strauss of contemporary science fiction scholarship. For instance, Jameson's complex and sometimes fashion-conscious contribution owes much to Suvin, as he declares freely.[27] Having articulated the terms within which learned argument has tended to be elaborated, Suvin's contribution has been absorbed so generally that it can seem transparently given – often a sign that a framework is due for drastic deconstruction, if not overthrow.

It might be said, for example, that Suvin's remote and abstract analysis misses the beating heart of sf's appeal to genre consumers. The link to Romantic tropes can be taken as a hint of much he scamps, in his failing, as

John Clute observes, 'to convey the experience of being a character (or an empathetic reader) in an sf world: eschewing, as it does, both nostalgia (for sf is a romance genre) and kinesis (because sf characters want something out of the worlds they inhabit, and act to obtain their desires)'.[28] Clute's characterisation of this oversight is darkly droll: Suvin's diagnosis – 'challengingly useful (though bats)' – is a 'menu for writing like Lem', whose fiction can be notably didactic, even parched.

Gregory Renault, offering a quite different kind of objection, invokes 'narrative strategies'[29] as a bridge between Suvin's model and Delany's. (We'll examine the latter briefly in a moment, returning for closer study in Chapter 5.) For Renault, Suvin's case is weakened once we see, and as he admits, 'that every semantic novum estranges (an insight denied by his basic distinction between naturalist and estranged fiction)' (1980, p. 117). What is more, 'Suvin's assertion of an oscillation between the author/reader's "zero world" and that of the SF novum confuses the crucial political issue of the tension between sign and referent, culture and society' (ibid., p. 118).

The problem with this criticism is the hazard any theory of the fantastic faces which finds its special character in 'difference', if one accepts some version of Jakobson's or Saussure's axiom (as Renault does) that *all* language use is rooted in difference. Clearly what Suvin is drawing attention to is sf's unusual *degree and kind* of difference, as Renault acknowledges, noting that Suvin 'claims that SF alone entails a change in the whole literary universe' (ibid., p. 114). Renault's own observation is implicit, I think, in Suvin's following words:

> Through its specific devices, combined in a unique narrative strategy, an *ensemble des tropes*, SF creates a fictional reality which powerfully enhances this distancing effect.
>
> As a figurative discourse itself estranged from the contemporary social reality signified by mainstream literature, SF is a fiction 'twice removed' from the significations of daily life, a figurative discourse with the imaginative power and potential of 'fiction squared'.
>
> (Suvin, 1979, p. 117)

Suvin's position, which I shall continue to draw upon, does seem to me too narrow, rather in the way Amis's myopic emphasis on the satirical function of sf, for example, occluded any real grasp of its access to the sublime. Yet it is praiseworthy for three features. The first is its historicity: 'All the epistemological, ideological, and narrative implications and correlatives of the novum lead to the conclusion that significant sf is in fact a specifically roundabout way of commenting on an author's collective context. . . . History has not ended with the "post-industrial" society'.[30] The second is its focus not so much on simple novelty, on technological or psychic gee-gaws, as on cognitive breakthrough.

33

The third, and most important, is its understanding that sf's mimesis – the *tactics* of its special narrative functions – subserve an unusual kind of metaphoric *strategy*. Semiotics has developed a useful specialised vocabulary to capture this kind of argument. When applied to the literary text, Terry Eagleton notes, semiotic theory distinguishes

> between the 'paradigmatic' (a whole class of signs which may stand for each other) and the 'syntagmatic' (where signs are coupled together with each other in a 'chain'). . . . Each word in the text is linked by a whole set of formal structures to several other words, and its meaning is thus always 'overdetermined', always the result of several different determinants acting together. . . . Each sign thus participates in several different 'paradigmatic patterns' or systems simultaneously, and this complexity is greatly compounded by the 'syntagmatic' chains of association, the 'lateral' rather than 'vertical' structures, in which signs are placed.[31]

The strategy of estrangement uses one thing as a figure or stand-in for another (as *metaphor* does: 30 Heads of State), which is the mechanism of poetry and allegory. Usually, prose fictions employ a strategy of *metonymy*, based on causality, contiguity, or 'combination' – the syntagm or unfolding word-string – or synecdoche (part standing for whole: 30 head of cattle).[32] The allegorising of sf, however, also differs from most poetry, which is both strategically *and* tactically metaphoric. Sf's special strategy yields a pre-eminent ontological saturation or intensity, of a kind that everyday metonymic narrative can never sustain – and yet it remains anchored in the natural or empirical:

> Probably the most important consequence of an understanding of SF as a symbolic system centered on a novum which is to be cognitively validated within the narrative reality of the tale and its interaction with reader expectations is that the novelty has to be convincingly explained in concrete, even if imaginary, terms, that is, in terms of the *specific* time, place, agents, and cosmic and social totality of each tale. This means that, in principle, SF has to be judged, like most naturalistic or 'realistic' fiction and quite unlike horror fantasy, by the density and richness of objects and agents described in the microcosm of the text.
>
> (Suvin, 1979, p. 80)

NEW WORDS, NEW SENTENCES

To Suvin's model of cognitive distancing, Renault opposes the textualist approach pioneered by Delany in an early pass at doctrines he has subsequently developed through several books of theory and theory-saturated fiction. Delany began by suggesting that

In a simple sense, what science fiction does . . . is to take recognizable syntagms and substitute in them, here and there, signifiers from a till then wholly unexpected paradigm. The occurrence of unusual, if not downright opaque, signifiers in the syntagm *focuses our attention on the structures implied.* . . . This focusing (or rather re-focusing) does not occur in mundane fiction.[33]

At a lexical level, science fiction contains and constantly generates novel terms, which fit into sentences and plots of varying degrees of alterity (Delany, 1978a, p. 256).

Consider how we read or decode a passage from a realistic novel, Robert Stone's contemporary *Outerbridge Reach* (1992), and compare that with reading the début science fiction by David Zindell, *Neverness* (1989). Without a moment's thought, we call on an astonishing amount of detailed knowledge of the known world to understand Stone's opening scene:

> When the last week of February came in mild and spring-scented as April, Browne decided to deliver a boat to Annapolis. He passed under the Verrazano Bridge shortly after dawn on the last Wednesday in February. With Sandy Hook ahead, he cut his auxiliary and hoisted the mainsail and genoa.
>
> (*Outerbridge Reach*, p. 1)

For me, as an Australian, the first remark sounds crazy, since I am used to thinking of April as early autumn, reversed from the Northern Hemisphere. The place names aid orientation, confirming that this is happening in America. The specialised nautical terms (opaque to one who, like me, hasn't a clue what a 'genoa' is) convey authority as well as fact. Above all, the text situates itself within the actual, recent world.

Contrast this with Zindell's very popular *Neverness*:

> My ship did not fall out into the center of the moons. Instead, I segued into a jungle-like decision tree. . . . Each individual ideoplast was lovely and unique. The representation of the fixed-point theorem, for instance, was like a coiled ruby necklace. As I built my proof, the coil joined with feathery, diamond fibres of the first Lavi mapping lemma.
>
> (*Neverness*, p. 66)

These star pilots, the sf-trained reader understands via a many-plied imaginative construction, are taking their ships through windows in hyper-space *by proving mathematical theorems*! How strange! And yet – don't today's pilots do something like that already? Mapping a course, by hand or by computer, is the application of mathematics to the shape of the world. These futuristic pilots happen to be doing it (somehow) *directly*! Feeling these sentences work on you, getting the point, is an audacious and shivery pleasure for those who know that the trick to decoding such sentences is not by way of the conventional dictionary and encyclopaedia. It is true, admittedly, that recognising the fixed-point theorem, which in mathematics governs the transformation of one set of points into an isomorphic set, helps one appreciate a sense of recursion in what is being described/constructed – but it is not crucial.

Hence, what is important for Delany is not the shock of the new but the web of signifieds these terms imply and constitute:

> That inmixing (or intrusion) restructures the web of signifiers that is
> ... the particular signifier's signified; as well, it restructures the web
> of signifiers that is ... that signified below the syntagm itself taken as
> signifier.[... F]or science fiction such inmixing ... works in a
> peculiar, unique, and identifying way.
>
> (Delany, 1978a, p. 257)

For Delany, the concept 'estrangement' is too tame to denote and articulate this radical process. The syntagmatic patterns in which sf is constructed are generally not very different from the grammar of standard fictive discourse. Nor are they simply distanced from 'ordinary writing' in the act of loading them with items from extended paradigm sets (or lists of synonymous words from which the sf writer can choose). Rather, their function is altered in what we might call a strategy-specific fashion, and this is Delany's quarrel with Suvin: that the discourse of estrangement oversimplifies the process, 'belies the complex structures, internal and external, of which the specifically science-fictional sentence is the signifier'. Ultimately, therefore, Delany casts aside the ladder of his original stipulation[34] which 'yields no insight into the structural web those signifiers form around themselves which is, finally, their signified, their meaning' (ibid., p. 260). This line of analysis is surely correct. I am not persuaded, however, that it is inconsistent with Suvin's sense of a textual micro-universe founded in a continuously creative act of distantiation from a given context of organised knowledge about the world (Suvin, 1979, p. 259). Indeed, it seems implicit in it. And because these differences are never gratuitous, that creative activity inevitably constructs an interlocked web or textus.

Renault also finds Delany's account flawed: 'he overlooks the determinate nature of the negation involved in SF syntagms' (Renault, 1980, p. 125). That is, sf's web of signifiers is not freely invented. It always, however unconsciously, kicks against some prick erected by 'the socio-cultural context of advanced capitalism' (ibid.). In a way this is self-evident. Where else could we get our new ideas? On another, it seems depressingly one-dimensional, for surely it is not true that 'the pleasurable shock of "difference" ... we get with the reading of SF signifiers occurs precisely because of the expectation of "similarity" which we bring to the discourse' (ibid.). Granted, for sophisticated readers the difference involved is often from expectations set up in the generic intertext, rather than by the mundane world. A coarse but amusing instance is Frank Herbert's 'raygens' – ray generators – which plays on the exhausted and despised 'rayguns' of an earlier era. Even so, I think readers always hope to find something *sui generis* in the mix.

But should we even be trying to analyse a body of texts, even those as governed by formulae as sf, in terms of a single, simple 'generic code'? Poststructural theories raise important questions about the salience of that programme. Before we turn in detail to Delany's semiotics of science fiction in Chapter 5, we must ask if the notion of sf as a genre needs to be replaced or expanded. I will suggest that it does, in two key respects: first, in Chapter 3, by seeing it as a 'mode' rather than a classical genre, and second, in Chapter 4, by exploring the key notion of a specialised sf 'mega-text'.

3

GENRE OR MODE?

[T]he question is whether genre is a so-called 'primitive', i.e. whether it is basic to the form of a text, or peripheral. . . . We do not, however, learn the 'content' of a game – whatever that could be – and then learn its rules. A game – and likewise a genre – is *constituted* by its rules and the techniques for implementing them.

(Anne Freadman)[1]

Genres, it is widely agreed, are not 'natural kinds' presenting themselves in a self-evident taxonomy. '[C]riticism by genres,' as genre-theorist Paul Hernadi acknowledged around the time structuralism was entering Anglo-American theory, 'has very little in common with the botanist's or the zoologist's unequivocal classification of species.'[2]

This is because, as philosopher Karl Popper argues, 'things may be similar in *different respects*'; 'any two things which are from one point of view similar may be dissimilar from another point of view'.[3] Likewise, any text may be reread in any brilliantly fresh or outlandish way by a suitable reframing. Nor can any reading ever be 'transparent', even the most apparently self-evident. As Jonathan Culler notes, even at the level of phoneme and rhythm choice 'we have all had the experience of seeing a text illuminated by patterns and echoes we had not previously noticed but which, once pointed out to us, seem thoroughly compelling'.[4]

Yet Hernadi's immediate qualification of his admission is no less compelling in its challenge: 'Popper's concept of similarity cannot fully explain why a rather small number of basic genres have prevailed, with important modifications to be sure, throughout the recorded history of literary criticism' (1972, pp. 4–5). Hernadi's search through this history leads him to less than a handful of major variants. '[T]actful critics,' he observes, 'can focus on any kind of generic similarity without losing sight of the limitations inherent in their preferred approach' (ibid., p. 7). Literary theory has provided several synoptic accounts of genre (such as those advanced by Douwe Fokkema and Robert Scholes)[5] which contest the typical poststructuralist disruption of coding protocols, the kind found in Roland Barthes's famous, endlessly elaborate study of a Balzac story, *S/Z*. (1974).

38

GENRE REGARDED AS A GAME OF TENNIS

The solution may be to accept genre less as a classificatory or 'essential' set of pigeon-holes and more as an analytic device for understanding the *moves* in the game of writing and reading, as negotiations in a social institution regulating the terms of the contract between reader and text. The semiotician Anne Freadman has proposed that

> the genre – the game of the text – is constituted by its ceremonial place, and this is appropriated by the full range of semiotic systems available as strategies or enablement conditions to that genre. . . .
>
> Knowing a genre is also knowing how to take it up: the manners are reciprocal. What do you *do* with a form, if you've never been taught to fill one out? . . . Using a text is primarily a matter of understanding its genre and the way it plays it – recognising it, certainly, but also reading its tactics, its strategies, and its ceremonial place.
>
> (Freadman, 1987, p. 120)

Frank Cioffi, for instance, admits that the formulae he identifies in the emerging sf corpus (Chapter 2) are not adequate to deal with most recent generic hybrids. He would agree with Jameson that

> we need the specification of the individual 'genres' today more than ever, not in order to drop specimens into the box bearing those labels, but rather to map our coordinates on the basis of those fixed stars and to triangulate this specific given textual movement.
>
> (Jameson, 1982b, p. 322)

Jameson's comment is from an enthusiastic review of a brief, concentrated survey of the sf field by Patrick Parrinder. That 1980 study 'triangulated' sf by reference to four grand generic species: romance, fable, epic, and the postmodern intertextual, construing this last as a sort of genre. Parrinder noted the dichotomisation of genre theory into taxonomic classification versus semiological coding. The first is a Todorovian 'pursuit in which *a priori* classifications are elaborated on purely logical grounds', the second a Barthesian approach, 'which views a literary genre as being constituted by a series of linguistic practices so that genre criticism may be reduced to a branch of semiotics'.[6] Parrinder urged that 'generic considerations . . . should come *before* any full-scale attempt to compile a "narratology" of science fiction' (1980, p. xviii). Neither approach has the merit I have granted to Cioffi's account, of taking historical context seriously, although Cioffi's history very often seems a straitjacket binding those who live it.

Parrinder's position is at variance both with Cioffi's and with a celebrated 'popular culture' estimate by John Cawelti, which conflates genre and formulae. Cawelti's model allows fiction to interact with its cultural matrix only conservatively: confirming conventions, resolving ambiguities, allowing controlled access to the tabooed, and reconciling new with old.[7] 'There is no place in such a scheme for genuine innovation,' Parrinder notes (ibid., p. 44). He insists that while genre is by definition a literary form governed by convention, sf is crucially a machine for thinking (p. 42). In a passage which might better be directed to Cioffi than to Cawelti, who pays little enough attention to sf in his study, Parrinder observes:

> The whole notion of a literature of ideas suggests a reader who, far from being invisibly manipulated, may be provoked into arriving at his own assessment of the arguments contained in the story. Fiction which has this effect cannot be viewed as merely diverting the audience with well-proven formulas. . . . Here we are not confronted by a 'mass medium' effect but by literature which makes a rather special appeal to a self-selected audience. [. . . I]f we wish to understand this genre we must consider it, not as a formulaic 'subliterature', but as an autonomous mode of writing with a history and traditions at variance with, and partly suppressed by, the dominant literary forms.
>
> (ibid., pp. 45, 47)

This valorising portrait draws upon Marc Angenot's claim that paraliteratures are 'literature's dialectical opposite [. . . and] bearer of the latent dreams, aspirations, and perceptions which it excludes' (p. 46).[8] Angenot in turn is employing a version of the Marxist criticism of Lucien Goldmann, which staged last century's popular romance, with its heroic men of action, as a dialectical contrary to high realism. Goldmann saw the latter as a fundamentally disenchanted and debunking mode of narrative, if ultimately an ideologically confirmatory one. Parrinder seeks to resolve the incompatibility between sf's clearly formulaic status and its condition as a poetics of ideas and novelty by insisting, finally, upon the specificity of 'particular texts and groups of texts', to be addressed 'by the methods of literary criticism' rather than by those of reductive sociologies (p. 47).

The immediate result is a suggestion that we construe sf in the first instance – as Wells did, after all – as a mutation of romance, the genre *par excellence* marked by its readers' hunger for pleasurable repetition. But Parrinder is not content to leave the matter there. Sf, on his account, operates also in the shadow of fable, the literature of knowledge and power (p. 87), and epic, a cognitive form linked with the dimension of history and change (p. 90).

Above all, science fiction textuality escapes the truly formulaic in its capacity – indeed, its dynamic need – for linguistic play and innovation. Angenot stresses that sf's lexicon constitutes a body of novel signifiers lacking actual signifieds outside their intertextual 'absent paradigms' (p. 113), using *paradigm* here in the linguistic rather than Kuhnian history-of-science sense to mean a list of interchangeable words with a common real-world reference.[9] Sf uses 'fictive words' of this kind plus innovative structures of playful parody and satire (pp. 115 ff.). Parrinder is typical of recent critics –

especially, as we have seen, Delany – in locating sf's special qualities here in rhetorical space.

If this case is accepted, as I think it must be, then the genre model, while illuminating in certain respects, proves finally too limited to deal effectively with sf's deformations of the linguistic and cognitive practices constituting both canonical literary and traditional paraliterary texts. Parrinder's call for close reading of individual texts and groups of associated texts has been echoed by Fredric Jameson's declaration that 'the generic effort to define SF or to characterise its specificity' strikes him as 'tiresome in a way which makes me wonder whether this line of inquiry is worth pursuing any longer'.[10] In a passage which seems to me a harbinger of sf criticism at the close of this century, Jameson speaks of

> the shift from a more static semiotic theory of the genre to what I have called a more poststructuralist framing of SF texts which tends, whatever the theoretical references – psychoanalysis, deconstruction, power, schizoanalysis, the simulacrum – to stage them in terms of the historical originality of our moment in our 'system'. This perspective obviously involves a shift away from the consideration of what all 'generic' SF texts have in common towards a more 'symptomal' attention to what certain heightened textual configurations show us about the contemporary conjuncture, and in particular about our own world of images and simulacra.
>
> (Jameson, 1987a, p. 242)

So while there remain benefits in parsing the acts of writing and reading into their notional components, as we shall continue to do, we need to keep in mind that this anatomisation can never be successful as pure reduction to simple unambiguous elements, that a moment of reconstitution is the goal of theory. Even if that moment, in turn, is always open to further deconstruction.

THE PERSUASIONS OF RHETORIC

Until quite recently, attempts at demarcation and definition of science fiction as a genre focused on sf's distinctive themes, formulae and tropes – imaginary science, superhuman abilities, extraterrestrial or apocalyptic *mises-en-scène*, time travel, robots, etc. – or its 'thought-experiment' strategies, marked by anthologist Judith Merril's advocacy of Heinlein's term 'speculative fiction'.[11] Against this tendency, Brian W. Aldiss has proposed that

> One of the difficulties of defining sf springs from the fact that it is not a genre as such, just as the absurd category 'Non-fiction' is not a genre. Taking my cue from Rosemary Jackson, I suggest that our problems in the area of definition will be lightened if we think of sf as a mode. Jackson says, 'It is perhaps more helpful to define the fantastic as a

literary *mode* rather than a genre, and to place it between the opposite modes of the marvellous and the mimetic.'[12]

Even so, Aldiss and his co-author Wingrove continue by and large to employ the customary term 'genre', and not just for convenience: 'The difficulty – the infinitude of SF – lies in the obdurate fact that it is both formulaic and something more than a genre. It is a mode which easily falls back into genre' (1986, p. 14).[13]

A TRANS-HISTORICAL TEMPTATION

Jackson herself – 'The term "mode" is being employed here to identify structural features underlying various works in different periods of time'[14] – derived her model from Fredric Jameson, who in his discussion of 'magical narrative' remarked:

> For when we speak of a mode, what can we mean but that this particular type of literary discourse is not bound to the conventions of a given age, nor indissolubly linked to a given type of verbal artifact, but rather persists as a temptation and a mode of expression across a whole range of historical periods, seeming to offer itself, if only intermittently, as a formal possibility which can be revived and renewed.[15]

This analysis of mode might suggest an ahistorical approach, although this is hardly likely in a model advanced by Jameson, who begins his principal opus 'Always historicize!'[16] Jackson repudiates such a reading in advance:

> Like any other text, a literary fantasy is produced within, and deter-mined by, its social context. Though it might struggle against the limits of this context . . . *it cannot be understood in isolation from it....* Recognition of these forces involves placing authors in relation to historical, social, economic, political and sexual determinants.
>
> (Jackson, 1981, p. 3; my italics)

Granted, it is not clear that this admission is fully consonant with her avowal that a range of different fantastic works 'have similar structural characteristics' and 'seem to be generated by similar unconscious desires' (p. 8). In any event, Jackson's fundamental model is useful:

> [F]antasy is a literary mode from which a number of related modes emerge . . . in different historical situations [. . . . T]he basic model of fantasy could be seen as a language, or *langue*, from which its various forms, or *paroles*, derive. Out of this mode develops romance literature or 'the marvellous' (including fairy tales and science fiction), 'fantastic' literature (including stories by Poe . . . Kafka, H. P. Lovecraft) and related tales of abnormal psychic states, delusion, hallucination, etc.
>
> (ibid., p. 7)

James Gunn, an sf writer as well as a literary academic, looks past the purely ideational toward textual strategies peculiar to sf. The reason sf is 'not an ordinary kind of genre' is because 'it has no typical action or place'.[17] Incorporative of other genres, it is a mode, although Gunn does not put it this way; he terms it a 'super-genre' (Gunn, n.d., p. 9). That mode yields a 'literature of discontinuity' (p. 4), founded in a break with the quotidian that marks either *change* (sf) or *difference* (fantasy). 'The reason we should make a distinction between fantasy and science fiction is that we read them differently, and we misread them if we apply the reading protocols of one to the other' (p. 9). Borderline cases may be distinguished by judging 'whether we get more out of the works by subjecting them to hard questions', to 'intellectual scrutiny' (ibid.). Sf, needless to say, is what answers better to hard questions.

Ursula Le Guin is considerably less positivistic:

All fiction is metaphor. . . . What sets [sf] apart from older forms of fiction seems to be its use of new metaphors, drawn from certain great dominants of our contemporary life – science, all the sciences, and technology, and the relativistic and the historical outlook, among them. Space travel is one of these metaphors; so is an alternative society, an alternative biology; the future is another. The future, in fiction, is a metaphor.

(Le Guin, 1982, p. 149)

Metaphor, yes, but for what? and why? Fredric Jameson has little doubt:

I would [base] the necessity of ideological analysis on the very nature of SF itself: for me it is only incidentally about science or technology, and even more incidentally about unusual psychic states. It seems to me that *SF is in its very nature a symbolic meditation on history itself*, comparable in its emergence as a new genre to the birth of the historical novel around the time of the French Revolution. . . . If this is the case, then, surely we have as readers not been equal to the capacity of the form itself until we have resituated SF into that vision of the relationship of man to social and political and economic forces which is its historical element.[18]

In its science fictional varieties, this modality systematically manipulates or deforms aspects of the industrial *episteme*'s categories of experience and 'reality construction'. These can be analysed within a multiplicity of contesting frameworks derived from Kant, positivism, Marxism, psychoanalysis, feminism, Foucault, Derrida or otherwise. Analytical parameters might range from noumena and phenomena to pleroma and creatura, from space and time to historical determinants, power, gender, work, etc. The sf mode performs these narrative manipulations in the interests of imaginative gratification, which can range from infantile fantasies of omnipotence and other regressive satisfactions or displacements, through an array of ideological mystifications, to the adult desire to open our hearts and minds alike as generously as possible.

Sf's modality uses characteristic narrative tropes, conventions and enabling devices. These usually preserve within each text a stabilised though variant world worked out in some detail. There is a premium on consistency and the experience of normality within the postulated frame. Individual actors are often backgrounded, while in the foreground loom striking features of environment or novel subject-position/s.

As we have seen, Fredric Jameson has posed science fiction's claims within an elaborate framework of literary and ideological analysis. In Part II we shall examine his reading of the postmodern.[19] It is worth noting two highly charged moments in his intellectual trajectory for their relevance to sf criticism. He has regularly addressed a variety of topics no less appropriate to sf criticism than to the literary canon – utopia as a locus of figuration,[20] 'generic discontinuity',[21] structural oppositions mappable on the Greimas semantic diagram,[22] simulacra, and so on.

DRAWING FROM LIFE

In an early paper entitled 'Metacommentary', almost his manifesto, Jameson instantiated his subtle Marxist programme with a bravura account of certain mass-media sf tropes. By contrast, his recent introduction to a volume of reprinted essays stages the act of critical readership in terms astonishingly salient to the project of a mature science fiction-cum-postmodernism.

The former spring from Sontag's much-admired essay 'The Imagination of Disaster' (1965; in Sontag, 1967) on B-grade sf movies. Jameson's impulse is unashamedly hermeneutical: the vocation of metacommentary is interrogation of the disguised, though not now the Freudian sexual wish but rather the repressed of the *political* unconscious, the hidden realities of our ideological construction and its daily enactment. We are reminded that however removed from the everyday an act of artistry (or even exploitative entertainment) might seem, its message 'may very loosely be described as a type of ... lived experience of some sort, no matter how minimal or specialised. The essential characteristic of such raw material or latent content is that it is ... already meaningful from the outset, being ... the very components of our concrete social life: words, thoughts, objects, desires, people, places, activities' (Jameson, 1988b, p. 14).

Sontag had suggested that sf's tropes of catastrophe enacted in displaced form narratives of psychic anxiety, viewed in psychoanalytic terms. Yes, but 'what if those terms were themselves but a disguise, but the "manifest content" that served to mask and distract us from some more basic satisfaction at work in the form?' (ibid.). Specifically, the fantasy of 'the mystique of the scientist'.

[U]ltimately none of this has anything to do with science itself but is simply a distorted reflection of 1950s male feelings and dreams about *work*, alienated and nonalienated: it is a wish fulfilment . . . of a peculiar type . . . for we do not deal here with the kind of direct and open psychic identification and wish fulfilment that might be illustrated . . . through the works of C. P. Snow, for instance. Rather, this is a symbolic gratifi- cation that wishes to conceal its own presence: the identification with the scientist is not here the mainspring of the plot, but rather its precondition only, and it is as though, in a rather Kantian way, this symbolic gratifi- cation attached itself, not to the events of the story, but to that framework (the universe of science, the splitting of the atom, the astronomer's gaze into outer space, and also, no doubt, some patriarchal guild system) without which the story could not have come into being in the first place.

(ibid., p. 15)

Even so lengthy a citation can hardly satisfy my wish to capture the complexity of Jameson's reading of an important sf mechanism, which in turn is the merest sketch of his developing though fragmented account built up over the ensuing couple of decades. More appropriate, due to its potential for providing a historical/scientific frame for the transcoding urged by Jameson, is the following polemical rallying-call. Perhaps its light spills from the same arc lamp out of which Brian Aldiss projected his magisterial Helliconia saga. It is as vivid and teleological, despite his express repudiation of *telos*, as Bernard Shaw's discredited Bergsonian vitalism. Jameson embraces what Jean-François Lyotard, propagandist of the *après*-revolutionary postmodern condition,[23] has dubbed 'the desire for Marx':

The time of individual human biology is radically incommensurable with the time of nature or the time of social history (or indeed, in capitalism, the time of the great economic cycles); nor is this some easily adjustable matter of *durées*, but rather a vision of interlocking, yet somehow also alternate, worlds, in which beings of brief life spans are also the components of enormous and properly unimaginable totalities which develop according to vast and inhuman rhythms, and in a different temporality altogether. . . . The 'desire called Marx', then, is not the will to reduce one of these dimensions to the other . . . but rather the effort to develop organs of perception capable of enabling us fitfully to position ourselves in that other temporality, that other story, over which we also hope – but now as groups and collectives, rather than as individuals – to assert some influence and control. The 'desire for Marx' can therefore also be called a desire for *narrative*, if by this we understand, not some vacuous concept of 'linearity' or even *telos*, but rather the impossible attempt to give representation to the multiple and incommensurable temporalities in which each of us exists.

(Jameson, 1988b, p. xxviii)

45

New organs of perception! Incommensurable temporalities! And spatial-
ities also, no doubt, when we recall the seductive if baffling hyperspaces of
postmodern architecture discerned by Jameson in contemporary architecture,
where the same biological/perceptual fantasia is projected: 'we do not yet
possess the perceptual equipment to match this new hyperspace. . . . The new
architecture, therefore . . . stands as something like an imperative to grow
new organs, to expand our sensorium and our body to some new, as yet
unimaginable, perhaps ultimately impossible, dimensions' (Jameson, 1984,
p. 80). It is even tempting to postulate here an echo from Jameson's sf
reading, of a classic sf story from 1953. In Damon Knight's 'Four in One'
the luckless but far from disconcerted scientist George Meister is absorbed
alive with three companions by an alien, and becomes the creature's
enhanced brain:

> he was sitting squarely in the middle of the most powerful research tool
> that had ever existed in his field: a protean organism, with the observer
> inside it, able to order its structure and watch the results; able to devise
> theories of function and test them on the tissues of what was effectively
> his own body – able to construct new organs, new adaptations to
> environment!
>
> (Knight, 1953, in Silverberg, 1988, p. 46)

This is precisely the ambition of that moiety of science fiction which is not
merely market fodder. It is fascinating therefore that one of Jameson's sf
readings is of Vonda McIntyre's superior space opera *The Exile Waiting*,
which he construes, entirely consistently, as an instance of a 'spatial genre':
'all SF of the more "classical" type is "about" containment, closure, the
dialectic of inside and outside'. He adds that the move

> from 'individual' SF to great SF epic histories of a new type is less a
> matter of the extrapolation of forms of individual destiny onto col-
> lective history (where 'peoples' or 'races' or 'species' would also be
> seen as knowing success or failure, etc.) than that of a planet, a climate,
> a weather, and a system of landscape – in short, a map. We thus need
> to explore the proposition that the distinctiveness of SF as a genre has
> less to do with time (history, past, future) than with space.
>
> (Jameson, 1987b, p. 58)

This is rather a leap from his earlier claim that 'SF is in its very nature a
symbolic meditation on history itself'. Under either interpretation, we may
locate the insight that science fiction is a narrative kind which importantly
foregrounds its schemata, maps that serve as territories. Sf offers maps
aplenty, not simply in the traditional cartographic sense of spatial plots, but
temporal mappings as well. The heroic and anti-heroic dynasties of the *Dune*
sequence are as crucial as its ecological flows and gradients. And on a
paradoxical metalevel, the strange loops of time-travel stories are maps which

seem designed to defeat, delightfully, the notion of mapping, as postmodern narratives seem designed to defeat determinacy.

A LITERATURE OF METAPHOR

We have examined, if only briefly, a substantial cross-section of current approaches to science fiction as a narrative mode or form, a practice, a problematic. Might this barrage of attempted definition, opinion, argument, speculation and schematisation be summarised and brought into focus? In a scholarly but elegant and confessedly enthusiastic essay, Peter Nicholls has identified a number of the most salient (and, to the sf aficionado, flattering) features which distinguish sf texts from more earthbound writings. He, too, stresses its enhanced analogical character:

> [I]t is the great modern literature of metaphor. Conventional literature has a limit, set by everyday realism, to the juxtapositions of imagery it can allow itself. Science fiction, which can create its own worlds, has access to new juxtapositions. . . . It is able to incorporate intellectually *shocking* material, partly because it is so pre-eminently the literature of change, as opposed to mainstream literature, which is the literature of human continuity [. . . . It] is the literature of the outsider, in the extreme sense. Traditional realist fiction observes its action from the viewpoint of a partaker. It shares the illusions of the society which produces it. So does all fiction, but it is science fiction which makes the conscious effort, sometimes quite successful, to stand outside [. . . . It] is pre-eminently the modern literature not of physics, but of metaphysics. It is in science fiction that we are now asking the deepest questions of meaning and causation.[24]

Perhaps we find here the answer, in capsule, to that severe refusal of the baroque metaphor expressed above so poignantly by Philip Larkin: 'I like to read about people who have done nothing spectacular.' The social world we inhabit in the twentieth century – especially at this its close, the close indeed of a millennium which, in its turning, figures 'the future' with all the terror and delight of discontinuity – is a world in profound internal rupture. Like the heat which drives the crustal plates across the globe, science works invisibly and ineluctably, brought to awareness for most of us only in abrupt quakes or vulcanisms. Even those people who live modestly, eschewing the spectacular, are participants in epistemic rift. Science fiction, Delany remarks,

> is no more a collection of themes than it is a collection of rhetorical devices. . . . It is a set of questions we expect to be answered about the relation of word and world, character and concept, fictive world and given world; and any given SF text can foil or fulfil those expectations in an infinite number of ways. [25]

47

It is perfectly possible, then, that the metaphors of science fiction, and the intertextually naturalised metonymic syntagms which link them in a sublime if sometimes infantile violence of proleptic imagery, are, in this moment of postmodernity, the privileged, pre-eminent mode of capture for such an epoch. To test that rather immoderate suggestion, we need to look at some of the innovative ways in which sf has learned to figure the new, the shocking, the *other*, and at the interlocking web of fictive worlds it has constructed in rhetorical space: what we shall call its 'mega-text'.

4

THE USES OF OTHERNESS

I have been wondering what it is about science fiction that so attracts its readers and writers. . . . I have been reading the stuff for thirty years, and writing it for twenty, until now it bores me almost to the point of insanity, and yet I can't leave it alone, and I really don't want to.

(William Atheling Jr [James Blish], 1960)[1]

It's not just physical laws that science fiction readers want to escape. Just as commonly, they want to escape human nature. In pursuit of this, sf offers comforting alternatives to the real world. For instance, if you start reading an sf story about some abused wimp, you can be pretty sure that by chapter two he's going to discover he has secret powers unavailable to those tormenting him, and by the end of the book, he's going to save the universe. . . . Having been an sf user myself, however, I have to say that, living in a world of cruelty, immersed in a culture that grinds people into fish meal like some brutal machine, with histories of destruction stretching behind us back to the Pleistocene, I find it hard to sneer at the desire to escape. Even if escape is delusion.

(John Kessel)[2]

To summarise the conclusions we have reached thus far about sf's inventions: unlike nearly all other literary projects, they are at once radically distanced or estranged from any collaborative effort of world construction outside their own modal intertext, yet they are carefully mimetic in address, and explicitly centred on systems of knowledge.

The function of estrangement in sf is thus not identical with the kinds found in certain other textual strategies, though it is related to them. With Roland Barthes, for example, we can value history 'for the strangeness of other epochs and what they can teach us about the present. . . . History is interesting and valuable precisely for its otherness'.[3] It is an ambiguous project, of course:

We need to develop the historical sense . . . into a real sensual delight. When our theatres perform plays of other periods they like to annihilate

49

distance, fill in the gap, gloss over the differences. But what comes then of our delight in comparisons, in distance, in dissimilarity – which is at the same time a delight in what is close and proper to ourselves?

(Bertolt Brecht)[4]

REALLY STRANGE BEDFELLOWS

Literal history, no matter how imaginatively rendered, cannot exceed its boundaries. Sf *may* enter into the truly other, as it does increasingly in repositing sexuality. It does so in Delany's fiction, for instance, especially his *Stars in My Pocket Like Grains of Sand*, to be discussed in Chapter 11. Speculative fiction ventures to perform rather than analyse the transgression surmised as a future possibility by Jacques Derrida:

> [Were we to approach] the area of a relationship to the other where the code of sexual marks would no longer be discriminating [. . . that relationship] would not be a-sexual, far from it, but would be sexual otherwise: beyond the binary difference that governs the decorum of all codes, beyond the opposition feminine/masculine, beyond homo-sexuality and heterosexuality which come to the same thing . . . this mobile of non-identified sexual marks whose choreography can carry, divide, multiply the body of each 'individual', whether he be classified as 'man' or 'woman' according to the criteria of usage.[5]

Yet even this rupture in the varieties of sexuality permitted in human cultures throughout history is modest compared with possibilities rehearsed in sf. Consider the sexual dealings imagined by John Varley in his Gaea trilogy,[6] where a moon-sized intelligent entity, almost a deity, constitutes an ecological environment for an entire creation of her own devising. Many of her aesthetic conceits, built into the living landscape, are drawn from human television programmes in the kitschest taste.

Humans find within Gaea a pre-Lapsarian species of 'Titanides': honour-able, strong, loving, similar in form to huge centaurs. The human torsos of all Titanides are at first glance massively female, although unlike the Greek original each has either male or female frontal human genitalia. As well, each has both male and female equine genitalia. The reproductive antics of these creatures are extraordinarily flexible and various. Twenty-nine distinct 'sexual ensembles', modelled on musical notation, permit conception, implantation of the egg, and bearing of the young by any of three partners. Humans are not cross-fertile with Titanides, but the possibility of sexual expression of inter-species love has been built in:

> Valiha was not like a human woman. . . . Her frontal vagina fitted him within lubricious tolerances too close to be the result of cosmic happenstance. . . . She was completely human – on a large scale – in

50

the caress of her hands, the mass of her breasts, the taste of her skin and her mouth and her clitoris. And she was at the same time wildly alien in her bulging knees, in the smooth, hard muscles of her back, hips, and thighs, and in the imposing slither of her penis as it emerged moist from its sheath. . . .

He was at first reluctant to admit the presence of most of her body. . . . Valiha led him gently to experience the surprising possibilities of her other two-thirds. [. . . S]he was an androgyne – though gynandroid was the closer of two words never meant to cover Titanides. Chris had never been homosexual. Valiha made him see that it meant nothing when making love with her. She was all things, and it made no difference that her anterior organs were so huge. He had always known that coitus was only a small part of making love.

(Wizard, pp. 298–9)

Does sf, then, above all else, write the narrative of the other/s? If this suggestion is taken in a spirit of description (though hardly of definition), a negating and demystifying alternative is instantly inscribed in its logical shadow: that sf writes, rather, the narrative of the *same, as* other.

Gregory Renault locates this co-opting move at the core of Darko Suvin's model: 'The claim is that naturalist fiction portrays the Same (author's empirical environment) by the Same ("exact recreation"), while estranged fiction portrays the Same by the Other' (1980, p. 115). But any act of signification 'selects from available potential signifiers. The strictest attempt at representation is therefore always an interpretation, an artistically mediated re-presentation or re-construction of "the real" (itself signifier as well as signified)' (ibid., p. 116). Sf's special character must therefore be in part to extend the range of potential signifiers. Citing Stableford, Renault observes that sf is reliant on 'an ever-changing supply of images which "gradually change so as always to appear novel while never becoming truly strange"' (ibid., p. 136).

PRETENDING TO SHOCK

Sf's amusing or shocking distortions and defamiliarisations of the present consensus world can be merely random, catch-penny. As Kim Stanley Robinson notes: 'when this is done regularly, as it was during the 1930s, then the distortions are meaningless individually, and cumulatively they tend to reinforce the assumptions and values of the dominant culture of our time, for assumptions and values survive this sort of distortion and are presented as existing unchanged, thousands of years into the future.'[7] Brian Aldiss has dubbed comforting post-holocaust adventures 'cosy catastrophes'. Extending that coinage, I once borrowed the Russian formalist Viktor Shklovsky's pre-Brechtian notion of alienation to name the 'mild aversive electric tingle' which brings bored sf readers, like laboratory rats, 'contentedly to the paperback shelves for a buzz of what we might term *cosy ostranenie*.'[8]

Unsympathetic commentators have regularly advanced this general point with a killing flourish, evidently in the belief that sf criticism has never thought of it. Gerald Graff, in his assault on poststructuralist and post-modernist trends in fiction and theory, is unmistakably of this view:

> Might not the effect of radical disorientation and cognitive estrange-ment be to confuse or disarm critical intelligence rather than to focus it? The question is never asked. . . .
>
> It does not follow that such a work induces its audience to see things more critically. [Estrangement effects] discovered by recent critics in the conventions of science fiction may result in a dulling of the audience's sense of reality, in shell-shocked acceptance rather than critical intransigence. The 'models for the future' celebrated by Scholes and other critics of science fiction may stimulate escapist fantasies rather than critical thinking – all the more probably if these models are inserted into an already uncritical, fad-worshipping mass culture. . . . Whether fantasy makes us more critical or merely more solipsistic and self-indulgent depends finally on whether it is accountable to something that is not fantasy.[9]

Graff's critique is not without force, the more so today as paperback racks replace traditional sf with an endless succession of 1500-page Tolkienesque or military trilogies and worse. He is quite wrong, however, in supposing that 'the question is never asked'. Suvin himself, for example, has summarised this aporia nicely:

> SF can be grasped as a genre in an unstable equilibrium or dynamic compromise between two factors. The first is its cognitive – philo-sophical and political – potentiality as a genre that grows out of the subversive, lower-class form of 'inverted world', within the horizons of knowledge and liberation. The second is a cluster of powerful upper and middle-class ideologies that has, in the great majority of texts, sterilized such potential horizons by contaminating them with mystifi-cations which preclude significant presentations of truly *other* relation-ships, with the horizons of power and repression.[10]

Vulgar manifestations of the sf mode are even more one-sided than this portrait of a narrative field struggling with internal tensions and antinomies might suggest. 'Sci fi' – which insider critics sardonically pronounce 'skiffy', like a toy or a breakfast cereal – is now more common than sf, for an opportunistic market has forced a return to the 1930s. A bad-tempered outburst by Aldiss is poignant:

The love of art and science I developed as a child was a rebellion against the smug bourgeois society in which I found myself. Art and Science were what *They* hated most. In this way, I reinforced the solitude I felt. This also: I merely wished to *épater* society, not overthrow it; the satirist needs his target. . . . During the 70's and 80's, sf has become widely popular, widely disseminated. Its sting has been removed. The awful victories of *The Lord of the Rings*, *Star Trek*, and *Star Wars* have brought – well, not actually respectability, but Instant Whip formulas to sf. The product is blander. It has to be immediately acceptable to many palates, most of them prepubertal . . . The nutritive content has been fixed to suit mass taste. Now the world, or the solar system, or the universe, or the Lord Almighty, has to be saved by a group of four or five people which includes a Peter Pan figure, a girl of noble birth, and a moron of some kind . . . In the old days, we used to destroy the world, and it only took one mad scientist. SF was an act of defiance, a literature of subversion, not whimsy.

(Aldiss, 1985b, pp. 108–9)

SF AND SUBVERSION

But ought sf to be subversive, rather than, say, bracingly uncomfortable? Subversive of what? Our political certitudes, our easy acceptance of current scientific and artistic paradigms? Ursula Le Guin's recent limp declaration does not inspire confident images of the barricades: 'My goal has always been to subvert as much as possible without hurting anybody's feelings.'[11] Still, the question seems perverse. After all, is not science fiction automatically the text of change, of unnerving prediction?

But as its 'prophetic' writers never tire of reminding us, sf is *not* prediction. In 'The Predictions of Science Fiction',[12] Isaac Asimov confessed, 'Actually, there is very little in the vast output of science fiction, year after year, which comes true, or which is ever likely to come true' (1983, p. 81). Listing some of his own most celebrated tropes, he added, 'I don't consider that any of these have predictive value; they weren't intended for that. I was just trying to write entertaining stories about the might-be, not at all necessarily about the would-be' (ibid., p. 84).

How could sf be predictive? On the effective case argued by Popper, the main reason for the future's cloudiness is the absolute unpredictability of scientific research itself. Who can tell what will emerge next from the lab? Moderate temperature superconductors were the major discontinuities of late-1980s technology. In fictional form they had long been the basis of 'hard-sf' from such specialists as Larry Niven, playing a pivotal plot role in his 'Known Worlds' sequence, especially the two books set on the Ringworld. For decades it seemed they were pure fantasy. Physics had no place for them. Abruptly physics as well as technology underwent an expansion as a result of these empirical findings, and we live in a slightly altered world of unknowable, though not unimaginable, consequences.

The best that sf can hope to provide us in the way of 'prophecy', if this line of thought is persuasive, is a scatter of possible futures or alternative life-worlds. Many narrative components of those alternatives that have become accepted as part of the common grammar and lexicon of sf writers seem plainly impossible in the real world – and not just empirically but logically impossible, or so our powerful and repeatedly corroborated paradigms insist. Transportation faster than light and travel back into the past both violate causality and relativity, and are shunned by science. Paranormal powers of communication and effectivity – reading minds, levitation, and other 'wild talents' – have at times been staples of sf storytelling.

These tropes are sometimes enabling devices. Superluminal travel allows tales of interstellar commerce and war. Sometimes they are metaphors of enhanced or decentred subjectivity, and of power or invasion. They are rarely offered as serious possibilities in the real world, outside the text. Fortunately, L. Ron Hubbard and A. E. van Vogt were unusual in turning a number of these fanciful idioms into 'dianetic' truth-claims about reality. On the other hand, research parapsychology continues to find a rather uncertain home at some universities, including Princeton and Edinburgh, and may yet provide a paradigm challenge of significant proportions.[13]

Leaving aside these suspect or counterfactual devices, sf is not theoretically or practically subversive in any obvious way. It is hardly even innovative (though, yes, Heinlein did invent the waterbed . . .). This does not diminish sf's role as a sort of cognitive shoehorn for the young. In a popular treatment of 'the new physics', Professor Paul Davies and Dr John Gribbin contrive a 'Confessions of a Relativist'. This working scientist recalls his difficulties in 'visualising' advanced scientific concepts.[14] The pragmatic method permits a scientist to manipulate equations and get appropriate answers, even when she deals with infinite dimensions. But how can we get a *feeling* for what curved higher-dimensional space, and dilated time, *mean*?

> In the end, my taste for science fiction helped me over these difficulties. By reading fiction you get used to picturing yourself in the place of the characters, seeing an unfamiliar world through their eyes, sharing their experiences. Even when reading about the impossible, you can still *imagine* what it would be like for certain things to happen.
>
> (Davies and Gribbin, 1991, p. 98)

Is this a scandalous confession from two accredited research scientists? Not any longer. One has become accustomed to learning that many significant theoreticians – Stephen Hawking is only the most notable – doted on sf in their precocious youth.[15] If anything, though, today's sf tends rather to borrow the speculations of these contemporary scientists. Indeed, those speculations often reach the lay public more swiftly via readable, sense-of-wonder-inducing popularisations written by articulate scientific practitioners such as Gribbin and Davies, or keen-eyed journalists like Dennis Overbye and Kitty Ferguson. The very idea of alternative or parallel universes, one of the prime instances of an sf trope rarely found in other narratives, is probably a vulgarised adoption from early quantum mechanics of superposition of states in the state vector.[16]

Yet significantly, conservative images of tomorrow tend to be valid only in the short term. In the longer term, they run foul of the prodigality of the universe and of human ingenuity and political inventiveness. This is especially true when the 'sciences' invoked are those of the humane (often the ideologically inculcatory) disciplines: psychology, economics, politics. It is precisely here that the greatest aperture is available for science fiction to subvert established values, which is to say, values legitimised by power and 'common sense' and operating to the benefit of sectional interests.

FEMINIST FUTURES

Isaac Asimov has argued, for example, that feminist aspirations, at least towards simple justice and equality, must be met perforce if we are to survive in this world created by the activities of science. The human world is breeding itself exponentially into devastation. Women will stop having too many children, on Asimov's analysis, only when they have free access to 'the traditional life of the man (outward-facing on the community and the world)'.[17] Until then biology will be perceived inevitably as destiny, a destiny which will drown us in human infants. While this argument is steeped in its own brand of sexism, it is the kind of liberal humanist or 'rationalist' thinking which sf might have been devised specifically to enact in the palatable shape of amusing or entertainingly frightening tales, rather than through hectic soapboxing or clinical postulation.

Sexual politics is, arguably, the most important and embattled form of struggle for freedom that humans have ever engaged in, more fundamental even than liberation from oppressions of class or race precisely because of its universality, its location at the source of those psychic and discursive processes which create and shape subjectivity. It is easy to see why sf is a natural arena for the vivid expression of sexual politics' hopes and fears, and the subversion of a patriarchal, heterosexist status quo. Sf's stock devices are, in the way of things, no less patriarchal than the rest of our cultural and ideological trappings. Nevertheless, they constitute a mechanism for exploring and questioning the ways in which 'woman' and 'man' are literally, and literarily, constructed within society. Science fiction's 'glorious eclecticism,' notes the feminist critic Sarah Lefanu, 'with its mingling of the rational discourse of science with the pre-rational language of the unconscious – for SF borrows from horror, mythology and fairy tale – offers a means of exploring the myriad ways' in which this social construction of feminine identity is accomplished.[18] What is more, it allows those ways to be put in question:

> it makes possible, and encourages (despite its colonisation by male writers), the inscription of women as subjects free from the constraints of mundane fiction; and it also offers the possibility of interrogating that very inscription, questioning the basis of gendered subjectivity.
>
> (Lefanu, 1988, p. 9)

Lefanu's pioneering investigation of how these two new ways of thinking about the world intersect in sf texts written by women painstakingly distinguishes 'feminist' writers and texts from 'women' writers who often remain complicit with hegemonic discourses. Following a ballistic of history from Mary Shelley, through 'James Tiptree' (Alice Sheldon) and Ursula Le Guin, to Joanna Russ, she maps out the several paths that have taken women writers from an exploration of their given condition to amalgams of plot and style which emerge as the aesthetic arm of a revolutionary feminist politics:

> Unlike other forms of genre writing, such as detective stories and romance, which demand the reinstatement of order and can thus be described as 'closed' texts, science fiction is by its nature interrogative, open. Feminism questions a given order in political terms, while science fiction questions in imaginative terms. . . . If science fiction demands our acceptance of a relativistic universe, then feminism demands, no less, our acceptance of a relativistic social order. Nothing, in these terms, is natural, least of all the cultural notions of 'woman' and 'man'.
>
> (ibid., p. 100)[19]

So it is clear that sf need not inevitably restrict its ambitions to the 'Instant Whip' whimsy which Aldiss detests. Implicit in the kinds of stories it tells, and the ways it tells them, is the clue we seek for the specific ways in which science fiction codes and transcodes the discourses from which it springs: the rhetorics and practices of the sciences and the humane arts, of wishful compensation fantasies which disclose the lacunae of our lives and the social order within which we live those lives, and of elaborate speculations which sometimes go beyond wish into aspiration and artistry.

METAPHOR AND METONYMY

In Chapter 2, I suggested that *sf operates metaphoric strategies via metonymic tactics.* Thus sf, in its very structure, constitutes a break from literature's cycle of formal polarities from metaphor to metonymy and back, avoiding what literary theorist and critic David Lodge sees as the alternative postmodernist traps of unchecked babble and tongue-tied silence.[20]

On Lodge's account, the strategy of realism is centrally metonymic. In its attempts to 'represent the real world', realist textuality enacts an epistemological fragmentation and reconstitution. It builds strings of signifiers which themselves are chosen for their contiguity, their actual connectedness, with interacting elements in the socially/linguistically constructed *Umwelt* or 'life-world'. Sf textuality is grounded in a distinctive *subjunctivity* (a useful borrowing from grammar by Samuel Delany).[21] Briefly: 'A distinct level of subjunctivity informs all the words in an s-f story at a level that is different from that which informs naturalistic fiction, fantasy, or reportage. [. . . Heinlein's] "the door dilated," is meaningless as naturalistic fiction, and practically meaningless as fantasy' (Delany, 1978a, pp. 31, 34). As sf, it confirms, while enacting, the text's radical 'futurity' or 'otherness'. In this special kind of text, metonymy passes first through cascades of suspended lexical paradigms, words regarded as metaphorically equivalent, which are then detached and sent aloft, freed from any last vestige of a supposed everyday *direct* reference to reality.

THE MEGA-TEXT

Yet on the face of it the process of decoding an sf text works by the same general principles of operation as any other reading. Christine Brooke-Rose provides a germinal account in several theoretical discussions of sf novels (most notably Vonnegut's *Sirens of Titan*), comparing their mechanisms with those of Tolkien's *Lord of the Rings*.[22] Her own poetics of the fantastic starts with a modification and compression of Philippe Hamon's 1973 study of the mechanisms of reading,[23] one parameter of which is the *parallel story* or *mega-text*:

> [T]he realistic narrative is hitched to a megastory (history, geography), itself valorized, which doubles and illuminates it, creating expectations on the line of least resistance through a text already known, usually as close as possible to the reader's experience. Exoticism is reduced to the familiar. This gives points of anchorage, allows an economy of description and insures a general effect of the real that transcends any actual decoding since the references are not so much understood as simply recognised as proper names.
>
> (Brooke-Rose, 1981, p. 243)

Regrettably, she blurs her most telling insight, slighting sf's own distinctive mega-text. Most of Hamon's literary parameters are shared by conventional sf but, Brooke-Rose believes, the mega-text or parallel story is not, or not to any great extent. Her reasoning is deceptively direct. The function of any parallel story is to evoke shared verities and commonplaces (however provisional and arbitrary these might be from the standpoint of a deconstructive critic, cultural relativist, or epistemological anarchist), providing behind every item in a syntagm a certified and secure paradigm of reference. How, then, could this procedure be mimicked in sf, where many of the lexical items have no 'real-world' reference?

There is no doubt that this lack of a predictable 'real-world' anchor threatens the security of sf's textual strategy with each new story. (Recall my comparison, in Chapter 2, of Stone's realism and Zindell's sf inventions.) Few readerly expectations are inviolable in sf. One awaits at every turn the piquancy and intellectual challenge of novelty, sometimes with absurd results. In his hard-edged cyberpunk novel *Halo*, for example, Tom Maddox shows us an operative with a 'memex', or machine-intelligence adviser, visiting the lavish home of his immensely rich employer,

> a Stately Home an idealized eighteenth-century English architect might have built for an equally idealized and indulgent patron. Off a golden domed center stood three wings of creamy stone, the whole in restrained neo-Palladian with no modern excesses of material, no foamed colored concrete and composites, just the tan and creamy sandstone and rose marble speaking wealth and taste. . . .
>
> Gonzales caught glimpses of side rooms through open doorways as they passed. One room appeared to front upon a night filled with swirling nebulae and a million stars, the enxt on sunshine and dazzling snows.[24]

In this 'lived-in future', we are not told directly about the standard architectural materials of the era (foamed concrete, composite) but learn by indirection. This works because we already have some picture of stately neoclassical homes (in this case, neo-neoclassical). But the peculiar shock of sf is to find discontinuities within that setting, as startling as stumbling upon a planetarium display in one of the rooms of Castle Brideshead. The 'memex' we have already absorbed, but what kind of machine or artificial environment (with its sunshine and snow) is an 'enxt'? In normative discourse we would automatically take this to be a typographical error, perhaps the word 'next' scrambled. For the seasoned sf reader there is a certain small shock of laughter, I think, in seeing that this is, in fact, the correct interpretation. In sf, we *expect* to read about memexes and enxts.

Brooke-Rose grants that an sf story or novel 'usually creates a fictional historico-geographico-sociological megatext but leaves it relatively vague, concentrating on technical marvels' (1981, p. 243). Thus, Tolkien's fantasy compensates for this lack of external referentiality by providing its own lumbering mega-text:

> [*The Lord of the Rings*], like SF but more so, is particularly interesting in that there is such a megatext, not pre-existent but entirely invented, yet treated with the utmost seriousness and in great detail, thus destroying the element of recognition and hence readability which this feature provides in the realistic novel, and causing on the contrary a plethora of information and the collapse of the referential code. . . .
>
> That is to say, it is treated *as if* it existed, except that instead of

allowing an economy of description and ensuring a general effect of the real, it needs on the contrary to be constantly explained (since it is unfamiliar).

(ibid., p. 243)

So its function is radically unlike that of any 'realist' mega-text. 'Since the megatext is not "already known", it cannot fulfil the readability requirement, but on the contrary, produces a pseudo-exoticism, much of which can be savoured simply as such, rather than tactically understood' (ibid., p. 248). Tolkien fans are not alone in savouring the details of invented worlds and peoples, quite a different pleasure from that found in relishing those invented 'realistic' biographies known as 'fiction'. Enthusiasts for the television programme *Star Trek* have for years gathered together garbed in the costume of starship crews of the twenty-second century, complete with weapons and 'Beam me up, Scottie' communicators. Manuals showing the design features of starships are purchased and pored over. Members of the Society for Creative Anachronism, who tend to be fans of both sf and 'heroic fantasy', not only dress in mock medieval garb but adopt appropriate personae and bash at one another with user-friendly blunt instruments. And of course the extension of sf and fantasy mega-texts into board and computer gaming has developed into a series of virtual cults, whose mega-texts, in a continuous state of communal expansion, are far more ornate than those once-and-for-all histories and genealogies which, in Brooke-Rose's tart words, 'have given much infantile happiness to the Tolkien clubs and societies, whose members apparently write to each other in Elvish' (ibid., p. 247).

ICON AND MEGA-TEXT

The element in sf which Brooke-Rose appears to have slighted, at severe cost to her analysis, is the extensive generic mega-text built up over fifty years, even a century, of mutually imbricated sf texts. When novelties like hyper-space and cyberspace, memex and AI (Artificial Intelligence), nanotech and plug-in personality agents are very quickly taken up as the common property of a number of independent stories and authors, we have the beginnings of a new mega-text.[25]

Using a strategy of *semiological compensation*, or redundancy and over-coding, similar to the one Hamon and Brooke-Rose discern in realism, the sf mega-text works by embedding each new work, seen by Delany as a self-structuring web of non-mundane signifiers and syntagms, in an even vaster web of interpenetrating semantic and tropic givens or vectors. Some of these have been dubbed 'icons' by Gary K. Wolfe.[26] Early candidates included the spaceship, the robot and the monster, as well as paradigmatic items shared with the 'real' world lexicon, such as the city, the wasteland and the barrier:

Like a stereotype or a convention, an icon is something we are willing
to accept because of our familiarity with the genre, but unlike ordinary
conventions, an icon often retains its power even when isolated from
the context of conventional narrative structures.

(Wolfe, 1979, p. 16)

It is, then, to be conceived as more nearly a narrative archetype; not an
archaic trace so much as a proleptic one, or at any rate one in a linguistically
unprecedented subjunctive state.

While Wolfe's suggestion is provocative, it is important to see what an
iconography of sf does *not* propose. None of the candidates (alien, robot,
spaceship, etc.) has a single, univocal conventional weight or meaning even
within a given generic time-frame or publishing regime. If robots are seen as
soulless and threatening in the 1930s, Asimov reconstructs them a decade
later as rule-governed and sweet-natured (though not every writer follows his
lead). Clarke re-reconstructs them two decades on as murderous (*2001*'s
HAL) or rather, on second thoughts, baffled by Hofstadterian aporia (the
version in *2010*). Lem, in Poland, makes them the allegorical focus of
comical but profound parables of 'cosmic constructors'. In the 1980s,
Benford and many cyberpunk authors blend human and machine into a
disturbing symbiosis. By the 1990s, Walter Jon Willams, in *Aristoi* (1992),
moves his posthuman characters through landscapes situated as often in
computerised virtual realities as in the real world, or in 'robot' teleoperated
bodies, a notion also used by Michael Swanwick in *Stations of the Tide*
(1992). Still other writers, like opportunistic Darwinian species, develop and
invest every possible modulation. Yet all these variants bear certain family
resemblances, and tend to cohere about a limited number of narrative vectors.
Wolfe was not unaware of this dissemination within his schemata:

such transformations and combinations of the favorite images of the
genre become like variations on a theme, with writers working from a
relatively limited number of consensual images to create a vast and
complex body of fiction that nevertheless often rests upon the assumption of reader familiarity with the fundamental icons of the genre.

(Wolfe, 1979, p. xiv)

But that familiarity, so necessary in alerting trained readers to the appropriate reception codes and strategies for concretising an sf text, maintains at
its heart a *de*-familiarising impulse absolutely pivotal to the form's specificity.
Basic to the very definition of most genres is stability in characteristic
situations, emblems, actions and types of conflict and personality-response –
it is why one chooses to discern/construct a category out of a catalogue. Sf is
different, being, as we have seen, at least by vocation a mode grounded in a
novum. Discussing the literal iconography of sf film, Vivian Sobchack
stresses this feature of sf by contrast to the gangster or the western genres:

[B]oth these genres are visually circumscribed by an awareness of history, the Western even more so than the Gangster film. This linkage of situation and character, objects, settings, and costumes to a specific *past* creates visual boundaries to what can be photographed and in what context. This historical awareness, which leads at least to an imaginative if not actual authenticity, demands repetition and creates consistency throughout these genres. This is not true, however, of the SF film, a genre which is unfixed in its dependence on actual time and/or place.[27]

THE ABSENT SIGNIFIED

The railroad, for Sobchack, has a quite different iconic weight to the spaceship. 'From its first silent chugging to the clangorous present, the railroad in the history of the Western film has not altered in its physical particularity or its specific significance; it is, indeed, an icon' (1987, p. 68). But 'there is no *consistent* cluster of meanings provoked by the image of a spaceship' (ibid.). From the sleek aerofoil Noah's Ark of *When Worlds Collide* to the sublime or celebratory UFOs in *Forbidden Planet* and *Close Encounters of the Third Kind*, from the clinical spinal column of *2001*'s 'Discovery' to the adventurous 'dog-fighting' modules of the *Star Wars* films which naturalise the future in the image of a glamorous and heroic past, the iconographical weight and density alters radically.[28] The spacecraft is a means of transportation which enables an entire cosmology of narratives, positive, negative and neutral in moral and aesthetic charge.

In what sense, then, can it be an icon? In the minimal sense, at least, that the spaceship is *not* a railroad, nor any other known, assimilated component of the quotidian – except, precisely, in its now-extensive iconicity. A vast range of connotations hang in generic phase space above or behind its manifestation in a given text, drawn together by association and practice into certain most-probable-use vectors, but the image or concept of the sf emblem remains parsable as a new noun or verb, a signifier which posts notice to us of an 'absent signified', an empirically empty but imaginatively laden paradigm.[29]

Still, there are constraints. Marie Maclean notes: 'The reader's development of the missing paradigm may be idiosyncratic, but it remains limited by the syntagmatic aspects of the narrative' (1984, p. 171), as does the use within any given text of any given iconic signifier by the grand exfoliating syntagm of the sf mega-text. At the very least, we can agree with Wolfe that sf's icons

> consolidate the 'sense of wonder' and offer readers some word or image that will assure them that what they are reading is in some way connected to the vast body of other science-fiction works.
>
> The use of conventional symbols or icons is one of the most

convenient methods for science-fiction writers to make this connection, for they embody not only the dialectic of known and unknown but also the germ of recognizable formulas. They are a message in code to the initiated reader and an emblem of dissociation to the uninitiated.

(Wolfe, 1979, p. 27)

It is the creation of such a shared, icon-echoing, redundant and inconsistent mega-text in the collective intertextuality of those works we name 'sf' which gives this kind of writing its power, a power verging on obsession or dream and only available elsewhere in other somewhat comparable varieties of textuality: myth, fairytale, surrealism. I am reminded of Gaston Bachelard's speculations on the elements (literally) of science and poetry, as well as the kinds of objections raised to them. Bachelard (1884–1962), at one time a tremendously influential historian and philosopher of science, proposed a 'psychoanalysis of matter', using a sort of proto-structuralist aesthetic of dream and reverie. He proposed water as wine's binary opposite, for instance (though Roland Barthes argued in *Mythologies* that milk rather than water had become the cultural 'other' to wine; in Australia, of course, it would be Foster's beer). Jonathan Culler has commented wryly on the psychoanalytic motifs Bachelard brought to literary studies 'as a way of analysing not authors but images, whose power is said to derive from their exploitation of a primordial and archetypal experience – not unlike that of a nineteenth-century village childhood' of the kind, by a curious coincidence, that Bachelard himself enjoyed.[30] Some of sf's favorite icons clearly work this way – one thinks of recurrent tropes in the sweet pastorales of Clifford Simak[31] – but Culler is not wholly dismissive. Bachelard's doctrine

has the virtue of falsifiability. We dispute it by showing that the force and significance of images depend more on specific ideological or differential functions within a text than on universal associations: that images of earth are not always 'stables et tranquilles' nor walls and houses welcoming and protective.

Moreover Bachelard's hypothesis leads us to argue that much poetry does not simply evoke or invoke an immediate and 'natural' experience of the world but works much as Bachelard claims science does; breaking down immediate intuitions, deconstructing a universe of archetypical clichés, and reinventing the world by giving it an order which is discursive rather than immediately affective.

(Culler, 1988, p. 101)

It is this same fulcrum upon which any theory of sf iconography teeters. Icons in a literature of cognitive estrangement must be intrinsically destabilised and multivocal, in a degree which outruns the always-already ruptured dissemination postulated by deconstruction for *every* act of language. That is, these icons are unstable at a higher level of discursive strategy, just as the always-provisional hypotheses of science must be, by contrast to the graven doctrinal character of traditional religious claims, for example. Yet they undoubtedly exist *as* discursive attractors, so to speak, about which narratives orbit in their contained but unpredictable paths. While it is important to grasp that they are not archetypes in any timeless and universal sense, their invocation of the known and the unknown, stressed by Wolfe, comes close to such a station. Yet this fact does not detract from their salience in helping account for the specificity and idiosyncratic coding of sf texts.

An immediate corollary of this postulate is that only readers inducted into the sf mega-text web or intertext – only 'native speakers' of its grammar, as it were – will be competent to retrieve/construct anything like the full semiotic density of a given text, most of which will overflow or escape the 'realistically' sanctioned definitions of the words in the fiction, not to mention their unorthodox schemata of combination.

This is certainly not immediately obvious to the inexperienced reader, and helps explain why many capable but uninitiated readers recoil in utter bafflement at sf-conventionalised rhetorical moves in the narrative, as well as from a textual surface which seems bizarrely under-determined. And this latter is precisely the difficulty usually experienced, by readers familiar only with the canonised literary modes, as defective characterisation. Yet we may now see that very gap or absence as the opposite of a deficiency: as one of sf's structural tools. This perspective has been well captured by Alexander Jablokov:

> The literature of science fiction is rich with modes that are immediately familiar to initiates, who understand the assumptions and proceed to the story, but require much thought and analysis, not to say puzzlement, for anyone coming from outside the field. . . . They are our equivalents of Georgics, Epics, and Bildungsromans, and have all sorts of hidden rules and assumptions. The outside reader is confused: who are all these Strephons and Phoebes? Why are they spouting iambic hexameters? We all know shepherds don't talk like this. What's going on?[32]

What's going on, as Jablokov says neatly, is a comprehensible mode. But only those who care to learn the articulations of the mode will ever discover why the shepherds are speaking in this strange way, and benefit from the peculiar coded beauty of their discourse. To theorise that knowledge is a task which has scarcely begun. One expert guide to this terrain is the American sf writer and semiotic-cum-poststructural theorist Samuel Delany, to whose extensive efforts in creating an adequate sf analytics we now turn.

5

READING THE EPISTEME

36. Omitted pages from an s-f novel:

'What I mean . . . is that my explanation would have been nonsense two hundred years ago. It isn't today. The episteme has changed so entirely, so completely, the words bear entirely different charges, even though the meanings are more or less what they would have been in –'

'What's an episteme?' Bron asked.

. . .

'An episteme is an easy way to talk about the way to slice through the whole –'

'Sounds like the secondary hero in some ice-opera . . .'

'Ah . . . but the episteme was *always* the secondary hero of the s-f novel – in exactly the same way that the landscape was always the primary one . . .'

37. Everything in a science-fiction novel should be mentioned at least twice (in at least two different contexts).

38. . . . . The episteme is the structure of knowledge read from the epistemological *textus* when it is sliced through (usually with the help of several texts) at a given, cultural moment.

(Samuel R. Delany)[1]

Samuel R. Delany is the most persuasive theoretician of sf as that species of storytelling native to a culture undergoing epistemic changes implicated in the rise and supersession of technical-industrial modes of production, distribution, consumption and disposal: which is to say, the epistemic fiction of Western scientific culture, the culture of the object.

Delany is anomaly and paradigm conjoined: black, gay, father, dyslexic college drop-out, multiple prize-winning and bestselling sf and fantasy novelist, film-maker, sometime fellow at the University of Wisconsin's Center for Twentieth-century Studies, deconstructive critic, now Professor of Comparative Literature at the University of Massachusetts at Amherst; in 1984, when the first part of his magnum opus *Stars in My Pocket Like Grains of Sand* appeared, he was just 42 years old.[2]

His concern with language is rare in an underpaid commercial entertainment field marked by slapdash or slick sales-staff-governed formulaic writing. In essays combining close reading, attention to the specific characteristics of sf, and original theoretical investigation, he has anatomised exemplary writings by Thomas Disch, Roger Zelazny, Joanna Russ, Ursula Le Guin, Robert Heinlein and Theodore Sturgeon.[3] Perhaps most importantly, he is one of the very few working sf writers of any theoretical sophistication. His familiarity with current theory greatly exceeds that of Brian Aldiss, for instance, in the latter's avatar as sf historian. One can trace through his essays a critical trajectory launched from a distrust of the content/form antithesis and peaking in an idiosyncratic blend of semiotics, Marxism, psychoanalysis and deconstruction.

DELANY'S CRITICAL PATH

Rising from such ground-breaking work as the 1968 address to the MLA Seminar on Science Fiction (in Hay, 1970, pp. 130–45), that trajectory passes via his collection *Starboard Wine* (1984), the appendices to the fantasy novel *Flight from Nevèrÿon* (1985), and certain important interviews, to university lectures and public addresses, and articles in critical journals such as the *New York Review of Science Fiction*: for example, a 1989 three-part series on sf and deconstruction, and in 1992 a presentation at the Whitney Museum in New York on the future of the body.

The 1968 paper reappeared in subtly rewritten form as 'About Five Thousand Seven Hundred and Fifty Words' in his first collection of essays, *The Jewel-Hinged Jaw*.[4] It is instructive to note the original line of argument and his subsequent attempts to improve on it. Professor Parrinder has referred to it, under its revised title, as a 'classic . . . familiar to SFS [*Science Fiction Studies*] readers', an indication of the impact of its initial fanzine appearance and subsequent reprintings.[5] 'Every generation some critic states the frighteningly obvious in the *style/content* conflict,' Delany begins, immediately declaring his own formalist position. At that time, certainly for an sf critic, it was a thoroughly heterodox stance: 'Put in opposition to "style", there is no such thing as "content".'[6]

This claim, so inoffensive to textually oriented criticism, is almost inconceivable in a folk-critical tradition which proclaims that sf is peculiarly a 'literature of ideas', a format which rises above its adventure-story packaging through a play of 'thought-variants', scientific and sociological extrapolations which burst through stale or conservative paradigms to stimulate cognitive wonderment.

Of course, Delany was not denying the cognitive novelties of sf. His definition of its singular level of subjunctivity was that it dealt with events that 'have not happened', which include 'events that might happen', 'events that will not happen', 'events that have not happened yet', and even 'events that have not happened in [our] past' but might have done so in some other parallel reality (1978a, p. 32).

How was this level tapped or evoked? '[W]hen spaceships, ray guns, or more accurately any . . . images that [indicate] the future appear in a series of words and mark it as s-f, the subjunctivity level' is established for the reader (ibid.). In short, Delany was proposing a rudimentary aesthetics of reception.

Certain codons manifested in the text, such as the narrative units Gary Wolfe was to identify as sf's icons, alert the reader to *a special way of actualising the words*. The text is then received in such a manner that the information density and texture of its discourse is appropriately decoded.[7] 'The particular subjunctive level of s-f expands the freedom of the choice of words that can follow another group of words meaningfully', since the worlds and actions available to the sf text exceed those with a terrestrial denotation, 'but it limits the way we employ the corrective process as we move between them' (Delany, 1978a, p. 32).

For Delany, sf's syntagmatic expansion, and its correlative set of new paradigmatic lists of word choices at each position along the evolving syntagm, is presented in the paper's first version as effecting serial changes in a kind of mental motion-picture:

'Words in a narrative generate pictures. But rather than a fixed chronological relation, they sit in numerous semantic relations.'[8]

In the revised version, additional sensory modalities and, more importantly, cognitive frames, are acknowledged:

Words in a narrative generate tones of voice, syntactic expectations, memories of other words, and pictures. But rather than a fixed chronological relation, they sit in numerous inter-and overweaving relations.

(Delany 1978a, p. 25)

In either version, the crucial premise is an unlikely but thoroughly engaging model of reading which Delany advances in some detail in the first part of his paper, showing with some subtlety how one might 'realise' or concretise[9] the line *The red sun is high, the blue low* (ibid., p. 28).

That 'The' which begins his line, and his notional 60,000-word novel, is said to evoke an image which will be 'corrected fifty-nine thousand, nine hundred and ninety-nine times' (p. 25).[10] Delany's picture of a 'the' is 'a grayish ellipsoid about four feet high that balances on the floor perhaps a yard away. Yours is no doubt different. But it is there, has a specific size, shape, color, and bears a particular relation to you' (pp. 25–6).

Recalling Delany's severe dyslexia, it is impossible to be sure that this figure is only a rhetorical heuristic, but I am not alone in finding preposterous its over-concreteness. The British wit and fan critic David Langford remarks: 'Imagine his images of words like "concatenation", "molybdenum" and "gleet".'[11]

Adding a second word brings about the first correction: *The red* causes Delany's ellipsoid to change colour. *The red sun* replaces the original 'The' with a luminous disc. *The red sun is* introduces a speaker, and that speaker's intentional stance; the text is tonally modified: 'The *red* sun is . . .' (Delany 1978a, p. 27). 'This,' notes Delany acutely, 'is my first aesthetic pleasure from the tale.'

By the time we reach *The red sun is high, the blue* – and all this assumes a 'cold' reading, without generic or modal cues from, for example, the author's name or the publisher's packaging – 'the repetition of the syntactic arrangement . . . momentarily threatens to dissolve all reality . . . into a mannered listing of bucolica. The whole scene dims' (ibid., p. 28). A tentative coding has been settled, and its banality, its predictability, flattens the psychological tension of the reading. But with the final (single word, but explosive) correction of the original grey blurry image – to *The red sun is high, the blue low* –

> We are worlds and worlds away! The first sun is huge; and how accurate the description of its color turns out to have been. The repetition that predicted mannerism now fixes both big and little sun to the sky. The landscape crawls with long red shadows and stubby blue ones, joined by purple triangles. Look at the speaker. . . . You have seen his doubled shadow.
>
> (ibid., p. 28)

Whether or not Delany's parable of the reading process is generally valid, or even valid for some people – its assumption that to understand written or spoken language we use a serial, additive algorithm flies in the face of contemporary linguistics and semiotics[12] – it nicely allegorises some of the processes of coding and decoding called up by genres and generic hybrids alike.

Taken as naturalism, the red sun high in the sky would strain against one's knowledge of the ordinary. It denotes a disruption of one's everyday *and* literary expectations, perhaps only of the order of smog, or perhaps of apocalypse, or simply of the narrator's perceptions. Or perhaps it signifies a shift from literal description to metaphor. By contrast, in the frame of an sf reading, the text has a quite violently specific and 'mimetic' denotation, but to an experience none of us has yet had, though it might have occurred to us in imagination, built up from astronomical data, or even from having seen paintings of double-star systems by such artists as Chesley Bonestell or David Hardy.[13]

SUBJUNCTIVITY AND MEGA-TEXT

In other words, the subjunctivity of sf calls upon a Hamon/Brooke-Rose 'mega-text' or vast intertextual 'hyper-text': part encyclopaedia of knowledge drawn from current scientific data and theories, part iconography established in previous sf, part generic repertoire of standard narrative moves, their probability-weighted variants, and their procedures for generating new moves.

This mega-text and its associated coding/decoding procedures accounts, as I noted in discussing Todorov, for a major difference in the way one reads sf compared with, say, fantasy. For the latter, the displaced functions ultimately serve psychodynamic ends. 'The corrective process in fantasy is limited too,' Delany observes; 'when we are given a correction that is not meaningful in terms of the personally observable world, we *must* accept any pseudoexplanation we are given. If there is [none], it must remain mysterious' (1978a, p. 33). Todorov would add: *because* we remain uncertain of its status, fantastic hesitation ensues. By contrast, sf's subjunctivity insists 'that we must make our correction process in accord with what we know of the physically explainable universe. . . . The particular verbal freedom of s-f . . . not only [throws] us worlds away, it specifies how we got there' (ibid., p. 33).

Plainly, this view hangs from a theory of signification, if a questionable one. Delany's original version of the paper was notably primitive; the revision attempts, without great success, to incorporate a Saussurean perspective. 'Consider meaning to be a thread (or better yet [he adds in 1977], the path) that connects a sound or configuration of letters called a "word" with a given object or group of objects (or better [he adds], memories of those objects)' (ibid., p. 22; the earlier version is in Hay, 1970, p. 132).

A story is not a paraphrase, Delany argues in a move familiar in traditional criticism, but he adds: 'The story is what happens in the reader's mind as his eyes move from the first word to the second', and so on.

Interestingly, the question of referentiality becomes a pivot in Delany's revised understanding. His earliest elaboration of the mechanism involved in that word-to-word process is this: 'Subjunctivity is the tension on the thread of meaning that runs between word and object' (Hay, 1970, p. 140). A decade later, this had become: 'Subjunctivity is the tension on the thread of meaning that runs between (to borrow Saussure's term for "word":) sound-image and sound-image' (Delany, 1978a, p. 31). The object in the world has gone; so too, perhaps surprisingly, has the signified. Now the elastic tension holds slippery Lacanian signifiers. One's suspicion that this glib replacement reduces the original metaphor to nonsense is clarified by Delany's subsequent rejoinder to Parrinder's *Science Fiction Studies* review:

[B]y 1972 the phrases *subjunctive tension* and *particular level of subjunctivity* had all but vanished from my thinking. . . . I abandoned the phrases because *subjunctive tension* seemed to suggest for the 'literalizing' phenomenon of certain sentences characteristic of science fiction an explanation based on a linguistic entity my current linguistic interests had all but convinced me simply did not exist: that entity would have to be a kind of semantic energy, loose in the language centers of the brain, flitting around 'tightening up' the meanings of the sentences.[14]

Thus, what one might have taken as figurative had always been a kind of neuro-mechanical hypothesis. Shades of Freud's psycho-physics! Significantly, Delany ascribed the shift in his views as much to cognitive science experiments by Jerry Fodor and his colleagues at MIT, and reception theory, as to his discovery of Saussurean structuralism:

> The theory of 'literal language' I now hold can be found in Professor Stanley Fish's essay 'Normal Circumstances . . .'. [Its gist] is that 'literal interpretation' is a set of learned language conventions no different in their basic workings from those conventions governing 'poetic', 'symbolic', or 'literary' interpretations. The conventions are called into play by contextual signs.
>
> (Delany, 1984, p. 217)

Such an account is of course in much closer sympathy with Delany's own developing reception aesthetic.

It is notable that this bias towards a strictly textual account of sf's specificity was readily located by one of his earliest explicators. In a book entirely devoted to Delany's fiction (up to *Triton*), Douglas Barbour observed:

> As anyone who has looked into the problem knows, sf has proved as recalcitrant to definition as that most open of genres, the Novel, and a vast number of competing definitions exist. . . . Delany, however, solves the problem by changing the nature of the question. Instead of asking 'how is science fiction different from other forms of fiction?' he asks 'how is the language of science fiction different from the language of other forms of prose?'[15]

LEARNING TO READ SF

Delany's model of the semiotics of sf is now increasingly being taken up, even popularised.[16] Introducing *The World Treasury of Science Fiction*, prepared for that bastion of middle-class readers, the Book of the Month Club, editor David Hartwell summarises the case precisely.[17] Canonical literary culture, he finds, tended to reject sf for its lack of canonical virtues, especially because it was 'unreal on the one hand (space travel and atomic power were considered fantastic and laughable . . .), and so concerned with the gritty realities of science and technology on the other' (1989, p. xvii). The result was not merely ostracism of the sf sub-culture but an impoverishment of 'a majority of educated readers' who 'had no interest in learning how to read the genre, a practice easily picked up by children and teenagers – by taking every detail literally at first, until given other directions by the text' (ibid.).

This moment of the interaction between text and reader does not, however, altogether accord with the disseminative, deconstructive account which increasingly sways Delany's theoretics. It is assumed by Hartwell that a specific modality of reading is encoded within the text, and within its generic intertextual virtual surround. These mega-textual cues, and their exercise, must be acquired by each reader through patient apprenticeship. The educated reader finds this a more difficult lesson to swallow than unsophisticated readers do, because sf requires

> just the reverse of the way we approach the prose literature of this century; we teach ourselves to read with a sensitivity to metaphor and subtext, assuming that that is the route by which the essential communication between reader and text will take place.
>
> (ibid.)

If a literary story tells us that a man woke to find himself transformed into a large insect, we do not look immediately for clues to his mutant genes, or to deleterious disruptions in the ecology or the spacetime manifold. To read Kafka's tale 'Metamorphosis' on this 'literal' level, by this blatantly 'referential' transcoding of his tropes, is entirely and vulgarly to miss the point. Granted, in one moment of the reading it must be done as it were *sous rature* ('under erasure'), since the 'realistic' level is also crucial to the tale's effectiveness. Kafka offers such details with an utterly straight face and a rigorous attention to detail, so that an entomologist like Nabokov can be certain that the 'vermin' was not a cockroach but a beetle.[18] But the traditions of sf demand, by contrast,

> that the reader first experience the text as a literal report of something that, by a thin thread of possibility, could be true, given a specified set of circumstances, at some other time, in some other place. . . . The vehicle, in other words, has just as much weight as the tenor in SF.
>
> (Hartwell, 1989, pp. xvii–xviii)

SF AS PARALITERARY

Following this critical trajectory has taken Delany to a controversial locus where sf is received as categorically other than 'literature': as a form of paraliterature. '[T]he differences between contemporary science fiction and other modes of writing are akin to the differences among, say, poetry, prose reportage, prose fiction, and drama; the differences, as I see it, are *formally categorical*' (1984, pp. 217–18).

> One *can* . . . speak of 'genres' and go on to characterize a genre as a set of texts sharing certain rhetorical similarities – but the taxonomic difficulties of such an approach are notorious. . . . A more fruitful way

to characterize the difference [. . . is] as a set of distinctions between reading protocols. . . . *The category is not a set of texts (or textual, i.e., rhetorical, figures)* but rather a complex of reading protocols: different writing practices involve different complexes.

(ibid., p. 218; my italics)

Demarcation 'becomes one with the problem of intention and richness: is it clear or unclear that the writer intended a particular complex to be employed; and is it clear or unclear that a text reads richly under a particular protocol complex? *The situation that continually contours our critical responsibility is this: we are free to read* any *text by* any *reading protocol we wish*' (ibid.; my italics). Likewise with critical discourse. 'The criterion is simply how useful and interesting the resultant discussion is, how it enriches our sense of the reading' (p. 219).

I suspect that this solution flirts with the supposed Intentional Fallacy even as its invocation of 'rich' versus impoverished readings seems to embrace disseminative free play. For one cannot, finally, posit a plurality of effective reading codes without supposing that readers *do*, and should, strive to adjust their coding protocols on the assumption that the writer knowingly put some detectable set or sets of codes into play in any given text, even if these codes are then pitted one against another in a self-reflexive novel by, say, Robbe-Grillet or John Barth.

Some of the cues will be declarative and extra-textual: generic markers placed by publishers, for example. Others will be embedded in the text but will only function effectively within a reader's awareness, conscious and otherwise, of the 'ecology' of textual and tonal variants it is played against. Irony especially is notoriously at risk of inappropriate reception as, say, bathos or reportage.

And the writer's modal intention is often crucial in establishing the most fruitful terms ('rich' readings) of that play, to whatever extent it can be recovered as encoded into the text and the text's available surrounds – and that extent is hardly ever nil. Patently, as Raymond Tallis remarks,

The wrong 'mental generic set' will prevent us from being able to assimilate or even make sense of [a text]. Anyone who reads, say, *Philosophical Investigations* under the impression that it is a detective story or *The Red and the Black* in the hope of learning the rules of snooker will simply read past what is essential in these works or find them incomprehensible.[19]

These reflections are important in any discussion of Delany's theory or evolving ensemble of theories, which make a great deal more use of an implied or encoded reader, interacting with the intentional generic set of the real reader, than some of his more deconstructive remarks would seem to permit:

The play of meanings, contradictory or otherwise, that makes up the SF text is organized in a way radically different from that of the mundane text. . . . When we read science fiction carefully,[20] we can see that practically any rhetorical figure operates differently in an SF text from the way the same, or similar, figure would operate in a text of mundane fiction.[21]

True, the rhetorically grounded imaginary worlds of mundane 'mainstream', usually 'realist', fictions are no less culturally constructed, no more 'real' (merely more 'given') (Delany, 1984, p. 49). 'The science fiction writer, however, *creates* a world – which [relates to both its] characters *and* the given world in a much freer way' (ibid., pp. 49–50). Although there are conventional expectations in sf, 'the reader of the SF story must create a new world that operates by new laws for each new SF story read'. I would argue, conversely, that the existence of an elaborate sf mega-text severely restricts the need for, and possibility of, major novelty from story to story. Even so, in terms of surface decoration at least, Delany's point stands.

> The various verbal devices SF writers use to lay out, sketch in, and color their alternate [*sic*] worlds, as well as the verbal constructs that direct the play between the world and the story, constitute the major distinctions between SF and the mundane text, altering the reading of the various rhetorical figures that appear in both texts.
>
> (ibid., p. 50)

This fundamental distinction, which parallels those which demarcate other problematic forms of writing such as allegory and myth, strengthens the case for treating sf as a kind of writing separate from 'literature'. By literature I mean, as previously, that body of texts constituted under canonised writing and reading protocols, which operate with their own ideologically 'naturalised' signifier lexicons and syntagm algorithms, although these are seldom perceived as 'generic' without an explicit act of defamiliarisation. This is not a claim for some privileged, transcendental status.[22] Sf is, of course, 'about the current world' (ibid., p. 48).[23] It is 'about' it in a special way:

> [Sf] is not a metaphor for the given world, nor does the catch-all term metonymy exhaust the relation between the given and science fiction's distortions of the given. Science fiction poises in a tense, dialogic, agonistic relation to the given.
>
> (ibid.)

And it does this precisely through the techniques of its textual codings, its insertion, as we sketched earlier, of new signifiers into new syntagmatic relations in order to construct a web of novel meanings. None of this makes for ease of reading for those unused to sf's genre-specific intertextual baggage. Citing Robert Scholes, Delany observes: 'Before you can deconstruct a text . . . you have to be able to construe it.'[24] And that is possible only after a reader has learned the codes and contexts of the genre/mode, which are embedded in the lexicons, the sentence paradigms, the varieties of syntagmatic strings available within that genre/mode. Once grant that perspective and

> I suspect there's little to say about writing, mine or anyone's that doesn't fall out of its sentences, or the codes which recognize and read them, the codes which the sentences are – and the sentences which are the only expressions, at least in verbal terms, we can have of the codes.
>
> (Delany, 1987c, p. 137)

Perhaps Delany's densest presentation of his perspective, apart from the remarkable *S/Z*-like discourse on Disch's 'Angouleme', *The American Shore*, is a paper given to the Conference on the Fantastic in 1982, *'Dichtung und Science Fiction'*.[25] The special defining characteristic of the writing/reading orientation which constitutes sf is here focused precisely:

> As a way of reading, the literary modes today, despite their numerous differences, tend to analyze, and finally to deconstruct the subject. As a way of reading, science fiction today tends to analyze, to critique, and finally to deconstruct the object. . . .
> Precisely because this aspect . . . is currently foreign to the literary modes, it is necessary that we pay attention to it just as astutely . . . that, today, we resist the temptation to reread the texts that richly exploit this way of reading as we would read those texts of the literary genre 'The Fantastic,' in which the literary priority of the subject obliterates the paraliterary priority of the object.
> [. . . Sf's] implications for representation alone make it of considerable importance to the history and philosophy of modern aesthetics.
>
> (Delany, 1984, p. 189)

The discourse of science is traditionally supposed to have as its priority the construction and deconstruction of the object. Anti-humanist assaults on the privileged position of the subject have entailed a revival and extension of both anti-positivist and anti-essentialist assumptions in the philosophies of science. For if the subject is constituted in social practice, the object which is constituted by the social practice of the subject tends to be even more distant from any ideal ontological solidity. Delany insists:

> The discourse of science fiction gives us a way to construct worlds in clear and consistent dialogue with the world that is, alas, the case. Literature's unitary priorities do not. And in a world where an 'alas' must be inserted into such a description of it, the dialectical freedom of science fiction has to be privileged.[26]

CRITIQUING THE OBJECT

It is plausible that a paraliterary discursive formation which has at its centre a critique of the object will present unusual challenges and benefits to both traditional and poststructural theories of literary and scientific texts. William Paulson's *cultural analysis* offers the obverse to Delany's meditation on the supersession of the subject, within the humane disciplines, in favour of attention to the object. Paulson's case is either stressful or exultant, according to one's estimate of its likely outcome:

> As science disqualifies the medium through which we have experienced and spoken the world, language and culture as we have known them are swept away at an astonishing rate. This may be a disaster, or it may be an opportunity, a chance to create a new culture whose language will be of science as well as of tradition, whose science will be of the subject as well as of the object. If we want to preserve something of our subjectivity, then we must open our texts to the new codes and messages and noises of science, begin to place science in the place of the cultural subject.[27]

But it is, of course, inevitably, both disaster and opportunity. Fredric Jameson has made it clear (as a veritable connoisseur of epistemological breaks) that it is precisely in the disasters which seam and fracture History that he finds the richest opportunities for a utopian outcome. If it was in B-movie science fiction especially that Jameson found these vectors recorded, these censored messages unmasked in 'a glance that designates, through the very process of avoiding, the object forbidden',[28] the transgressive texts of 'postmodern' sf are an exemplary locus for its best attempts to look with a fierce directness, via the subjectivity of character, at the forbidden: the object, the culture, the world, that is, alas, the case. And to posit, in imaginative enactment, its negating or fulfilling alternatives.

Before we advance to the postmodern in Chapter 8, however, let us first turn these theoretical gains to advantage, examining in detail a variety of texts characteristic of good and ill from sf's modern moment, and several more located at the cusp of this new way of writing and reading sf.

6

DREAMS OF REASON AND UNREASON

How often do you reach the last page of a book . . . to find that the spacemen beat the aliens with a spark of irrational genius? The aliens may be clever and ruthless but the humans win through because they have feelings and intuition – qualities no bug-eyed monster could ever understand.

(John McCrone)[1]

As we have seen, the jargon, the icons, the tropes of 'Modern sf' – which is to say, post-*Astounding Science Fiction* sf, most of it commercial, usually published and written in the USA, and drastically influenced by that milieu even when it comes from other sources – are simply the most visible features of what virtually constitutes a unique cultural dialect, whether its texts are notated in English, Polish or Japanese. Yet despite the ambitious agendas of its theorists, even the best sf continues to be disparaged. For the uninitiated, sf's syntax and lexicon appear to diverge only a little from standard narrative – and then chiefly in the 'Buck Rogers' or 'fake technical' jargon that tends to be deplored by those beyond the sf ghetto.

My developing case is that sf's special language, clichéd and flattened as many of its routine moves have now become, remains a tongue uniquely shaped for the articulation of the subjunctivity of our current *episteme*. (Recall my definition of 'episteme': 'the complex of discursive templates active within a given space and epoch'.) It is, in short, a distinctive and paradoxically apt variety, in an age ruled by the instrumental diction of technology and management, of that radically *subjunctive* art which Ursula Le Guin has apostrophised with her usual grace:

In recent centuries we . . . have reduced the English verb almost entirely to the indicative mood. But beneath that specious and arrogant assumption of certainty all the ancient, cloudy, moody powers and options of the subjunctive remain in force. The indicative points its bony finger at primary experiences, at the Things; but it is the subjunctive that joins them, with the bonds of analogy, possibility, probability, contingency. . . . We cannot ask reason to take us across the gulfs of the

75

absurd. Only the imagination can get us out of the bind of the eternal present, inventing or hypothesizing or pretending or discovering a way that reason can then follow into the infinity of options, a clue through the labyrinths of choice, a golden string, the story, leading us to the freedom that is properly human, the freedom open to those whose minds can accept unreality.[2]

OUT OF THE KINDERGARTEN

So, against the urgings of Thomas Disch cited earlier, it is clear that sf is hardly restricted to playing out unchecked the embarrassing fantasies of the kindergarten, even though it is willing, like science in the act of hypothesis-formation, to 'accept unreality'. Consider the structural framework of a typical winner of the Nebula and Hugo awards, Orson Scott Card's impressive if perhaps overly slick fable, *Speaker for the Dead*.[3]

In the similarly well-liked and award-winning *Ender's Game*,[4] to which *Speaker* is the first of two sequels, Card placed a child at the focus of an excruciating programme of military training. Andrew 'Ender' Wiggins is a brilliant child with the potential of a Napoleon. To defeat the alien Buggers (*sic*!), infants like Ender are harrowed in the ultimate military school, a project which culminates in young Ender exterminating the sole known non-human species, a hive-race mistakenly at war with Earth.[5] The redemptive, sentimental ending might moisten some eyes; the book is beyond doubt as expertly done in this respect as any traditional three-handkerchief movie. In the sequels, set thousands of years later, a penitent Ender and his equally gifted sister carry a healing message from world to world, protected from ageing by the time-dilatation of relativistic transport.

The same megalomania is at work here, then, which undeniably surfaces in much canonical sf: precisely the iconography of omniscient phantasy of which Disch despaired. Drastically extended lifespan, superhuman competence, personal intervention on the most supra-global scale by pleasing figures we can more or less identify with. Is this, after all, no better than the stuff of childish dreams?

Yes and no. Card has been a Mormon missionary, and remains a faithful member of the Church of Jesus Christ of the Latter-day Saints, drawing powerfully upon the metaphors and ethical dilemmas of that 'humanistic' and regulated religion. Ender, 'speaker for the dead', is a kind of lay priest or large-scale social therapist whose task is to reconcile the living with the dead. This duty fetches him to Lusitania, a world licensed to Catholics of Brazilian background. Here a second non-human intelligent species has been found, the 'piggies', who are protected from culture shock and depredation in the wake of Ender's infamous Xenocide. When they begin murdering the ethnologists who study them, the piggies become one of sf's celebrated cases of conscience.

If this outline resembles some *Star Trek* script, Card's treatment does not. He writes cleanly, with intelligence and sensitivity enough to match his material. He invents tools for thinking about problems we do not yet face, yet some day surely will, and it is to this apparatus that I wish to direct particular attention. Adapting Nordic terms, he distinguishes the *utlanning*, or local human stranger, the *framling*, human of another world, the *raman*, human of another species, and *varelse*, the truly alien (such as animals). His problem of conscience, then, is this: are the piggies raman or varelse? Card tightens the screw by introducing another trope familiar to sf readers of such texts as Heinlein's *The Moon is a Harsh Mistress* (1966), David Gerrold's *When HARLIE was One* (1972, revised 1988), Budrys's *Michaelmas* (1977) and Maddox's *Halo* (1991): what is the moral status of a computer not only intelligent but conscious?[6]

To the literary sceptic, these are questions only an sf devotee might conceivably find diverting, let alone urgent. In our world, it cannot be denied, they seem the sheerest twaddle. Like the myths of *utlannings* (Australian Aboriginal sacred dreamings, say), sf's lacework of ideas and images can seem the merest froth to the uninitiated. Yet I would argue that they are metaphors for what should, perhaps, trouble us all; for what, perhaps, *does* trouble us all.

FAMILIARISING THE ESTRANGED

Consider Phillip Mann's *The Eye of the Queen*,[7] an extremely effective dramatisation of the central sf notion of *alienness*: neither the metaphysical alienation of existentialism nor the economic dispossession central to Marxist critique, but the quiddity of some postulated non-human but self-aware consciousness. What exactly does the existence of this kind of novel, this kind of narrative conceit, tell us readers about our socially/historically/scientifically/mythically constructed selves?

Vladimir Nabokov chided those who worry the bones of allegory: 'we say "stop, thief" to the critic who deliberately transforms an artist's subtle symbol into a pedant's stale allegory'.[8] Poststructuralist Paul de Man, by contrast, built his literary theory on it.[9] And how else are we to understand why grown men and women patiently read a book about contact with 3.5-metre-tall aliens who shed their skins, reproduce without sex, and spend much of their time patched into the spiritual broadcasts of beings resembling angels (another trope echoed in Card's *Xenocide*)?

On reflection, Mann's alien Pe-Ellians look rather like a child's idea of human adults: very large, very mysterious, custodial but selfishly dedicated to the incomprehensible, and of course, perhaps above all, the focus of enormously confusing thoughts and feelings about gender and sex, usually dealt with at the conscious level (for the child) by repression.

So yes, science fiction, like fairytales before it, on Bruno Bettelheim's account, does clearly transform and subdue elements of our experience apparently forgotten but which linger to trouble our dreams, and more than our dreams.[10] At the same time, like therapy, sf allows us to articulate these repressed perceptions. Perhaps, then, in this regard, it is *ostranenie* in reverse. It familiarises the estranged.

The most effective sf, though, is not bluntly declarative, overt, schematic. Mann means to show us the impact of the non-human on the human, and though he does so with a certain directness, using twin viewpoints, these perspectives are not simply parallel, stereoptic. In a hermeneutic move that undermines its own credentials, to the reader's benefit, Mann sets a modest, sensible, rather stolid scholar to editing and annotating the increasingly bizarre diary entries of his mystical mentor, a 'contact linguist' who shares this first contact with the Pe-Ellians. Editor and edited are peeled apart by the shared alien experience, but locked together by the novel's structure. It is a startling and rewarding experience, one which could hardly be duplicated outside the generic possibilities and enabling codes of science fiction.

MONSTROUS DREAMS

Taken together, the science fiction novels I shall now mention, all too briskly, comprise a piquant tapestry of ideas, images and treatments in science fiction's growth from the 1940s to the present, offering an unusual glimpse of the twentieth-century underbelly.

Whether chosen by academy, connoisseur, or ideological criterion, any catalogue of the 'best' science fiction (as with all fiction) risks farce. Nevertheless, such informal lists exist, constituting a series of overlapping canons. If, let us say, feminist critics constitute an alternative canon which for political reasons flies in the face of their predecessors, still they honour writers who have been singled out even in previous unregenerate epochs: Joanna Russ, Ursula Le Guin, Angela Carter, Vonda McIntyre. If a predominantly rightwing *lumpen* libertarian readership hails Heinlein and Niven, still it will probably countenance Delany and Lem.

Such lists include the tallies of winners of the Nebula award, given annually by the membership of the Science Fiction and Fantasy Writers of America, a somewhat less chauvinistic assembly than its name suggests, and of such popular awards as the Hugo and the Locus Poll,[11] both chosen by collectivities with more than a passing interest in the form but not especially qualified to make either literary or scientific judgements. Annotated scholarly guides include the Nicholls/Clute *Encyclopedia* and the Barron *Anatomy of Wonder*,[12] or the contents pages of such vast collections of readings as the Magill Survey in five volumes.[13] I shall take as indicative the selection by David Pringle in his book *Science Fiction: the 100 Best Novels*,[14] which explicitly mimics Anthony Burgess's *Ninety-Nine Novels: the Best in English since 1939*.[15] Pringle's boundary dates are 1949, chosen to coincide with

George Orwell's great marginal sf novel, *Nineteen Eighty-Four* and, in a neat if dated touch, 1984. His choice is limited to works written in English, obliging him to ignore Stanislaw Lem and the Strugatski brothers. Of his hundred, three-quarters are by Americans, all but one of the rest are British; only nine are by women. His list can be parsed in many possible ways. Perhaps the most obvious feature is that some years are dense with candidates, others altogether barren. This does not necessarily reflect annual productivity, since many of the early years are graced in book form by fiction appearing earlier as magazine serials. For all that, it is interesting to note that Pringle's favourite year is 1953, with eight books, followed by 1964, with six, 1968, again with six, and, perhaps surprisingly to those who fancy the genre to have been in the doldrums, 1980, with seven novels.

If we divide the span into decades, beginning at the end, we have the partial decade 1949–54 with 16 novels, the equivalent for a true decade of about 27 books; 1955–64 is the most remarkable period, with 30 novels; 1965–74 has 29, and 1975–84 has 25. This evenness seems suspicious. Has Pringle shuffled his preferences to balance matters out? Perhaps, but it is difficult to fault most of his choices. Some seem implausible at first blush, such as *The Unreasoning Mask* (1981), a Sufi space opera by Philip José Farmer and *Oath of Fealty* (1981), a sort of hymn to corporate Fascism by Larry Niven and Jerry Pournelle, reminiscent in that respect of *A Torrent of Faces* (1967) by James Blish and Norman Knight.[16] But Pringle demonstrates that even these have some exemplary character. Some few of his choices are clearly privately motivated, which is not surprising in a paraliterature where powerful impacts are felt in childhood and adolescence (Heinlein's *Have Spacesuit, Will Travel* (1958), Simak's *Way Station* (1963), John Christopher's early eco-doom novel *The Death of Grass* (1956)). Very few are indefensible. (I have to admit that I was astonished to find my own *The Dreaming Dragons* (1980) listed.) Certain absences are difficult to tolerate (Asimov's *Foundation Trilogy* (1951–3), Heinlein's *Stranger in a Strange Land* (1961), Poul Anderson's *Brain Wave* (1954)); others are imposed by the cut-off dates (for instance, Brian Aldiss's magisterial *Helliconia* (1982–5) trilogy was not yet complete). For all that, an informed observer such as Pringle can offer a sounder list, provide a more useful cartography to the landscapes we are exploring, than the usual default solution: a list of the fan-selected Hugo winners.

Such informed catalogues help pinpoint the changing contours of the field. Consider the volumes chosen by David Wingrove, Brian Aldiss's collaborator in the sf history *Trillion Year Spree*, in his 'SF Alternatives' set of 'Classic Science Fiction'.[17] In a series of graphic ten-year jumps, the seething power fantasies of an age are nowhere better revealed. A. E. van Vogt's *The World of Null-A* (1945) – where the teleporting Gilbert Gosseyn (go-sane) is a cloned superman of reason – is followed by Alfred Bester's brilliant *Tiger! Tiger!* (1955), a cascade of satirical invention, Apollinaire *calligrammes*, romantic compulsions and compulsive Romanticism. A decade later, Roger

Zelazny's adroit poet's pen combines these images of driven mythic demigods in *This Immortal* (1966), a tale of post-holocaust renewal. One might compare this first of Zelazny's novels with Pringle's choice, the superb *The Dream Master*,[18] and his later *Eye of Cat*,[19] a drastically 'literary' adventure using Navajo Indian mythology: somehow the verbal pyrotechnics in the latter strike one as tawdry, brought forth mechanically, as they do in Alfred Bester's late works *Golem-100*[20] and *The Deceivers*.[21]

CYBERPUNK

Such lists and publishing ventures have a tendency to superannuation. By the mid- and late 1980s, the genetic line from Van Vogt and Bester had yielded William Gibson's award-winning first novel *Neuromancer* (the last of Pringle's hundred)[22] and its successors *Count Zero*[23] and *Mona Lisa Over-drive*.[24] The first of these effectively launched cyberpunk's new 'New Wave'. In less than a decade, it had been cloned a hundredfold by inferior copyists and abandoned by its inventors.[25]

The early cyberpunk texts remain a telling embodiment of sf's self-renovating paraliterary contrivances. Set with tense validity in a tacky, scintillating future of computer hacker *idiots-savants*, *Neuromancer* (a knowing wink here to a 'new romanticism') plugs us directly into that universe of dream satisfactions and images – virtual reality – which may well replace television and the ballot. At a cutting edge of sf style innovation, drawing on Raymond Chandler and other 'dirty realists' *avant la lettre*, Gibson's *noir* surface is often brilliantly hard and apt, though any critic sensitive to fashion had to fear for its shelf-life. Andrew Ross has offered the sarcastic opinion, reminiscent of Foyster's cited earlier, that

> Cyberpunk's idea of a counterpolitics – youthful male heroes with working-class chips on their shoulders and postmodern biochips in their brains – seems to have little to do with the burgeoning power of the great social movements of our day: feminism, ecology, peace, sexual liberation, and civil rights. . . . However modern the zeitgeist of cyberpunk, it was clearly a selective zeitgeist.[26]

For all that, Gibson's sleazy hypertech future was a quintessence, for the knowing sf reader, of every crystalline pen from Alfred Bester in the fifties, through Philip K. Dick's paranoia in the sixties, and John Varley's glacial holograms and brain-transplants of the seventies,[27] to a whole ensemble of prestidigitators in the early eighties: Michael Swanwick, Bruce Sterling, John Shirley, some of these latter acknowledged in an afternote. In the late eighties and the nineties, Gibson's peers would carry this trajectory toward an even newer romanticism, employing the latest speculative tropes of nanotech-nology and virtual reality. Especially notable are Swanwick's Varleyesque *Vacuum Flowers*,[28] and *Stations of the Tide*,[29] veritable Lacanian meditations on decentred subjectivity, rendered literally as the fragmentation of neural 'wetware', John Varley's own *Steel Beach*,[30] and Walter Jon Williams's *Aristoi*,[31] a narrative *tour de force* in which the eponymous superhumans each comprise an exquisite notional ego coordinating specialist sub-personalities or 'daimones'.

Gibson himself is fluent in gutter poetry and mock-computerese, his future no less pre-lived-in than Heinlein's. Yet it is revealing that despite a broad consensus hailing the cyberpunk innovations, certain competent critics soon disagreed with this estimate. George Turner claimed that 'the steam-heated prose serves mainly to obscure the novel's deficiencies'.[32] Turner rejected a bid in favour of its 'poetry' made by Russell Blackford, who identified a

> kind of high-tech short-attention-span poetry . . . befitting the high-tech punk future described. Like the movement of the story itself . . . the movement of the sentences is often swift, elliptical, sometimes confusing, occasionally outrunning the capacity of the reader:
>
> > Cold steel odor and ice caressed his spine. And faces peering in from a neon forest, sailors and hustlers and whores, under a poisoned silver sky . . .
>
> Articles, auxiliaries, whole verbs are crushed out. Sentences fragment and sometimes collide.[33]

Turner's traditionalist reading rebels against both text and commentary:

> *Cold* steel odor? Hot steel has a false odor, cold steel has none. Poetry, even as mere poeticism, has to make sense. . . . '. . . a poisoned silver sky . . .' What picture does that create that will make visual sense of an Earthly landscape?[34]

Interestingly, Blackford has already answered Turner's question: no 'picture', but a syntax which performs and emblematises the interior and exterior worlds of the novel, in which the data stored in 'cyberspace' are perceived and manipulated synaesthetically.[35] But the complaint is too narrow in any case. 'Poisoned silver sky' is as much a cognitive image as a visual one, and conveys meaning in several dimensions. It denotes an almost terminally polluted Japanese sky, which is doubtless literally poisoned and silvery in hue. As well, it works by connotation: for example, 'silver sky' = 'silver sea', recalling the mercuric poisoning of edible fish by heedless Japanese industry.

Neuromancer is a dance of death inside the notional space of a computerised data-matrix, a consensual hallucination shared and created by machines and hackers jacked into circuits of astounding power and interconnection. It essays to have us feel – through the violence it does to our syntactic and semantic expectations, which as we have seen is one of the key conditions of effective sf – what the future might be, now that we await autonomously intelligent and even conscious computers. The motivating event of the book is an almost incomprehensible love/hate contest between two machine intelligences, Neuromancer and Wintergreen. In the sequels, these titanic minds are fragmented, but manifest to humans as Voodoo *loa*, a metaphoric move which seems to me as regrettably arbitrary as the poetic devices designated above seem inevitable.

Perhaps the most effective gambit in Gibson's armoury draws on the central implication of formalist criticism: if fiction is not life, neither is life – all is text. If a computer simulation is absolutely compelling, how may its artifice be detected?[36] And how may this truth best be conveyed in a written fiction which tells us of a world that does not exist, outside the link between our programmed brains (our 'wetware') and the lines of text? It is perhaps at this crux that cyberpunk's romantic modernist heritage gives way to drastic ontological doubt, shifting its texts into postmodern territory.

The medium is here almost wholly the message. *Neuromancer* has a story, a sort of hard-boiled gangster plot with Yakuza in place of mafiosa, Tokyo-Chiba instead of downtown San Francisco, the Sprawl spread from New York to Atlanta, the decadent rich Oedipal and Southern-Gothic in a baroque space habitat, dreadlocked Rastas instead of crack vendors – but such itemising denatures the text. Complaints by Foyster, Ross and feminist Nicola Nixon[37] that Gibson relies on male teenagers' fantasies is accurate enough, but irrelevant to what is most impressively at work in these texts: an interaction between novel signifiers and cliché-derived syntagms which create, in Delany's terms, a new 'web' of signification.

VALUE-ADDED TRASH

Gibson deploys his minimalist (*not* skimpy) characters through swift, barely comprehensible plots and counterplots in a century of Japanese super-computers and biotechnology, implants and urban decay. He is the Robert Stone[38] of *gomi*: tomorrow's glistening garbage, reprieved into a kind of cynical art. Lem's defence of Philip K. Dick was exactly that he redeemed trash into value.[39] Collage and pastiche are also, of course, the pre-eminent feature of postmodern textuality, as theorised by such commentators as Jameson (and, indeed, as I use it in this book).[40]

Witness the interpenetration in Gibson's text of vehicle and tenor, of signifiers sliding to signifiers in an hallucinatory attempt on an as-yet (in our 'real' world) unrealisable signified:

Bodiless, we swerve into Chrome's castle of ice. And we're fast, fast. It feels like we're surfing the crest of the invading program, hanging ten above the seething glitch systems as they mutate. We're sentient patches of oil swept along down corridors of shadow. . . .
We've crashed her gates disguised as an audit and three subpoenas,

but her defenses are specifically geared to cope with that kind of official intrusion. Her most sophisticated ice is structured to fend off warrants, writs, subpoenas. When we breached the first gate, the bulk of her data vanished behind core-command ice, these walls we see as leagues of corridor, mazes of shadow. Five separate landlines spurted May Day signals to law firms, but the virus had already taken over the parameter ice. The glitch systems gobble the distress calls as our mimetic subprograms scan anything that hasn't been blanked by core command.[41]

Virtually incomprehensible as this might seem at first blush, it is actually highly redundant, each mention of the concept 'ice' enhancing the reader's preliminary guess at its neologistic meaning. Strictly, a definition has already been offered (Intrusion Countermeasures Electronics: Gibson, 1986a, p. 178), but in such formal terms that it probably does not signify strongly until a second reading; the action sequences concretise this strange usage. What is more, much of the texture is hardly futuristic: 'hanging ten' is even now somewhat old-fashioned surfer cant, conveying, perhaps, the grubby revanchist character of the 'console cowboys' who are attempting to raid and reassign Chrome's Zurich account.

The metaphors which are here actualised perform or enact in miniature the science fictional programme itself. 'Disguised as an audit' is the sort of figure previously found only in some absurdist play by N. F. Simpson or Eugène Ionesco, and carries over from that phantom context some measure of absurdist humour within its *Blues Brothers*-style imposture. Metonymies draw on present-day computing languages (glitches, virus, parameter), immunology and evolutionary theory (virus, mutate), literary theory itself ('mimetic subprograms').

Exposition in such a generic regime becomes implicated in the innovative language itself. New signifieds are constructed within our apprehension that these oddly aggregated signifiers must reflect and not construct *ab initio* some unprecedented collective core meaning: namely, Gibson's 'lived-in' future:

There was a trode-net plastered across the guy's forehead; a single black cable, jacked into a socket behind the left ear, was lashed along the edge of the stretcher. . . . Some kind of cyberspace rig? . . . People jacked in so they could hustle. Put the trodes on and they were out there, all the data in the world stacked up like one big neon city, so you could cruise around and have a kind of grip on it, visually anyway, because if you didn't, it was too complicated, trying to find your way to a particular piece of data you needed. Iconics, Gentry called that.

(*Mona Lisa Overdrive*, p. 19)

Now clearly this is an imagined extension of computer GUI (graphical user interface) 'shell' applications, the kind of thing that Apple Macs or DOS Windows provide with their nested arrays of 'pull-down menu icons'. Or *is* such a description clear, and to whom? It must be highly opaque to any reader without hands-on experience of modern microcomputers, just as metaphoric reference to 'entropy', whether in Heinlein or Pynchon, is inevitably opaque to anyone still ignorant of the fundamentals of thermodynamics or information theory. Obviously it is not necessary to know or even understand the relevant heat equations (I don't) to have some rough sense of what is meant by 'entropy', but C. P. Snow was correct in taking concepts of this order as a shibboleth for separating the scientifically literate from their purely literary kin.

But once the hypothetical circuit is established, the semantic jump achieved, Gibson's text can be read with a minimum of bafflement, mimicking on a kinetic level the transitions of understanding which the reader is making. The theory and practice of reception allegorises the human reader of print as a computer read-head, text as spinning data disk, the almost instantaneous electronic passage of bytes through the circuit as the phantasmatic movement of consciousness through both the iconic realm of cyberspace *and* the iconic economy of science fiction:

A gray disk, the color of Chiba sky.
Now –
Disk beginning to rotate, faster, becoming a sphere of paler gray, expanding –
And flowed, flowered for him, fluid neon origami trick, the unfolding of his distanceless home, his country, transparent 3D chessboard extending to infinity. Inner eye opening to the stepped scarlet pyramid of the Eastern Seaboard Fission Authority burning beyond the green cubes of Mitsubishi Bank of America, and high and very far away he saw the spiral arms of military systems, forever beyond his reach.
(*Neuromancer*, p. 52)

To parse this single, fairly simple dramatisation of cybernetic interface is first to follow all the standard moves of literary address, noting the overall generic slickness, almost kitsch surface common to much popular culture textuality, then the deft syntagmatic progression of 'flowed, flowered for him, fluid' broken, at least in vocal principle, by 'neon', a hard drawn-in bright word disrupting the soothing outward glide, and the crisp primary colour symbolism, halfway between metaphor and metonymy (the bank is the green of money, the Fission Authority scarlet with hot energy and danger), the jousting archaism of 'leagues of corridor' from the earlier quote, and so on.

Beyond these customary analytic moves, common to the anatomising of conventional prose and poetry in all its manifold variety, we are obliged to take a further step: to see in this verbal display the creation of something new under the sun. The logic of the passage is this: a computer is a simulation of certain mental processes, as an electric motor simulates adenosine triphosphate energy sources in muscles. Hence, its inner workings are in *some* sense homologous to our own, or will be when technology has developed to the generation of self-aware computers and beyond; hence we can imagine accessing this inner life by something like the procedure we use to access the consciousness of others. We do *that* by semiotic (iconic and less transparently motivated) forms of imaginative construction of the viewpoint/s of the other. Gibson simply takes this recognition and builds a story from it. And while on some level that story is merely an adventure in an entertainment medium derived from the hard-boiled thriller, on another it is a genuine contribution to the armamentarium of art in its ability to confront aspects of an *episteme* which in many important respects, while we lack the iconic registration to signify it, evades *our* authority.

BEYOND SATIRE

This Besterian conjoining of satire and startling imagery recalls an alternative line or, to borrow an evolutionary figure from the cyberpunk writer Bruce Sterling, a 'clade' of science fiction descent. Kingsley Amis found sf attractive partly because 'it provides a field which, while not actually repugnant to sense and decency, allows us to doff that mental and moral best behaviour with which we feel we have to treat George Eliot and James and Faulkner, and frolic like badly brought-up children among the mobile jellyfishes and unstable atomic piles'.[42] His choice for best sf novel of all time remains what it was in 1960, *The Space Merchants*,[43] Frederik Pohl and C. M. Kornbluth's classic 1953 dystopia about a world run by mad-dog advertising. Amis dubbed this variety of frenetic, intelligent satire 'comic-inferno'.

But the importance of satire in science fiction ought not to be over-emphasised. A quality of wonderment approaching the sublime is central to most memorable science fiction, a quality which requires some deeper engagement than mockery. Consider *Hothouse*, a 1962 fix-up by Brian W. Aldiss.[44] It contrives an anti-Stapledonian destiny for humanity and the world which at once shames our pretensions and arouses a kind of astonished reverence.

Diminished, almost mindless, our descendants scurry or drowse in a global greenhouse where the moon hangs in Earth-Sun Trojan orbit and vast vegetable spiders cross the circumlunar gulf on their mighty cobwebs. The dwarf human Gren attains a degree of poignant consciousness only after invasion of his nervous system by a parasite, the sardonic morel. 'The long afternoon of eternity wore on, that long golden road of an afternoon that would somewhen lead to an everlasting night' (*Hothouse*, p. 43). This is the perspective which afflicts and energises the morel:

> The life forms of the great hothouse world lived out their days in ferocity or flight, pursuit or peace, before falling to the green and forming compost for the next generation. For them there was no past

and no future; they were like figures woven in a tapestry, without depth. The morel, tapping human minds, was different. It had perspective.

It was the first creature in a billion years to be able to look back down the long avenues of time. Prospects emerged that frightened, dizzied, and nearly silenced the harp-like cadences of its voice.

(ibid., p. 92)

What is the morel, if not a figure of humankind, marooned in the symbolic order of our self-constitution in all the great slow cycles of a life-sustaining but mindless and entropic universe? Elegiac as Elgar, witty as Debussy, the conceit leads us at last into Aldiss's 'wonderful gladness' (p. 253).

Is there some common factor in these works, these tales, these intertexts? Certainly it is not the simple assertion that their characters dwell in the future, or that the world is other than we suppose it to be. A suitable test case is Raymond Federman's metafiction *The Twofold Vibration* (1982), a tale ostensibly about people being removed to space colonies.[45] Whatever its merits as *nouvelle vague*, it is markedly weak as sf. Of course, the text wishes strenuously to deny such lineage, but it cannot that easily be let off the hook:

> what do you mean science-fiction, not at all, it's not because one wanders into the future that
>
> call it exploratory or better yet extemporaneous fiction, that's right, a question of more space, room to expand forward and backward, a matter of distanciation if you wish, room to turn imagination loose on the spot and shift perspectives unexpectedly, sounds interesting, damn right, but no futuristic crap, I mean pseudoscientific bullshit, space warfare, fake theories of probabilities, unsolvable equations, strange creatures from other planets, ludicrous busybodies with pointed ears . . . none of that, a way to look at the self, at humanity, from a potential point of view, premembering the future rather than remembering the past, but no gadgetry, no crass emotionless robots that crush the shit out of you . . .
>
> as for the space colonies, they are conquered planets, moons, satellites in the solar system, and even beyond, in the galaxy, the Milky Way, which were explored and civilized during the last part of the 20th century, and where
>
> of course I have to invent the future, all right the near future only, move about among new forms, new concepts, project ourselves into the potential cosmological layout, but obliquely. . . .

(Twofold Vibration, pp. 1–3)

I cite this feverish disclaimer at some length precisely to heighten its overwrought character when compared with the best sf. Aldiss's *Hothouse* plays all the tricks which Federman's narrative voice abominates, delighting in invented creatures with odd names (the tummy belly man, the sodal, speedseeds, pluggyrugs, the radiation-hungry traversers), but the Wellsian perspective Aldiss seeks and attains is hardly less worth winning.

But Federman is surely not attacking the likes of Aldiss, whom I suspect he has never heard of. His foe, the idea he has of sf, is rather some unschooled amalgam of *Star Trek* (the pointed ears), comic-book robots, and that other postmodern sf fellow traveller, William Burroughs. His affected distancing from the devices of sf, the halfhearted handwaving of the penultimate paragraph above, signifies above all his contempt for the medium which he wishes to colonise, which he conceives to be vulgarised beyond endurance.

It would be dull to chide him for the truly stupid error of supposing that the Milky Way – its 100,000 light-year extent, the worlds of its trillion stars – might be 'colonised' in less than two decades, for that would be to miss the fact that he is debunking this level of verisimilitude. . . . But what, then, is gained in his imposture of 'premembering the future'? The vulgarities of sf are sidestepped, true, but a new coarseness, a kind of highbrow philistinism, is the cost.

Professor Federman is, as it happens, a notable Beckett specialist; he owns, the jacket notes inform us, a dog named Sam and a cat named Vladimir.[46] In bite-size paragraphs lacking periods, his narrator tells the tale of The Old Man, who is neither and both Federman and Beckett, and his attendants Moinous (me-us) and Namredef (the author mirrored). The Old Man is to be deported to the space colonies on New Year's Eve, 1999. For some crime? For old age? For not being a new redeemed person, it seems. Utopia has been attained, and the old people have to be put down quietly. Is the novel about new technology, then? No. Clearly, like other Federman writing, it is not about the future but about that past which lingers like a wound in the guts of the twentieth century, the German death camps.

Nightmares and dreams again. Can we persistently hold the Holocaust, the Gulag, the evils of Left brutalities and Right death squads alike, all this horror, at some pivot of awareness? No. Can it be expelled from art, or indeed through art, perhaps from that kind of art which toys with large angelic aliens and non-existent space colonies? No, but a total obsession with ruin and evil is psychologically insupportable, or absurd. D. M. Thomas's *The White Hotel* built the horror right into the core of his tale of self-discovery through fantasy, as Rod Jones's *Julia Paradise* has done more recently.[47] Federman attempts the same transformation, without Freud, at a further remove. The first two approximated their artistic goals. I doubt that Federman has done so.

Why is that? It is telling that he declares a need for an 'exploratory or better yet an extemporaneous fiction . . . room to turn imagination loose on the spot and shift perspectives unexpectedly . . . a way to look at the self, at humanity, from a potential point of view, premembering the future rather than re-membering the past'. Federman is right in this. Sf has given writers and readers access to new metaphors and metonymies. But for all Federman's learning and postmodernist nuance, it is not he but the genre-rooted and fertilised Besters, Gibsons and Aldisses who make these tropes bear fruit.

I have mentioned Aldiss's vast dreamscape *Helliconia* several times already. In some respects it is the epitome of modern science fiction, a kind of last hurrah for a modernist impulse already overtaken by the postmodern. Yet it stands against a tide of inconsequential consumer produce like a bulwark. It is at once a rich revelling in free invention and a sort of thesis novel, a three-decker of extravagant ambition. Let us spend some time exploring this remarkable text which, like its contemporary cyberpunk, links sf's modern and postmodern moments.

7

THE STARS MY DISSERTATION

[A]t the far end of the smoke-filled room was a guy leaning over a typewriter as big as an upright piano. He just sprawled there, taking no notice of anyone, tapping out a few sentences on the keys. And [a] man in [a] sharp suit said, 'What you turn out that fantasy stuff for? Play something happy, something familiar.'

And the guy looked up . . . and kind of smiled . . . 'I believe in what I do. This is where I sing the science fiction blues. This is my kind of music. I work in an under-privileged, under-valued medium, sure, and even within that medium my style offends a whole lot of people . . .'

And the man in the sharp suit said, 'People want to be cheered up. They want to hear about real things.'

'One or the other you can have. Not both. See, my stories are about human woes, non-communication, disappointment, endurance, acceptance, love.'[1]

So wrote Brian Aldiss in a barbed Author's Note prefacing his short story collection *Last Orders* (1977). He portrays himself running off bitter-sweet arpeggios of fantasy to the uncaring ears of a noisy, drunken crowd who await only that ultimate fantasy, that final reality, the dropping of the Bomb.

An extravagantly gifted writer poised always between facility and felicity, Aldiss had written wistfully, four years earlier, of a day to come 'when writers who invent whole worlds are as highly valued as those who recreate the rise and fall of a movie magnate or the breaking of two hearts in a bedsitter. The invented universe, the invented time, are often so much closer to us than Hollywood or Kensington'.[2] On this reckoning, sf prestidigitators are typically short-changed on two counts: earnings, and the esteem of peers from the dismissive realm of 'literature'. If to a small extent things have improved in the interim, sf's inventiveness, by an unhappy irony, has tended to fall inversely with the rising stock of imagined worlds.

LEARNING THE TROPES

The faults of most well-liked consumer sf are those of fiction-as-product, written by those who have gone to school with the experts for those who insist on nothing more demanding. This weakness in genre readers for a reliable 'mixture as before' helps explain that repugnant marketing phenomenon of the 1980s and 1990s, the sf or fantasy 'trilogy'. Nor should one forget that for sf's annual batch of fresh apprentices, the mixture has *not* been tasted before. As Canadian commentator Andrew Weiner put it in 1993:

> The real business of sf is sci-fi (that is, entertaining action-adventure books, with a sympathetic protagonist pursuing a clear-cut goal through a series of escalating crises, preferably packaged in series and with appeal to adolescents). Perhaps it always has been, although never so single-mindedly as today.[3]

The impulse behind extended multi-volume texts is not, however, automatically discreditable, though it is most easily understood in Barthesian 'readerly' terms. Consumers become attached to their favourite escapist settings and characters. Sf writers, too, obliged with each new work to conjure entire ecosystems and social orders, find increasingly attractive the possibility of lengthy exploration in a trademarked domain. But intellectual and artistic laziness, the lure of the ideological comforter, is not always the motive in either case, though these are patently the constant risk and temptation.

Sf's revival of the Victorian three-decker is a borrowing less from Proust, Powell, Durrell and Waugh than of radio and television narrative techniques: the soap, the big-budget mini-series. Instead of a leisurely stroll through the transparently reassuring stability of a nineteenth-century imperial social landscape, sf offers brisker jogs through entirely constructed settings of outer and inner space (plenty of the former, admittedly, just as imperial). This opportunity can meet fair ends as well as foul. If 'Doc' Smith made full use of it, to sf's artistic cost, with his endless adolescent galactic adventures, which Asimov bureaucratised and sanitised within an allegorical frame of history, Ursula Le Guin chanced her hand and made the Earthsea and Hainish universes for our instruction and delight, our pleasure and gain.

After many years of abundant diversity in voice and plot, Brian Aldiss himself turned finally to the creation of a whole world and the millennial cycles of its civilisations. In the *Helliconia* sequence, Aldiss avoided the usual difficulty in producing part-works, that of either creating false climaxes or leaving his readers dangling between volumes. Broadly delimited in advance, it took advantage of new scientific perspectives (such as the nuclear winter threat and the Gaia hypothesis) which arose during its writing. The structure of his trilogy's universe solved the problem by meeting it head on. Its time scale is so great that Aristotelian unities are burst before we begin.

And if the work can be seen as a tribute to both the realist tradition of the last century and the modernism of the early part of this one, it is also curiously self-deconstructing. To judge from his magnum opus (nearly half a million words long), Aldiss is no stranger to aporia. While the three books teem with invention and undisguised creative generosity, these are paradoxically propelled by a profound pessimism.

In our own remote future, after the near death of the Earth, an evolved humanity muses that for us today 'aggression and killing had been an escape from pain: in the end, the planet had been murdered by its own sons' (*Helliconia Winter*, p. 234). That bone-deep gloom is ostensibly reprieved, in the final volume, by mystic apprehensions of Gaia. But one could be forgiven for supposing that Aldiss is reaching for hope like a street-wise Pandora who should know better than to look for comfort at the bottom of a jar of bad news.

TIME'S ARROW, TIME'S CYCLE

Two great metaphors govern temperate-zone human life, at mutual odds. One is the annual round, the endless rise and fall of the sun in the sky, the mercury in the thermometer. The other is a linear measure, the individual's passage from conception to death and dissolution. How we see and weigh the world's fate and our moral implication in it depends, perhaps, on which of these images stings most deeply into our hearts. Aldiss raises a complex, audacious structure upon this dichotomy. Helliconia is an imaginary world a thousand light years from Earth, spinning about a sun dimmer than ours. For eight million years it has followed a vast ellipse around an intruding distant hot giant star which once snatched Helliconia's moon out of its sky, a catastrophe which seems to have spurred humanoid life into consciousness (a notion with interesting Jungian undertones). Every 1,825 lesser years, these epicycles fetch Helliconia from glacial centuries of winter through a season of spectacular spring metamorphosis to a cruel summer basting under two suns high in the same sky.

Nor is Aldiss content with doubling the number of suns. His world is inhabited by two major conscious species, one humanoid, the other distinctly not. These latter 'phagors' or 'ancipitals' are creatures suited to a glacial world, the world which was Helliconia before the hot sun gave the upstart mammals a chance at equality. An authentically disturbing feature of the invented phagors is the nature of their consciousness. They do not think; apprehensions move like curdled milk in their 'pale harneys', a haunting phrase which captures for sf something of Princeton psychologist Julian Jaynes's poetic vision of pre-modern 'bicameral' humanity.

Jaynes's ponderously titled *The Origin of Consciousness in the Breakdown of the Bicameral Mind* was a literary if not a scientific *succès de scandale* in 1976, proposing that as recently as the singing of the Iliad human minds were literally split, the wisdom of the race introjected as 'gods' who audibly spoke their commands and temptations.[4] The *thumos*, or emotional soul, was originally figured as a sort of abdominal organ, though even a raging ocean also has *thumos*. Achilles fought, according to Diomedes, 'when the *thumos* in his chest tells him to and a god rouses him!' Rather similar was *phren*, located in the middle of the body and generally plural. Aldiss catches this shivery hypothesis exactly and amplifies it. His ancient phagors 'in tether', sinking ever more profoundly into moribund semi-life, gain a condition halfway between household god-totem and embodied collective unconscious.

These two species, 'human' and phagor, pursue an ancient cycle of renewal and forgetfulness. One important theme of the trilogy (recalling Asimov's 'Nightfall') is the human search for a scientific social order robust enough to carry formal knowledge through the scourges of high summer and dread winter, to wrench cyclic time into linear progress.

What is more, Helliconia rejoices in an abundance of well-conceived beasts, birds, semi-sentients, cultures, languages, climates, religions, political systems, and indeed verifiable afterlives: not merely the tether of the phagors, but a similar state for the humanoids, who sink under the earth as 'gossies' and 'fessies'.

As if all this is not enough, Helliconia's ecological drama is observed from orbit by the Earth-human *Avernus* crew, who transmit detailed real-life soap operas of Helliconian life back home, before falling prey in turn to corruption, boredom and savagery. And on Earth, in *its* turn, great changes are taking place. Aldiss reveals these in reverse, showing us first the peaceful and highly evolved people of the eighth millennium, only to track remorselessly backwards to the holocaust and nuclear winter which all but exterminates linear society on Earth even as the seasonal societies of Helliconia grind through their own pitiful and exultant trajectories.

FLAWS IN THE PATTERN

For all this godlike perspective, Aldiss spares his reader the lofty pretensions of Frank Herbert's prescient superfolk, the soothing whimsy of sword-and-sorcery heptalogies by Piers Anthony and his epigones, the flattened affect of most routine sf. Yet for whole stretches, curiously enough, the result is boredom rather than cognitive excitement. With a few obvious late exceptions (*Enemies of the System* (1978), for example, or *Moreau's Other Island* (1980)), Aldiss has rarely been tedious. Baffling and enigmatic, certainly, as befits a writer working at the boundary of modernism and postmodernism; pedestrian, no. His language dances. Early forays in *Helliconia* might suggest that the weight of a new seriousness crushes the usual sportiveness. Yet several conceits redeem the first volume, especially those portraying psychic descent into the underworld of the dead 'fessups' and 'gossies'. It is as if the shade of Philip K. Dick has taken possession of Aldiss's hand:

There was no smell except terror. Every death had its immutable position . . . This was the realm of entropy absolute, without change, the event death of the universe. . . . In the original boulder . . . the gossies and fessups were stacked, like thousands of ill-preserved flies. . . . They resembled mummies; their stomachs and eye sockets were hollow, their boney [*sic*] feet dangled; their skins were coarse as old sacking, yet transparent, allowing a glimpse of luminescent organs beneath. Their mouths were open like fish, as if they still recalled the days when they breathed air. Less ancient gossies had their mouths stuffed with things like fireflies which issued forth in smokey [*sic*] dust. . . . The gossies emitted a noise of unceasing complaint.

(*Spring*, p. 206)

The whingeing iteration of grievance which Aldiss goes on to create is more horrifying still, a vision of hell from some bad-tempered suburban spiritualist. Yet in this evocative stretch of writing, certain depressing flaws of the whole are evident: a carelessness, perhaps, or a blurring of focalisation. Through which consciousness (in a world straining, as the first volume's is, for the astronomical insights of a Galileo) does the narrative compare the afterlife with the second law of thermodynamics? Our own century's, of course; Aldiss's. And do fish really hold their mouths open to breathe air, even on Helliconia? A more startling lapse is found at the very beginning: on p. 3, 'Yuli was seven years old'; by p. 15, a few hours later, he has become 'a nine-year-old human being'. Does this reflect the differential between Batalix and Solar years? No, for that ratio is 1.42 to 1. While this detail is entirely trivial, it suggests a surprising heedlessness. Perhaps this rupturing of scrupulously limited focalisation is desirable in what is plainly an allegorical construct, but it constitutes a clumsy dissonance (and not an effectively deconstructive one) with those techniques of the sf mega-text on which it otherwise depends.

Worse yet, intrusive lumps of exposition repeatedly loom in italics on the page. Their scientific validity is vouched for, we are told insistently in the apparatus which surrounds these books, by leading scientists and linguists, friends and advisers to Aldiss. Likewise, too much hangs on coincidence in a work which lacks the self-undermining *joie de vivre* of, say, Barth's *Sabbatical* (1982). Shay Tal's 'ice miracle', echo of a dozen Boy's Own adventure books, is a wonderful image, quite nicely executed:

Then the transformation. Then the moment that ever after in the annals of Oldorando would be referred to as the miracle of Fish Lake.
. . . The whole group of marauders, sixteen in number, had entered the lake, led by the three mounted stalluns. Their rage drove them into the alien element, they were thigh deep in it, churning it up with the fury of their charge, when the entire lake froze.

One moment, it was an absolutely still liquid, lying, because un-
disturbed, unfrozen at three degrees below freezing point. The next
moment, disturbed, it became solid. Kaidaws and phagors all were
locked in its embrace.

(*Spring*, pp. 175–6)

It is so improbable, however, in the good luck of its timing, that it ejects
readers up out of the text at the very moment when we are meant to applaud
this proto-scientist's cleverness, not Aldiss's.[5] Besides, who measures these
degrees below freezing? What has gone awry in his sf-specific artistry?

Aldiss once observed: 'When sf writers began taking themselves seriously,
they tended to abandon their imagination and rely instead on the predictions
of think-tanks or on extrapolations from scientific journals and population
statistics, resulting in a descent into greyness, a loss of the original driving
force, an espousal of literalism.'[6] In *Helliconia Spring*, this unattractive fate
began to overwhelm Aldiss himself, undercutting what would prove nevertheless to be one of his finest achievements.

THE HAZARD OF DIDACTICISM

At its most ambitious, science fiction aspires to the achievement of civilisation's great learned crackpots: Gibbon, Marx, Spengler, Wells, Jung, Lévi-
Strauss, Lacan. Wells, after all, was himself the greatest of sf's progenitors.
The impulse is to catch up all the world's bounty in a single equation. A
formula for generating freewheeling adventure stories is recast to fuse the
rigorous claims of the laboratory with the heart-pulse of myth.

Climbing high for perspective, left foot on the physicist's shoulder, right
on the shaman's, such visionaries are foredoomed but exhilarating. So
Asimov plots the dynamics of empire out of Gibbon into the galaxy, Blish
sends entire immortal cities aloft, borne up by Spengler's ghost, peevish as
any fessup or gossie. Aldiss is one of the few truly able representatives of
this impulse, favouring the generous over the austere, the drone, or the shriek.
Clearly, in the enormous thought-experiment of the trilogy, he has followed
a trail blazed by Wells. He has expressed his credo, evident from *Non-Stop*
and *Hothouse* on, that

my fiction should be social, should have all the laughter and other
elements we associate with prosaic life, yet be shot through with a sense
that our existence has been overpowered (not always for the worse) by
certain gigantic forces. [7]

He means the forces of intellect coupled to energy unleashed in the
Industrial Revolution. On Helliconia, those gigantic forces are emblematised
by the terrible cycles of seasons beyond our ready comprehension. Still, one
can discern in *Helliconia* a hint at least of what Aldiss found in Wells: 'He

took to making the message clearer and clearer. His characters became mouth-pieces, the fiction became lost in didacticism. Wells gained volume and lost quality' (Aldiss, with Wingrove, 1986, p. 131).

The second volume, *Helliconia Summer*, goes much of the way to reprieving Aldiss from this edifying fate. Its compass is restricted to a few months, and it is possible, as it was not in the first volume, to follow across the landscape a handful of fifteenth-century-style kings and queens, ice traders, and proto-scientists, human and otherwise, without suspecting that they might on any page be snatched from us and cast abruptly into the narrative's antiquity.

Even the segments of laboured exposition are renewed by embodying their principal viewpoint in the person of a young man from the Earth observatory, the *Avernus*, which has circled Helliconia for 3,269 years. A further haunting resonance is established when we also witness the response, a thousand years later again, of viewers on a radically altered Earth. Aldiss has experimented with this dislocated perspective before, most notably in his *nouveau roman*, *Report on Probability A* (1968), in which watchers watch watchers who watch other watchers. . . . This recursive voyeurism is now mediated by communications technology limited to the speed of light-transmission. The expedition which launched the *Avernus* left our future in 2108. Those on Earth who read the new world through its lens, as a vast soap opera, do so in AD 7877. The cultures of our home planet ebb and alter to a cycle slower but no less ineluctable than that which racks Helliconia.

In a typical Aldiss reversal, the voyage in the underworld of fessups is replayed in summer garb – and now we find the dead cloyingly sweet, forgiving, and hence more irritating than previously. Moreover, with advances in scientific insight in the principal Helliconian culture, the 'original boulder' that was previously the heart of its ontology has become the 'original beholder' – a sort of quantum theoretic jest, or perhaps merely a Berkeleian one.

Elsewhere, the language remains little better than drab. The canvas becomes so broad that we lose hold on any commitment to its figures. Arguably, of course, this is less an artistic failure than a suitable extended metaphor for the multi-layered text Aldiss offers us.

We are returned, in these questions of evaluation, to the fundamental issue: what is the merit in making such an imaginary object as this trilogy's multiple worlds? When we might read Tolstoy and Proust on the one hand, or Kafka and Calvino on the other, do we really wish to hear about flawed nervy kings and their beautiful betrayed women strutting a wholly contrived but (perhaps vulgarly) circumstantial *mise-en-scène*? When I raised some of these doubts publicly after the appearance of the first two volumes, Aldiss responded with some vehemence:

I derived this particular bit of the Helliconia story from the Nemanija

dynasty which ruled a medieval Serbian state until the Turks over-
whelmed them. Milutin, in particular, married a child bride for dynastic
reasons. [Another] answer to the rhetorical question, and the best one,
would be that while you are reading about this flawed king and his
betrayed queen, you are also reading a drama of human lust and
possessiveness. The story makes it clear that the queen really can't let
go of the king, even when dismissed, any more than he can of her. . . .
In a sense, the whole book [i.e. the trilogy] is 'about' our fever to
possess one another: the happiness it brings, the misery. I'm glad
Damien didn't consciously observe this, since it absolves me from the
charge of didacticism . . . No, I'm cheating saying it that way: for in
the end of Winter I do almost step forward and deliver my message to
the camera. You can't write three slogging great novels like these
without having something to say about which you feel strongly.[8]

This is certainly a curious apologia for so literate and self-conscious a
writer, especially one specialising in fanciful constructs. Do we wish to hear
X in sf, the domain of the freely invented? Yes, since X is based on a true
story (the sales pitch more typically heard of made-for-TV movies). What is
more, X can teach us, perhaps in allegory, timeless truths about human
ambivalences. But is this not brute didacticism, the enemy of art, the stars as
dissertation? No, but then again yes.

The afterword to *Helliconia Winter* is an open letter to Aldiss's son Clive,
where we find a most explicit address to the camera (p. 283, but significantly
unnumbered), which comes closer to resolving the matter:

it occurs to me that the question to ask is, Why do individuals of the
human race long for close community with each other, and yet remain
so often apart? Could it be that the isolating factor is similar to that
which makes us feel, as a species, apart from the rest of nature?

Aldiss wishes us to search out biological links with the remainder of
creation, rather than dwell on our essence-free construction as 'subjects'
within ideology. It is as distressed a cry against the isolation which consciousness works in us (and, whether or not Aldiss means this, also against the anti-
humanist project of poststructuralism) as one might find. The Avernus, that
orbiting entrance to Hell, plainly represents the ruin culture may wreak upon
us, the very contrary of the condition observed so poignantly in *Hothouse*:

The Avernus was an embodiment, cast in the most advanced technology
of its culture, of the failure to perceive the answer to that age-old
problem of why mankind was divorced from its environment. It was the
ultimate token of that long divorce.

(*Summer*, p. 74)

While such declarative passages fail to illustrate the richly embroidered texture of the trilogy, they do show the courage of Aldiss at his best (his willingness to say something about the largest possible scheme of things human and otherwise) and at his worst, when rude summary tilts into egregious failure of tone, as in this fall from literary tact:

> Everything depraved flourished. The laboratories were encouraged to bring forth more and more grotesque mutations. Dwarfs with enlarged sex organs were succeeded by hybrid sex organs imbued with life. . . . These reproductive leviathans publicly aroused and engulfed each other, or overwhelmed the humans thrown into their path. . . . In their later stages of evolution, these autonomous genitalia grew enormous; a few became violent, battering like multicoloured slugs at the walls of the glass tanks wherein they spent their somewhat holobenthic existence. (p. 76)

So, again: might sf writers such as Aldiss be best advised, purely on artistic grounds, to stick with the mundane world and have their say without the obscuring tricks of a cosmic costume-drama genre? One might have posed a similar question to, say, L. H. Myers, whose *The Near and the Far* (1940) adopted as setting a largely fanciful sixteeth-century India. 'My object,' Myers noted, 'was to carry the reader out of our familiar world into one where I could – without doing violence to his sense of reality – give prominence to certain aspects of human life, and illustrate their significance.' Myers wrote under the explicit threat of Fascism, but stood firm in his belief in the virtues of imagination:

> It has certainly not been my intention to set aside the social and ethical problems that force themselves upon us at the present time. On the contrary, my hope has been that we might view them better from the vantage-ground of an imaginary world.[9]

Aldiss's achievement in the Helliconia sequence is to develop a genuinely wondrous world without, indeed, violating our sense of reality. What the text means to teach us seems to be a tragic acceptance, a conservatism spelled out thus by one of the characters: 'Culture may flourish better under old injustice than under new' (*Summer*, p. 330). One recalls Fredric Jameson's Marxist assessment of *Non-Stop* (*Starship*): 'it makes little difference whether the reader chooses to take Mr. Aldiss's own rather reactionary political interjections at face value . . . en route to space and to galactic escapism, we find ourselves locked in the force field of very earthly political realities'.[10] And indeed Jameson has praised the Helliconia trilogy for its fecundity, the ambitious scale of its artistry:

> [A]bove all I admired the *intelligence* of this series – its marvellous narrative inventiveness being taken for granted – but here on top of it is a literature for grown-ups and a very intelligent man asking *mature*

questions about the span of history and a range of landscapes and experience normally furnished us in the mode of adolescent fantasy. It is a renewal of history in a new way. [11]

One sees how this is possible. Aldiss's conservatism is not wholly defeatist: it is close to dialectical. His work seems obsessively to return to the principle he terms 'that chastising enantiodromia' (*Summer*, p. 388): a force in mind and brute matter alike which ceaselessly changes each thing into its opposite. It is the axis upon which the great wheel of the seasons of Helliconia, world and novel, turns. In the final volume, the topic recurs on pages 43, 221 ('Enantiodromia once more. Just when the ranks were closing, a gulf opened; when unity was within reach, the divisions became widest'), and 271 ('Sunrise was enantiodromic sunset'). What is more, Joseph Winter in *Forgotten Life*, a non-sf novel drawing very closely on Aldiss's own life, speaks of 'that fatal phenomenon at the heart of the sodding world, enantio-dromia, the incessant and inevitable turning of all things into their opposites' (Aldiss, 1988, p. 182). This definition might profitably be matched with Jameson's account of dialectic:

> The basic story which the dialectic has to tell is no doubt that of the dialectical *reversal*, that paradoxical turning around of a phenomenon into its opposite. . . . It can be described as a kind of leap-frogging affair in time, in which the drawbacks of a given historical situation turn out in reality to be its secret advantages, in which what looked like built-in superiorities suddenly prove to set the most ironclad limits on its future development. [12]

It is hardly surprising, then, that Jameson so greatly admires the Helliconia trilogy, or that his early study of generic discontinuities found its example in Aldiss's *Starship*.

A FATAL INNOCENCE

The third volume, *Helliconia Winter*, follows the Tolstoyan wanderings of young Luterin Shokerandit, citizen of Sibornal (a northern land strongly reminiscent of eighteenth-century Russia) and son of a man even more powerful than Luterin appreciates. Scarred by a 'fatal innocence', an inability to face evil which makes him both saint and sinner, convenient victim of a politics he loathes, Luterin ends an outcast, screaming useless but exhilarated defiance at the sunken sun of winter.

While Aldiss's writing *qua* writing remains in this concluding volume less pleasing than usual, much *is* genuinely powerful and beautiful, particularly his evocation of an iced landscape stretching from north Tropic to polar circle. In one vividly realised and quite terrifying sequence, luckless Luterin escapes his tormentors by entering a cell inside a gigantic rotating stone zodiac which completes its own cycle only once in ten years. Luterin's loathing and desire for his snail's-pace-shifting cell is no less convincing than Oriana Fallaci's account of the immurement of Alexis Panagoulis, the Greek patriot imprisoned and destroyed by the Colonels and his own anarchic soul.[13]

The mythic inevitability of this final tale of a culpably innocent son at once fleeing and seeking the father he loves/hates, and his quest's Oedipal resolution, carries the trilogy to a general success on both metaphors of change, linear and cyclic. Regrettably, it carries as well the gratuitous weight of a somewhat lumbering mystic component Aldiss adds – rather opportunistically, one might think – to his parable. What one tends at first to read as wicked sarcasm in the portrayal of the dead in the post-mortem condition of 'pauk', initially bitter and complaining and later saccharine in their summer forgiveness, is inverted once more, this time (allegedly) to our metaphysical hearts' ease:

> Dreadful though the phagors are, they are not estranged from the Original Beholder, the Helliconian Gaia figure. So they are not tormented by the spirits about them. . . . How happy . . . if [Helliconia's 'humans'] could have comfort from their gossies in the midst of all their other troubles.
>
> (*Winter*, p. 139)

So Gaia (the ecological totality of life on Earth), recovered from nuclear holocaust, uses massed human empathy to awaken her equivalent tutelary deity on Helliconia. It is a belated note of redemptive uplift damaging to Aldiss's fundamentally sceptical and tragic realism. In Doris Lessing's clumsy mythoderivative 'Canopus in Argo' sequence of pseudo-sf novels, hailed everywhere for their imaginative daring except among apprenticed sf fans, humans have suffered a kind of von-Danikenesque expulsion from the Garden of Eden. Aldiss's closing figuration is almost as tiresome, as unrelated to reality, as Lessing's bathetic and literal-minded SOWF ('Substance of We Feeling'), to which we postlapsarian humans have lost soothing access.

For all that, the *Helliconia* trilogy constitutes a major text in the emerging sf canon. Despite its flaws it is perhaps the pinnacle of Modern (and modernist) sf to date. This category within sf's mode, we recall, is marked by its emphasis on knowing the universe and capturing that knowledge in some variety of prose appropriate to its epistemological assumptions: not always 'transparent', but in some measure confident in its purchase on an external reality. The postmodern branch of sf is altogether less secure. Simulation and reality are liable to bleed into one another, which is why Fredric Jameson (as we shall see in the next chapter) finds cyberpunk so richly emblematic of both postmodernism and late capitalist culture with its ontological *angst*, its ceaseless questioning of the 'being' of the world. I do not mean that Aldiss is complacent, only that his artistic emphasis is always focused on the utterance of his text rather than its subversion, even when he is building entire worlds in notional contrast to our own quotidian.

Helliconia fails only and precisely in the degree to which it attempts to escape its own strategic location as a node in a specialised mega-text. Its worst moments are its lapses into explication; its finest are those where it takes for granted a readership keyed to the usages of its generic coding (but a readership alert, as well, to the overlaid codes and connotations of authorised 'literature').

DEEP IDENTITY

I have attempted in the first part of this book to convey something of the extent and mechanism of contemporary science fiction. The major result of such explorations has been a growing recognition, I think, that in sf the impulses of science and fiction do indeed overlap, not as opposed variant forms of human understanding but in sharing a deep identity, rather as the four drastically different fundamental forces of physics are now theorised as having sprung from the broken symmetrisation of a single Ur-force.[14] In this case, that deep identity is the discursive unity noted in Fredric Jameson's gesture towards 'one of the newest and most profound tendencies of contemporary thought in general, namely, the increasing foregrounding of narrative itself as a fundamental instance of human understanding.[15]

Sf has been located, in short, at the intersecting knot between the two great discursive fields known in shorthand for 30 years as 'the two cultures' – a knot suffering a torsion that arguably must twist Western civilisation from one *episteme* to another not yet quite born.

Now I mean to take description and analysis further, invoking post-modernist challenges to literary and paraliterary traditions, especially as these models and challenges are articulated through Jameson's theoretical constructs and Delany's theorised fictions and fictive theories.

Part II

POSTMODERN SCIENCE FICTION

8

MAKING UP WORLDS

[T]he dominant of modernist fiction is *epistemological* . . . the dominant of postmodernist fiction is *ontological*. . . . What happens when different kinds of world are placed in confrontation, or when boundaries between worlds are violated? What is the mode of existence of a text, and . . . of the world (or worlds) it projects? . . .

Science fiction, like postmodernist fiction, is governed by the ontological dominant. Indeed, it is perhaps *the* ontological genre *par excellence*. We can think of science fiction as postmodernism's non-canonized or 'low art' double, its sister-genre in the same sense that the popular detective thriller is modernist fiction's sister-genre.

(Brian McHale)[1]

Contemporary sf, especially when it follows strategies pioneered by Kurt Vonnegut and Samuel R. Delany, intersects and even overlaps the postmodern in crucial respects.

Diagnoses of the postmodern have become endemic in the last couple of decades. For clarity and economy, and by reason of its general persuasiveness, I shall follow Fredric Jameson's synoptic account, 'Postmodernism, or The Cultural Logic of Late Capitalism',[2] while noting my twofold unease: first, at Jameson's unmodified faith in Marxism as the highest stage of practical philosophy, a view I do not share; and second, despite this, at an ecumenical inclusiveness he manages to manifest toward incompatible theories (though this is, it's true, a mark of the postmodern).

Moreover, Jameson is too often hortatory and minatory by turns precisely where one wishes to see hard analytic bridgework. In one impassioned and absurd strophe, he espies, like some Preacher of the End Days, 'an imperative to grow new organs, to expand our sensorium and our body to some new, as yet unimaginable . . . dimensions' (1984, p. 80). This resembles nothing so much as the utopian – even the somewhat crackpot – voice of a Bernard Shaw if not a Timothy Leary. Yet it is in exactly this perilous register that Jameson's theories come closest to illuminating science fiction at its most audacious, silly, ambitious and indispensable.

What Jameson would term a dialectical relationship, and I would prefer to characterise as complexly interactive, obtains between the postmodern condition – roughly, the sociology of our epoch – and those cultural objects which critics have come to group together as sharing certain 'postmodern' sites, tropes and strategies.

WHAT IS THE POSTMODERN?

Is this analytic category *the postmodern* an artistic or social one or indeed finally historical, as its periodising name – though timidly indefinite – implies? All three, no doubt, in a mutually modifying loop of texts and contexts. Hence it is feasible for a theorisation of textual kinds to feed back into empirical readings even as those readings help to reframe the definitions of the objects under scrutiny.

Modernism and postmodernism, for Jameson as for McHale, are best construed as *cultural dominants*, Roman Jakobson's notion, rather than single styles: so to speak, as modes rather than genres (Jameson, 1984, pp. 55–7). Not everything produced today is postmodern, but postmodernity remains 'the force field in which very different kinds of cultural impulses . . . must make their way' (ibid., p. 57). (Jameson's borrowing of 'force field' from physics, albeit rather superannuated physics, is typical, and refreshing.) The principal features associated with this dominant, or perhaps constituting it, though its source is elsewhere than in culture proper, are:

- 'a flatness or depthlessness . . . – perhaps the supreme formal feature of all the postmodernisms' (p. 60);
- a waning of affect, or feeling, linked to the (alleged) loss of discrete subjectivity, (p. 61) and
- the replacement of affect (especially alienated *angst*) by 'a peculiar kind of euphoria' coupled with a loss of memory (p. 64);[3]
- the end of personal, unique style and a sense of history itself, and their replacement by *pastiche* (not parody, but the transcoding of modernist idiolects into jargon, badges and other decorative codes) and nostalgia (pp. 64–5);
- the fragmentation of artistic texts after the model of schizophrenic *écriture*, which takes the form especially of *collage* governed by 'differentiation rather than unification' (pp. 71–6);[4]
- and most of all, the 'hysterical sublime', a theme developed in Lyotard, in which the 'other' of human life surpasses our power to represent it and pitches us into a sort of Gothic rapture (pp. 76 ff.).

In this last feature, Jameson's attempt at a transcoding between the arts and the cultural determinants or the dominant which focuses them in our analysis is at once most traditionally Marxist and yet provocative even in an era when Marxism is widely regarded as discredited.

104

Following Ernest Mandel (p. 77),[5] he sees recent capitalist history as a succession of technological and concomitant economic ruptures. Human and animal labour is replaced by steam machinery, those by electric and petroleum engines, and those in turn by 'machine production of electronic and nuclear-powered apparatuses' in the latter part of this century. In this era of the First World post-industrial society,[6]

> networks of reproductive process . . . afford us some glimpse into a post-modern or technological sublime. . . .
>
> [O]ur faulty representations of some immense communicational and computer network are themselves but a distorted figuration of something even deeper, namely the whole world system of present-day multinational capitalism.
>
> (ibid., p. 80)

Inevitably, the sf theorist thinks of William Gibson's cyberpunk world, and those of his followers and colleagues. Of course even in the early 1980s Jameson was aware of such rising fictive vectors even if most of his academic readers were not (and still are not):

> This is a figural process presently best observed in a whole mode of contemporary entertainment literatures, which one is tempted to characterize as 'high tech paranoia'. . . . Yet conspiracy theory (and its garish narrative manifestations) must be seen as a degraded attempt – through the figuration of advanced technology – to think the impossible totality of the contemporary world system.
>
> (ibid., p. 80)[7]

Jameson himself explicitly extended this linkage to recent sf in his 1991 book on the postmodern,[8] singling out cyberpunk's prime mover for special praise:

> Such narratives . . . have only recently crystallized in a new type of science fiction, called *cyberpunk*, which is fully as much an expression of transnational corporate realities as it is of global paranoia itself. William Gibson's representational innovations, indeed, mark his work as an exceptional literary realization within a predominantly visual or aural postmodern production.
>
> (Jameson, 1991, p. 38)

It is of course Marxism's vocation – one of Jameson's useful phrases – to think impossible totalities of this kind. Such totalities might not be identified by participants at the structural level we inhabit; might not, indeed, exist. Jameson's reaction to this challenge is watertight but, by the same token, frustratingly monadic. That 'global world system', he remarks, has not been portrayed as 'unknowable, but merely . . . unrepresentable' (ibid., p. 91). Gödel turned, as it were, on his head! Cyberpunk, thus conceived, essays to represent the 'unrepresentable'.

Finally Jameson is not without confidence in his power, or at any rate that of a community of committed scholars, to engage this new episteme. And his move is strikingly salient to the suggestion that science fiction might compose an interface between the traditionally segregated cultural practices of literary and scientific discourses. What he proposes is 'an aesthetic of _cognitive mapping_'. Arguably, this is just the sort of mapping and aesthetic that sf's ideational narratives and enabling tropes offer.

Such a suggestion, developed in what follows, does risk vulgarising Jameson's reverberant phrase. 'The problem with this particular slogan clearly lay in its own (representational) accessibility,' its coiner noted in 1991. 'Since everyone knows what a map is, it would have been necessary to add that cognitive mapping cannot (at least in our time) involve anything so easy as a map; indeed, once you knew what "cognitive mapping" was driving at, you were to dismiss all figures of maps and mapping from your mind and try to imagine something else' (ibid., p. 409).

This clarification is not, one feels, entirely successful. Jameson adds in a typical flight of paradox: 'A new sense of global structure was supposed to take on figuration and to displace the purely perceptual substitute of the geographical figure; cognitive mapping, which was meant to have a kind of oxymoronic value and to transcend the limits of mapping altogether, is, as a concept, drawn back by the force of gravity of the black hole of the map itself . . . and therein cancels out its own impossible originality' (ibid., p. 416). Indeed, we learn finally that it 'was in reality nothing but a code word for "class consciousness" – only it proposed the need for class consciousness of a new and hitherto undreamed of kind' (p. 418) – specifically, 'a new international proletariat (taking forms we cannot yet imagine)' (p. 417).

MAPPING UTOPIA

Jameson's former graduate student, novelist and critic Kim Stanley Robinson, offers just such cognitive maps in several fine novels that blend sf's Modern and postmodern impulses and strategies. In _Pacific Edge_,[9] his limpid, sunny prose builds the most ordinary of utopias, as befits an imagined southern California in the summer of 2065. Green politics suffuses every minute of domestic life, which means that it is an uphill battle against inertia, special or corrupt interests, global poverty, the forgetfulness born of happiness in a land 'like a garden run riot' (Robinson, 1990, p. 1).

In its midst, a brooding note obtrudes from the first sentence: 'Despair could never touch a morning like this'. Like a Möbius strip closing upon itself, its twist skewing what we knew, it ends thus:

> If only Ramona, if only Tom, if only the world, all in him all at once, with the sharp stab of our unavoidable grief; and it seemed to him then that he was without a doubt the unhappiest person in the whole world.
>
> And at the thought (thinking about it) he began to laugh.
>
> (ibid., p. 280)

Kevin Claiborne is an artisan in a fairly brave new world, not very intelligent, lacking the nous of his grandfather who helped make the revolution back in 2012. *Pacific Edge* is a modernist domestic study, a couple of months in the life of that most difficult feat, the *believable* utopia. No cosmic mysteries burst across its sweet tale, but a shadow falls ever and again across its bucolic ordinariness: the incipient Fascism of an earlier cruel day, still in our own future, the world of excess and terror we are making at the end of the twentieth century. Robinson's achievement is to present both realities. If we never quite learn how one grew from the other, that is where the novel regains the actual, beckons us (in a political claim upon our sympathies) into making it true.

The very best sf, Modern or postmodern, does not repudiate extremes, the sublime, the utopian. It appeals to something eager and open within the crustiest adult heart even as it dazzles the mind with the riches of abstract knowledge and the hard, constrained ambitions of scientific practice. So there is often something joyfully exuberant and romantic in sf, fatally kitschy to the cultivated literary intellectual. Like those heightened screen epics that star Charlton Heston or Kirk Douglas – Anthony Mann's *El Cid*, Kubrick's *Spartacus* – sf may play with the consequences of huge historical change through the rhetoric of melodrama. Indeed, in Robinson's astonishing *Red Mars* (followed by *Green Mars* and *Blue Mars*), he shows us in detail the building of a utopia in the wastes of a dead world, and its corrupting by the old order. In the early years of colonisation by the 'first hundred' scientists and technologists, a programme of careful exploitation is begun by a largely capitalist Earth of the 2020s. Ironically, these representatives of the home planet live in a kind of monastic, socialist order, outside the realm of economics. It is a human ecology based on the design of scientific research settlements. When it breaks down in a polyphony of special interests and imported xenophobias, the Russian anarchist Arkady offers a rich explanation that recalls something of Jameson's redemptive impulse:

'When we first arrived, and for twenty years after that, Mars was like Antarctica but even purer. We were outside the world, we didn't even own things – some clothes, a lectern, and that was it! ... This arrangement resembles the prehistoric way to live, and it therefore feels right to us, because our brains recognise it from three million years of practicing it. In essence our brains grew to their current configuration in response to the realities of that life. So as a result people grow *powerfully attached* to that kind of life, when they get the chance to live it. It allows you to concentrate your attention on the real work, which means everything that is done to stay alive, or make things, or satisfy one's curiosity, or play. That is utopia, John, especially for primitives and scientists, which is to say everybody. So a scientific research station is actually a little model of prehistoric utopia, carved

107

out of the transnational money economy by clever primates who want to live well.'[10]

This intriguing analysis explains why scientists work cheerfully on devastating weapons systems, why many men and women find their happiest billet in the peacetime armed services, indeed why wartime is remembered so fondly by those who have not actually been maimed (and some who have). It also captures one of the lures of sf's typical sociological foregrounds: a happy band of brothers (and, latterly, sisters) outside the circuit of *realpolitik* and economics, paid by the Culture or the Galactic Survey 'to boldly go where nobody has been before', and have intellectual fun there.

However pleasing and intelligent Robinson's novels are, they are not quite postmodern by Jameson's criteria, although they do fit Colin Greenland's account of postmodern sf, in *The Entropy Exhibition*:

> It illuminates our enslavement to the idea of the future and to our own technology. It subdivides reality and adds provisional worlds, each flickering unsteadily, whose reflected light does not always draw our attention back to the source we know to be there.[11]

At any rate, science fiction seems to me undoubtedly the expert domain for imagining what 'we cannot yet imagine'. The most audacious possible claim would be, therefore, that sf constitutes the possibility, if hardly ever yet the reality, of a vellum and a set of cartographic techniques and tools – Robinson's deep utopias, cyberpunk's 'paranoid' iconography, Delany's renovated or altogether new signifiers strung on webs of previously unarticulated syntagms – which might transcend the exhausted, the seductively transparent, the cosily mimetic:

> the new political art ... will have to hold to the truth of post-modernism[12] ... at the same time at which it achieves a breakthrough to some as yet unimaginable new mode of representing this last, in which we may again begin to grasp our positioning as individual and collective subjects and regain a capacity to act and struggle which is at present neutralized by our spatial as well as our social confusion.
>
> (Jameson, 1984, p. 92)

It is clear that Jameson's sensitivity to the overdeterminations of art saves his account from falling into reduction, into a vulgar Marxist attribution, via some step of transcoding, of certain economic or political categories directly to their instantiation in the texts, even such 'texts' as hotel buildings. In this sense his style of aesthetics is at least somewhat vulnerable to falsification (a plus, in my terms); or if that is too strong, to assay. If his terms of reference have any validity or utility, they will cast light on phenomena not adduced in their development. He offers this web of relationships as a kind of modular calculus (Delany's useful term, to be discussed in Chapter 10) for the artistic texts of late capitalism.[13]

Perhaps, therefore, it is ironically regrettable that Jameson is an astute and up-to-date reader of sf, since an austere critic might fear that his theory is contaminated in advance by empiricism. I do not regard this feature as a drawback. Theory should constantly test itself against the real, batter itself if need be, until it anneals its lesions. At any rate, it is desirable that a model of such audacity, especially one which has been taken up in the most high-toned cultural forums, in respect of painting and architecture as well as writing, should illuminate less privileged realms as well. Since Jameson is exactly the commentator or metacommentator best positioned to extend this claim on behalf of science fiction, his failure to do so in a systematic fashion is, in fact, somewhat daunting. Nevertheless, it is astonishing how closely a roster of his extant studies in science fiction matches this postmodern agenda.

JAMESON'S POSTMODERN AND SF

All these features are drawn in contrast to notionally 'typical' modernist or even pre-modernist texts. The first parameter is a certain flatness, a lack of mimetic or illusory 'depth'. Now this is precisely the attribute Jameson discerns as one of science fiction's special strategies, in this case at work in Ursula Le Guin's *The Left Hand of Darkness* (1969), a notable interrogative utopia. He calls it 'world reduction',

> an attempt to imagine an experimental landscape in which our being-in-the-world is simplified to the extreme, and in which our sensory links with the multiple and shifting perceptual fields around us are abstracted so radically as to vouchsafe, perhaps, some new glimpse as to the ultimate nature of human reality.[14]

The second parameter is loss or attenuation of discrete subjectivity and memory, yielding an odd blend of flattened affect and 'a peculiar kind of euphoria'. It is signalled in general by the replacement of time by space as the favoured or hegemonic dimensionality. Jameson's proposal of 'Science Fiction as a Spatial Genre'[15] confirms this identification as common also to sf. So too does his praise of Aldiss's *Helliconia* trilogy where, as we've seen, diachrony on the largest scale is figured almost wholly in vast ebbs and flows of populations and kinds across a world, and between worlds. Vonda McIntyre's space opera, the subject of his 'spatial genre' paper, is also notable for its typical invocation of disordered or ambiguous subjectivity ('pseudosibs' and telepathy play crucial roles), permitting Jameson's nuanced and ingenious accounts of what 'can be said or shown in the figural (SF) narrative which it is impossible to encode in the psychological language of a realistic one'.[16]

The third parameter is the abandonment by the artist of any pretence to a unique style localised in history, in favour of *pastiche*, jargon and nostalgia. This is at least foreshadowed in Jameson's valorisation of 'generic discontinuities' as a source of the greatest pleasure and success in sf by Aldiss and Le Guin. While Jameson has not yet addressed cyberpunk texts in detail, it is clear that they capture these particulars in a most calculated and even somewhat theorised fashion. In the very first footnote to his *Postmodernism*, Jameson remarks: 'This is the place to regret the absence from this book of a chapter on cyberpunk, henceforth, for many of us, the supreme *literary* expression if not of postmodernism, then of late capitalism itself.'[17]

The fourth postmodern parameter is schizophrenic *écriture*, especially jumbled *collage* and a radical breakdown in reality-testing. Even the slightest familiarity with sf since the 1950s pinpoints this trope as the patented territory of Philip K. Dick, and not surprisingly one of Jameson's earliest published investigations into the mode was a complex Greimasian study of a Dick work, the phantasmagoric *Dr Bloodmoney* (1965). It must be admitted, though, that his reading in this case is ruthlessly rationalising, perhaps more so than he would now approve, laden with ingenious semantic rectangles. Other Dick novels, from *Time out of Joint* in 1959 to quite literally psychotic writings in his last works, *A Scanner Darkly* (1977) and *Valis* (1981), more adequately instance Dick's mastery of blurred reality and staggering subjectivity, projected with the most sustained ambiguity into the ontology of the universe. Eerily, Jameson's rendering of Duane Hanson's postmodern simulacra precisely captures Dick's characteristic effect, not least in his novel *The Simulacra* (1964):

> Your moment of doubt and hesitation as to the breadth and warmth of these polyester figures . . . tends to return upon the real human beings . . . to transform them also for the briefest instant into so many dead and flesh-coloured simulacra in their own right. The world thereby momentarily loses its depth and threatens to become a glossy skin, a rush of filmic images without density. But is this now a terrifying or an exhilarating experience?[18]

For devotees of Dick, it has always been both. Compare this with the bleak, utterly unpretentious prose of Dick's *Time out of Joint*.[19] The ontologically devastating fact to keep in mind through this passage is that luckless Ragle Gumm's experience is *not*, at the diegetic level, a metaphor, *not* a psychotic hallucination. This is the stuff of his being-in-the-world. It is a postulate possible only in an sf text, the concretisation of what elsewhere, even in the postmodern, would almost inevitably *have* to be read as figurative:[20]

> Reaching around in his pockets, he found some change. A line of kids waited at the soft-drink stand; the kids were buying hot dogs and popsicles and Eskimo Pies and orange drink. He joined them.
> How quiet everything was.
> Stunning desolation washed over him. What a waste his life had been. . . .

The soft-drink stand fell into bits. Molecules. He saw the molecules, colourless, without qualities, that made it up. Then he saw through, into the space beyond it, he saw the hill behind, the trees and sky. He saw the soft-drink stand go out of existence, along with the counter man, the cash register, the big dispenser of orange drink, the taps for Coke and root beer. . . .

In its place was a slip of paper. He reached out his hand and took hold of the slip of paper. On it was printing, block letters.

SOFT-DRINK STAND

The final parameter in Jameson's catalogue of postmodern tropes or loci is the 'hysterical sublime'. Utterly repellent to the well-behaved canonical bourgeois text, except in carefully pruned moments of 'epiphany', this is surely the very mirror of science fiction's convulsively appetitive 'sense of wonder'. Arthur C. Clarke's Rapture in the climax of *Childhood's End*, for instance, misunderstood by Rabkin as a fall back into myth, is actually a figure of transcendental paradigm crisis. The sublime is figured again and again in Jameson's principle of utopian hope, borrowed from Ernst Bloch: 'the unexpected emergence, as it were, beyond "the nightmare of History" and from out of the most archaic longings of the human race, of the impossible and inexpressible Utopian impulse here none the less briefly glimpsed: "Happiness for everybody! . . .".'[21]

SCREEN TEST

For all that my brief survey suggests the continuity in Jameson's own critical work between the registers of the postmodern and the science fictional, so far it has been left to others to develop at least the preliminary groundwork in a Jamesonian theory of postmodern sf. While such efforts seem fated to be always questionably *post hoc* – do they ever predict directions, or merely pack into tidy boxes what has already been catalogued roughly by the order of the empirical? – they have the merit of condensing that plenty of the empirical into schemata which are not too unwieldy for further theorisation. Vivian Sobchack's recently expanded study of American sf movies, *Screening Space. The American Science Fiction Film*, is a convenient test-case.[22]

At the outset I declared that I would avoid discussing motion-picture sf, principally because most of what purports to be science fiction in the cinema is starved fare in terms of the rich gravies of cognitive estrangement available in print form. It is not hard to see why this should be so, by and large. The grammar of commercial narrative is almost obliged to present us, as John Clute claims, with a depressingly limited *combinatoire* of clichés:

Most of the generic moves in *Them* [for instance], and it should be kept in mind that there are literally thousands of them, will have been recognized by most viewers of the film, who will have counted on this sort of high profile genericness for much of their pleasure. Indeed, an intense visibility of moves, or trope exposure, does arguably distinguish not only the generic film but maybe cinema as a whole from other narrative arts. Industrial, sociological, historical and ontological reasons for this – as well as obvious ones about the sensorium film addresses – can be brought forward by the film critic.[23]

Arguably this is less true since the dawn of what Sobchack terms the 'second Golden Age' of sf movies. After 1977's *Star Wars* and *Close Encounters of the Third Kind*, with the exuberantly compulsive storytelling of the former and the technically dazzling simulations of the sublime in the latter, it seemed that box-office movies had begun to match in filmic form many of the satisfactions of print sf from the 1940s and 1950s. Granted, *Cocoon* (1985) or *Starman* (1984) were feeble attempts on the luminous, numinous effects which climax such novels as *Childhood's End* or *Tiger! Tiger!* And *Blade Runner* (1982), for all its brilliantly sleazy surface, was a thin echo of Philip Dick's hallucinatory paranoia, even if it was a foretaste of, and perhaps influence on, cyberpunk's trashed-future iconography.

Yet it is not the big-budget *son et lumière* extravaganzas which Sobchack finds compelling. Her attention is directed for the most part to 'marginal' movies like *Repo Man* (1984), *The Brother from Another Planet* (1984), and *Uforia* (1986), though she finds evidence for her postmodern thesis even in such 'mainstream' sf successes as *Alien* (1979), *Tron* (1982), *The Last Starfighter* (1984), and other (at least mechanical) triumphs of special effects and computer simulations:

> The popularization and pervasiveness of electronic technology in the last decade has reformulated the experience of space and time as expansive and inclusive. It has recast human being into a myriad of visible and active simulacra, and has generated a semantic equivalency among various formulations and representations of space, time, and being. [. . . I]n a culture where nearly everyone is regularly alienated from a direct sense of self . . . the once threatening SF 'alien' and Other become our familiars – our close relations, if not ourselves.[24]

Borrowing Jameson's and Mandel's economic-technological schema of recent epochs, Sobchack plausibly finds sf's generic variants at first 'flourishing as a symbolic representation of the new intersections of science, technology, and multinational capitalism', a novel reality of the 1950s with its 'expansive promise and threatening unfamiliarity' (Sobchak, 1987, pp. 299–300). From the late 1970s on, by contrast, sf films familiarised the future and the Other, conscripting their potential estrangement effects to the accommodating maw of a multinational hegemonic consumer culture, marked by nostalgia, 'euphoria and a totalised "pluralism" – both of which are realised in space and do not logically admit the temporalizing of a future' (ibid.).

These marks of a postmodern schema at work are notable for manifesting Jameson's two principal themes of this sensibility: *inverted millenarianism* and *aesthetic populism*.

> Both these themes are nowhere so blatantly addressed as in the contemporary SF film. [The former] is consistently figured in . . . the visual 'trashing' and yet operative functioning of what used to be shiny 'futurist' technology. . . . Predominantly independent productions . . . not only announce and celebrate their own existence as the simulacra of grade-B 'schlock' movies [. . . but] also foreground and locate themselves in a culture that is 'schlock'. . . . Recent mainstream and big-budget SF is no less fascinated by the landscape of contemporary popular culture. These more conservative films either wholeheartedly and transparently absorb and displace it, or explicitly foreground and wonder at it.
>
> (ibid., pp. 246–50)

What is lost in this nostalgia, pastiche and simulation is depth and historicity, precisely in line with Jameson's sense of the postmodern impulse – though one might wonder whether Hollywood had ever been notable for adhering to high artistic and cultural values. Sobchack's elaboration of these hints is provocative, if sometimes irritatingly trendy in expression (she favours the false etymology; 'co-Here-nce' is one of her less agreeable coinages, p. 269), and far too detailed to be deployed fully here. In brief:

- a simultaneous *deflation and inflation of space* (Jameson's 'depthlessness');
  - *deflation* being a replacement of deep or indexical spatial volume by an iconic register of hyper-real surface (p. 256);
  - *inflation* captured either in
    - *excess scenography*, such as the laden collage-surface of David Lynch's *Dune*, also a feature of Herbert's books, or
    - *emptied terrestrial space*, a denuded landscape co-ordinated only by exhausted real-world icons, reminiscent at its limit of the Dick passage cited above (p. 262);
  - these two mapped together into an *absolute* space, 'concentrat[ing] spatial value as autonomous [. . . and] characterised by the discontiguity of a busy, eclectic, and decentered mise-en-scène' which mocks narrative coherence (p. 269);
- a *collapse of time* or 'weakening of historicity' (a tendency 'to conflate past, present, and future – in decor constructed as temporal pastiche', p. 273);
- a 'new emotional ground tone' in *special affect/effect* (where Jameson's 'peculiar kind of euphoria'[25] 'is structured and represented not as the intense feeling and expression of a *centered subject constructed in time*,

but rather [that of] a *decentered subjectivity objectified in space*',[26] and hence readily externalised in wonderful display); and

■ our postmodern introjection of otherness in, quite literally, *the embrace of the 'alien'* (p. 254).

If this last, embracing the alien, seems an advance on previous xenophobias, it is largely illusory. Borrowing from a distinction well drawn by Michel Foucault,[27] Sobchack cautions:

> the most postmodern SF does not 'embrace the alien' in a celebration of resemblance, but 'erases alienation' in a celebration of similitude. . . . The 'alien' posited by marginal and postmodern SF enables the representation of alienation as 'human' and constitutes the reversible and nonhierarchical relations of similitude into a myth of homogenized heterogeneity.
>
> (Sobchack, 1987, p. 297)

This is precisely the accommodating move, as we shall see, which Delany's fiction has been at pains to circumvent. But for Sobchack, these observations do not imply a simple denunciation. 'Not only do these articulations negate the genre's earlier xenophobia, but they can also be seen as an attempt at what Jameson calls "disalienation". . . . This is a progressive move. It at least allows for the possibility of some new form of empowerment' (ibid., pp. 301–2).

Beyond this, if Jameson's hopes are valid, lie radically new forms, his 'invention and projection of a global cognitive mapping, on a social as well as a spatial scale', a 'post-postmodernism' which Sobchack, not surprisingly, identifies with a certain tendency in feminist film. Without such a move (in cinema, at least) postfuturist sf, in Sobchack's view, might simply dissolve in its auto-deconstruction:

> [W]hile their subversion of the boundaries between inner city/outer space, estranged/alien, male/female, familiar/novel [etc.] 'deconstructs' the hierarchical relations that ground capitalist notions of power, desire, and value, this subversion also 'dissolves' the very structure and notion of the film genre as a bounded category of texts valuing the market and hierarchical difference between signs of 'science' and signs of 'fiction'. When 'science' and 'fiction' are no longer visualized and narrativized as oppositional, the genre . . . dissolves.
>
> (ibid., p. 302)

Sobchack finds this prospect is at once liberating and catastrophic, removing cinema's capacity to 'imagine and image our possible futures' (ibid., p. 302). Now, in terms of any nuanced analysis of the function of sf, this is a primitive account. Sf, as we have seen repeatedly, has never really tried to 'imagine the future'. Sobchack does recognise the inevitable tension in any genre between 'invention' and 'convention', and knows perfectly well that while the sf movie 'ostensibly strives to transcend the conventional and, perhaps, reach toward the avant-garde "and beyond" to the radical, the demands of the genre's commodification also compel it to inscribe itself as familiar, unthreatening, unrevolutionary, and easily understood' (p. 303).

In short, cinematic sf is free to elaborate any number of decorative 'local universe' intertexts, especially if they allow profitable franchising spinoffs like *Star Wars* computer games and toys, but they cannot be permitted to tap into the kind of mega-encyclopaedia which mobilises sophisticated print sf – or to begin, move by move, to construct one. Even if they were, it is arguable that such mega-texts are always more likely than not to promote and entail reactionary values, disguised though these might be behind momentarily blinding shocks of cognitive estrangement. The history of American commercial magazine and paperback sf, despite its peaks of achievement, is hardly encouraging on this score.

A NEW DOMINANT

Sobchack's attempt to identify the vectors of recent science fiction and the postmodern, in cinema at least, is in any case unnecessarily reductive. My discussion of Jameson's path through twenty or more years of theory illustrates how certain general global features of an episteme can have similar effects in a variety of narrative forms, including the 'narratives' structured into architecture. I agree with Teresa Ebert that

> [t]he 'dominant' of postmodern science fiction . . . has shifted, and a
> new aesthetic and thematic hierarchy has been established within the
> genre according to which the very 'fictivity' of science fiction is its
> primary element [. . . although] none of the (older) components of
> science fiction is completely lost.[. . . T]he very texture and substance
> of the fictive worlds and even the language and narrative structures of
> the fictions, whether of Delany or Sukenick or Pynchon, are woven out
> of the complex and multiple web of science and technology.[28]

Behind this easy adoption by some innovative sf writers of certain expansive possibilities now seen to be available from metafiction, magic realism and 'textualist' writing[29] in general, it is true that one may discern in modern science fiction and postmodern writing a comparable positioning toward language which is in many ways closer to scientific discourse than to traditional literature. We can see this by parsing both kinds of writing according to the emphasis they give, according to Roman Jakobson, to the six main components of any communication act. An Addresser sends an Addressee (or Receiver) a Message about the World, in a common Code, along a Channel checked for reliability by shared, standardising procedures. This picture is too simple, but serves our limited purposes. My argument is that literary fictions give these components different emphases from both paraliterature and postmodern fiction.

Abolishing literature's stable subjectivity shifts fictive discourse away from the Addresser, and perhaps relocates it in the communal or dispersed Addressee/s, if not indeed within Code proper. Pastiche is the figurative domain of the Channel (where I place algorithm and generic trope), albeit distanced, renovated not by the kind of sarcastic superiority with which modernism appropriated the quotidian but in a 'euphoric' embrace akin to science's articulation over algorithms and paradigms. And in their emphasis on the technological surround, the density of new signifiers bursting up especially from the consumer-oriented market productivity of post-industrial science, both new forms of writing privilege *context*, reference to the World: in a word, the *object*.[30]

It is Samuel Delany's emphasis on the Other and the object, in fiction and theory alike, that singles him out for the special attention we shall pay his texts in the remainder of this book.

9

ALLOGRAPHY AND
ALLEGORY

I am interested in reading recent science fiction ... in terms of its relation to the dominant episteme and aesthetics of advanced techno-logical societies – a stylistic and epistemological development that I have called the 'aesthetics of indeterminacy'. . . . The middle of the generic spectrum in mainstream fiction today [. . . employs] an orderly, resolvable linear plot (indicating the writer's belief in a causal, rational and orderly universe) and deals with fully developed characters (an expression of the writer's faith in a coherent human identity and integrative selfhood) in a very clear and transparent language (which is a sign of the author's trust in ordinary language as a mediator among all members of a speech community). The major epistemological function of this type of fiction is ... to 'totalize' human experience. [. . . 'Transfiction'] heralds a new break-up and a new synthesis in narrative in post-industrial communities. . . . It is the narrative of the consciousness that has moved beyond the 'two cultures'.

(Teresa L. Ebert)[1]

From his earliest novels – and he wrote a number of book-length fictions before he tried the shorter forms – Samuel Delany has followed the vocation of what we might call 'allographer', one who writes the Other.[2] Even more than other sf writers, he inscribes in his texts' signifiers and syntagms the elusive face of the excluded, the unadmitted . . . the other.[3] If his first published novel was a gaudy exercise in romantic quest, by his eighth he was writing a veritable mythology of undecidability, and this in 1966, before Derrida had arrived in America with the first tidings of decon-struction. A richly metaphoric attempt at a self-subverting pastiche of myth, *The Einstein Intersection* combined blatantly autobiographical epigraphs (the first revelation that he was black, in this previously white enclave) with a denial of closure designed to confound generic expectations. It was a meditation on difference and a manifesto for textual and cultural dis-semination that might more accurately have been entitled *The Gödel Asymptote* than its publisher's choice.[4]

117

From its opening epigraph, drawn from *Finnegans Wake*, the book makes claims beyond its generic packaging: 'It darkles, (tinct, tint) all this our funanimal world'. If it is not yet postmodern, still it is directly within the American tradition of pop modernism from Faulkner to Salinger. But already in its first paragraph it exceeds that system of codes as well, postulating excessive ambiguities, differences, hints of that genuine aporia sounded in the borrowed word 'funanimal':

> There is a hollow, holey cylinder running from hilt to point in my machete. When I blow across the mouthpiece, I make music with my blade. When all the holes are covered, the sound is sad, as rough as rough can be and be called smooth. When all the holes are open, the sound pipes about, bringing to the eye flakes of sun on water, crushed metal. There are twenty holes.
>
> (*The Einstein Intersection*, p. 1)

Reread, at the book's end, and then a couple of decades later, this passage is compellingly overdetermined. Its narrator is Lobey, one of the non-human inhabitants of the Earth some 50,000 years in the future. More precisely, he is Lo Lobey, a male, but his masculine status is inscribed already within his proper name.[5] His form is human, but only just, and although he gives a circumstantial account of his appearance in the second and third paragraphs, anomaly is structured into the text as early as the fifth sentence: there are twenty holes in his lethal musical instrument . . . because he has perfectly prehensile toes.

It is a poignant and aporetic abnormality. Apes have this functional stigma, and Lobey does compare himself to a gorilla (ibid.), but dextrous hands are one celebrated marker of *homo faber*. Like both mutually contradictory terms of some Lévi-Straussian myth schema, Lobey is thus simultaneously inscribed as both subhuman and superhuman, as indeed he proves to be.

His music has the same double character: sad/ bright, brought forth from a hacking, even a killing, tool, at an indefinite boundary between rough and smooth. Moreover, the sentences enact a science fictional trope which Delany admires in Bester, *synaesthesia*: the machete's sound provokes a visual figure, the ear transduces to the eye. And even that image has a slightly sf tonality, one often found in Delany's prose, of reference to metal shards, crushed foil, 'flakes of sun'. The natural world is invaded by the machined.

So it is with all the world of *The Einstein Intersection*, where the myths of us vanished humans, or our technologically advanced descendants, are being run like demented computer programs, under the aegis of an actual computer complex called PHAEDRA, in the life-narratives of the beings which have been drawn from the other side of the universe into our mysterious absence.

SF AS ALLEGORY OF READING

The book is, in short, an allegory of reading – to be precise, of reading science fiction. Its Lo's, Le's and La's (that is, characters gender-marked in their names as either masculine, undecidable/androgynous, or feminine) explicitly colonise the myths of our last 3,000 years. The most recognisable mythemes are Orpheus and Eurydice; Theseus and his wife Phaedra, daughter of Minos; the slaying of the Minotaur; Christ crucified; Billy the Kid; Jean Harlow; dragons. . . .

Science fiction stories often rehearse and colonise those same mythemes, bungling them, recasting them, sometimes merely filching them for exploitation, sometimes renewing them into a redemptive openness. Smashing the rigid structuralist machine, Delany might say, and liberating the deconstructive imp of uncertainty. And doing all this within what amounts to a display of how to write a science fiction text: how to appropriate the discourses of science and meld them into the discourses of literature and pulp alike. The yield, as Teresa Ebert suggests above, is a portrait of a consciousness that has moved beyond the two cultures.

The tale's propositional basis, if it can be so dignified (it is strictly a *parti pris*, a handwaving axiom, like the pseudoscientific cognitive enabling devices of most sf, though not less interesting for that) is precisely an enactment of Gödelian undecidability, recast as what philosopher of science Nicholas Maxwell would term a scientific 'metaphysical blueprint':[6]

Wars and chaoses and paradoxes ago, two mathematicians between them ended an age and began another for our hosts, our ghosts called Man. One was Einstein, who with his Theory of Relativity defined the limits of man's perception by expressing mathematically just how far the condition of the observer influences the thing he perceives. . . . The other was Gödel, a contemporary of Einstein, who was the first to bring back a mathematically precise statement about the vaster realm beyond the limits Einstein has defined: *In any closed mathematical system* - you may read 'the real world with its immutable laws of logic' – *there are an infinite number of true theorems* – you may read 'perceivable, measurable phenomena' – *which, though contained in the original system, can not be deduced from it* – read 'proven with ordinary or extraordinary logic.' . . . There are an infinite number of true things in the world with no way of ascertaining their truth. Einstein defined the extent of the rational. Gödel stuck a pin into the irrational and fixed it to the wall of the universe so that it held still long enough for people to know it was there. And the world and humanity began to change. And from the other side of the universe, we were drawn slowly here. The visible effects of Einstein's theory leaped up on a convex curve, its productions huge in the first century after its discovery, then leveling off. The productions of Gödel's law crept up on a concave curve,

119

microscopic at first, then leaping to equal the Einsteinian curve, cross it, outstrip it.

(*The Einstein Intersection*, pp. 120–1)

The technological figure for this moment of paradigmatic intersection and equilibrium, and its consequence, was instantaneous transportation 'to the limits of the known universe' (p. 121). Beyond that point, the victory of the Gödelian paradigm sent humans into a transcendental state, 'to no world in this continuum' (p. 122),[7] abandoning their empty cities to their myth-entrapped successors. But those Lo, Le, La heirs of the manipulators of ultimate undecidability are not static: prey to genetic disorders, the new beings teeter at the fulcrum on which every culture in epistemic disequilibrium oscillates:

'. . . must preserve,' Lo Hawk.
'. . . must change,' La Dire.

(ibid., p. 6; ellipses in original)

DIFFERENCE

The signature of this disequilibrium is *difference*, at once necessary and despised, inevitable and feared. As a black gay writer in the mid-1960s, Delany was writing his marginal experience. He chose to do so in a heightened way, in a metaphoric structure which cast a Gödelian shadow over our own culture:

Two women gazed idiotically from swirling colors. The caption: 'THESE TWO IDENTICAL TWINS ARE NOT THE SAME.'
The youngsters giggled and shoved another.[8] Obviously I missed something about the sign. . . .
He had freckles and a prosthetic arm. He scratched his head with plastic fingers. . . .
'What's so funny about that picture?'
First disbelief: then he grinned. 'If they're not the same,' he blurted, '*they're different!*' They all laughed. Their laughter was filigreed with the snicker that let you know when laughter's rotten.

(ibid., p. 116)

Such typical bigotry from those themselves marked by arbitrary difference is emphasised by the text in its doubled reference to prosthesis. The snigger when laughter is rotten befouls that signifier of pleasure, recalling its innocent other, mute Friza's laughter – 'the one sound she did make, loving it in her mouth' (p. 9)[9] – while the rottenness of bad teeth falls as a shadow behind the metaphoric filigree of dental fillings. By contrast, Lobey's ambiguous mentor Spider valorises difference:

'[S]omething new is happening to the fragments [of the human world], something we can't even define with mankind's leftover vocabulary. You must take its importance exactly as that: it is indefinable; you are involved in it; it is wonderful, fearful, deep, ineffable to your explanations, opaque to your efforts to see through it; yet it demands you take journeys, defines your stopping and starting points, can propel you with love and hate. . . . If I could tell you, or if you could understand from my inferences, Lobey, it would lose all value.'[10] (p. 120)

Perhaps a 'Gödelian' explanation, then, like a New Critical poem, should not *mean* but *be*? This is altogether too simple a dictum for Delany, even prior to his interest in deconstruction. If *The Einstein Intersection* is like a poem, and flagged as such for the reader, it is the kind epitomised in John Ciardi's epigraph to the sixth chapter:

'A poem is a machine for making choices.'[11]

REMAKING MYTH

No univocal verbal icon, a Delany prose poem is structured to challenge unities, to disrupt univocities, even when it is spoken by the single voice of Lobey who, like all the characters, is infested by multiple mythic overlays and temptations. Myth is an ideational and affective ensemble of stories which at once, for their native culture, articulate schemata of expected behaviours and, if Lévi-Strauss is right, specify and defuse the antinomies of that culture: a machine for *restricting* choices. While, on this account, they contain multitudes, their aim is not self-contradiction but the coercive institution of order, regularity, harmony, even if those ends are met through controlled passages into frenzy, carnival and hysteria.

Delany borrows many of the trappings of myth, thus understood, and embroiders them in a 'Gödelian' fashion, promoting myth to the status of a text in need of endless reinterpretation: a poem, in fact. He is explicit. In an epigraph from his 'Writer's Journal', taken from its early pages, we read: 'The central subject of the book is myth. [. . . O]rpheus had a very modern choice to make when he decided to look back' (1981b, p. 72). In another, jotted down halfway through the book's writing, he remarks: 'Endings to be useful must be inconclusive' (p. 129).

The wise woman of his village, La Dire, positions Lobey's culture's conventional wisdom on mythology, a mythology borrowed like some Derridean trace from the reverberant absent presence of the missing humans. 'In myth things always turn into their opposites as one version supersedes the next' (p. 13).[12] When Lobey revolts against her retelling of the Orphean myth, she adds: 'All life is a rhythm. . . . All death is rhythm suspended, a syncopation before life resumes' (ibid.).

For us readers, this may be true only for a family or a society. In Lobey's world, as in the world of many myths (so he learns in the course of the book's diegesis), it is also literally true for certain individuals who actually return from the dead. Hence, if even the primordial fact of death is capable of being suspended, it is clear that no mythic archetype can be stable.[13]

In a revelatory discussion near the close, the Lord Lo Spider asks Lobey what he knows about mythology, demanding 'a Gödelian, not an Einsteinian answer' (pp. 119, 122).[14] He adds, in a rhapsodic passage as vulgar and delicious in its heightened pulp manner as anything in Sturgeon's sf:

> 'I don't want to know what's inside the myths, nor how they clang and
> set one another ringing, their glittering focuses, their limits and genesis.
> I want their shape, their texture, how they feel when you brush by them
> on a dark road, when you see them receding into the fog, their weight
> as they leap your shoulder from behind; I want to know how you take
> to the idea of carrying three when you already bear two. Who are you,
> Lobey?' (p. 123)

A kind of declaration of the decentred or many-centred self, this is closer to Poe than to Freud or Lacan, even Freud the poet rather than the scientist. Spider does not deny the validity or utility of a structural analysis of myth, merely its salience. From this valorisation of some pre-Raphaelite essentialist *given* one might not have anticipated Delany's subsequent intoxication with theory. Even so, Lobey rebels in equally Gothic dread at what he takes, on our behalf, for normative imposition.

> 'It's fixed! . . . I'll fail! . . . You're trying to tell me that these stories
> tell us just what is going to happen. [. . . T]his is all schematic for a
> reality I can't change!' (p. 124)

MYTH RE-COMPLICATED

Spider refutes such fearful determinism. 'The world is not the same. . . . It's different.' Myths, like Lobey's musical machete, are two-edged. Indeed, they may be made by those who embody them. 'One wonders if Theseus built the maze as he wandered through it. [. . . Y]ou can either fail that goal, succeed, or surpass it.'[15] In the book's cosmogonic plot, the Christ-cum-Odin Green-eye can create *ab initio*, Lobey can order the chaotic, but Kid Death can only control. He can reverse even mortality, but only in those he has killed, such as Friza.

Posit this text, then, as an allegory of reading and writing texts. No other figurative schema fits so well in a tale so strangely, deliberately uncoupled from the quotidian. It is true that Spider insists: 'You're living in the real world now. . . . Myths always lie in the most difficult places to ignore. . . . You shy at them on entering or leaving any endeavor' (p. 125). On the other hand, despite Delany's taste in this text for schemata and their refutation, he ought not to be accused, I think, of any such simple matching as Green-eye = Superego, Lobey = Ego, Kid Death = Id, in principle a possible reading; let alone God, Everyman and Devil.

If the text is allegory of reading, Green-eye is perhaps *langue* or textuality proper, cultural and impersonal. He is, therefore, by a necessary paradox, mute, except when Lobey 'speaks' or sings on his behalf, by resonance, in a sort of telepathy of the phatic.[16] Lobey is the scriptor ordering the chaos of life into the music of letters.[17] Perhaps Kid Death, craving difference only to obliterate or colonise it, is the rule-bound, genre-governed '*lisible*' editor or reader, even critic, who requires the former two but consumes their labour and pays back in a coin of pain and derision.

This reading flies in the face of Delany's own developing aesthetic and theory, but it is curiously disturbing as a possible decoding of his story's narrative unconscious.[18] Swaggeringly evil in the fashion of Delany's artist-criminals (even when this villain was a child of ten, 'everybody got quiet. He already had quite a reputation', p. 77), Kid Death is too attractive to embody dreary moralism, rote work ethic, racism, any of the other nay-saying institutions or vices we might expect of a villain in the allegorical texts of a marginal writer like Delany.

THE MUSIC OF WORDS

More compelling than this thematic level is the use Delany makes of music, especially polyphonic melody, as textual metaphor. It is Lobey's special gift (his *difference*, in part) to resonate to the music in another's brain, and beyond that, I take it, to express through his own inventions a musical portrait of the conscious and unconscious activities of life. He reveals this curious gift by playing one of the melodies of Kodaly's 'Sonata for Unaccompanied Cello', captured *en passant* from Spider's idle mental rehearsal. Even insects and dragons utter their simple lives as tune:

A fly bobbed on a branch, preening the crushed prism of his wing (a wing the size of my foot) and thought a linear, arthropod music. I played it for him, and he turned the red bowl of his eye to me and whispered wondering praise. Dragons threw back their heads, gargling.
There is no death.
There is only music. (p. 87)

Music, says Spider, is 'patterning, relation, the knowledge that comes when six notes predict a seventh, when three notes beat against one another and define a mode, a melody defines a scale' (p. 125). On this account, music is very like science, or algorithmic grammar, or genre: 'the pure language of temporal and co-temporal relation' (ibid.). We might usefully compare this with a much later account Delany gives of writing's deep structures:

I do know that just under the verbal layers there is a layer that seems to me much more like numbers than words. It is a layer controlling pure pattern, where, among other things, places are set up for words that are going to be the same (or very much alike) and [the reverse]. Frequently these places are set out well before the actual words that will fill them are chosen.[19]

But this schematic remains to some extent mutable, especially when editing is interspersed with writing: choosing, striking out, re-choosing. 'The differences will probably have little or nothing to do with your plot, or the overall story shape – though they may. . . . But making these changes the moment they are perceived keeps the tale curving inward towards its own energy source' (ibid., p. 11). The interactions of these levels is what makes writing, and music, creative.

But Delany insists that this process is not auto-referential. When the verbal icon falls into total self-absorption and self-reflexion, it approaches madness. His texts give clear contrasting instances of both these modes. Lobey's music echoes and summates the 'music', the rhythms of life and death about him. *Babel-17*'s poet Rydra Wong, too, in a much-cited passage, makes poetry from the given, *trouvaille*:

'I listen to other people, stumbling about with their half thoughts and half sentences and their clumsy feelings that they can't express, and it hurts me. So I go home and burnish it and polish it and weld it to a rhythmic frame, make the dull colors gleam, mute the garish artificiality to pastels, so it doesn't hurt any more: that's my poem. I know what they want to say, and I say it for them.'[20]

If this model is surprisingly conservative (poetry soothes away the pain of reality) and elitist (poetry speaks for the inarticulate), nevertheless it approaches a poststructuralist sense of writing. Roland Barthes claims that 'discourse, or better, the language, speaks: nothing more'.[21] Yet Lobey knows that this is not the full story. In a carnivalesque nightclub of illusion, suspended literally over Hell, he forces his polyphonic rhythms on the patrons, as no doubt theirs are forced on him:

I let one melody go on without my playing it, and played another instead . . . and threaded a third above them. I shrilled my rhythms at them down the hollow knife, gouged notes down their spines the way you pith a frog. They shook in their seats. I put into the music a fourth line, dissonant to lots and lots of others. Three people had started dancing with me. I made the music make them.

(*The Einstein Intersection*, pp. 135–6)

Orpheus in his Dionysian avatar dances a rhythm at once imposed by the situation, responsive to it and dictating to it, as mute Friza, in a mythic

124

reversal of the sort announced by La Dire, commanded beast, tree and stone: the Orphic Apollonian aspect. It is a kind of Salome's treacherous dance, for Green-eye, ignored, is about to die on the cross. In any event, the music is pre-eminently a social act. A contrast to this 'dialectical' discourse is given in one of Delany's finest early passages, when the street poet Vol Nonik, bereaved like Lobey in the murder of his beloved, howls inside the cage of his own dementia. 'I don't want to talk any more. I just don't want to . . . speak.'[22] But telepathic Arkor overhears this autarkic babble, redeeming it, perhaps, to a social marginality:

> echo and re-echo, caught, held, and released, the cry of wild pigeons . . . and the first words come back, a cupric gleam, the walls of perception shaken, this vile voice not art, but madness trapped by ritual patternings of sound, lying because the ritual is bound by the limp nerves' response, the total matrix trying to contain realities of heart and bone and brain, knowing this working realness is only a machine constructed to apprehend the real; and the existence of leaf, sand, light, and good flicker out as they are named by the beast before me . . . the mirror breaks, again the beast awakes, stepping lazily from the splinters . . . whispering weights age old, lisping death deeds that cringle, garsh, shock new speech from the struck tongue; I will walk down the muscular anger of my voice, I will trample silence under the leaves. . . . (pp. 389–90)

French psychoanalyst Jacques Lacan proposed that the unconscious is an effect of language. Each child passes from the 'imaginary', or de-centred, pre-Oedipal state of symbiosis with the mother, a stage associated with the body, into the 'symbolic' or post-Oedipal social roles which comprise the self, a stage associated with 'logos' or the mind.[23] So in certain respects, this passage is strikingly Lacanian, if not *avant la lettre* at least ahead of translation. Vol Nonik (lacking volition?) appears trapped between the imaginary and the symbolic orders, the body speaking a doubled tongue: one not perfectly socialised, uttering a primordial babble, the other all too overmastered by the social, the mythic. The outcome is glossolalia combined with muteness, extreme fates Lobey and Rydra tend to avoid, while risking, in their several assaults on semiosis.[24]

THE INTERPRETATIVE CONTEXT

Speech and music, both forms of what Derrida (and Delany, today) would insist is a generalised writing of texts, are uttered within the force field of an interpretative community by subjects constituted in its utterance. Even the body's genetic givens are always interpreted within a social context. Kid Death's eerie attractiveness did not save him from expulsion, because he was born into the wrong context: '"I broiled away childhood in the sands of an equatorial desert kage with no keeper to love me. . . . Functional? To be born on a desert, a white-skinned redhead with gills?"' (*The Einstein Intersection*, pp. 56–7).

And Kid Death's motivation is the avoidance of history via its obsessive embrace. He is a cowboy outlaw in a land of dragon-drovers. 'We have to exhaust the past before we can finish with the present. . . . The past terrifies me. That's why I must kill it . . .' (p. 78). In fact, Kid Death targets not the past but the *different*, harbingers of the future. It is he who is condemned to repetition. His shark teeth, like his gills, are the stigmata not of difference simply, but of regressive persistence: of the same, in fact, endlessly repeated, out of context.[25]

Delany's text is telling us that the temptations of myth, cliché, generic algorithm share that fatal instruction to repeat. If it is to be (L)obeyed, it must be only on the proviso that the tropes are shuffled, recombined, generically engineered. If there are to be dragons and roses in today's text, they must be *different*, metaphors concretised or literalised to build new syntagms:

> Attacked by flowers, a dragon was dying. The blossoms jeweled his scales; thorns tangled his legs. . . .
> A blossom creeping to attack emptied an air-bladder inches from my foot. '*Sssss* . . . ' in surprise.
> I hacked it, and nervous ooze (nervous in the sense that its nerves are composed of the stuff) belched greenly to the ground. Thorns flailed my legs. (pp. 59–60)

The first line is authentically poetic. The rest is increasingly embarrassing, the kind of gaudy stuff the dreams in *Planet Stories* were made on. A quite deliberate generic mosaic (Parrinder dubs the book a 'generic hybrid'),[26] the text announces a programme more successfully instantiated in such later works as *Nova* (1968) and the deeply subversive *Triton: An Ambiguous Heterotopia* (1976). If it often falters, as in the feeble joke about 'nervous ooze', at once a play on gun-slinger's sweat and the sf writer's pseudoscientific explanation, it works as often to expand and expound the possibilities of the genre. After Delany, no serious sf can simply appropriate mythic patterns. It is the mark of the failure of so promising and fluent a contemporary as Roger Zelazny that his bricolage with mythemes has been increasingly exploitative, parodic and banal.[27]

For all its faults, then, *The Einstein Intersection* is a model of at least one kind of writing and reading science fiction. Its most notable failure as an adequate allegory of reading sf is, absurdly enough, its lack of science, either as plot motivation or decorative iconography – unless one is prepared to accept as pivotal the epistemological-cum-ontological pretext of Spider's lecture on Gödel. This proves finally no better than a pretext: the same end might have been reached by an invocation of paranormal phenomena, say, or the disruptive interpenetration of 'another dimension'. Still, the discourse of reductive science is clearly under attack, no less than the discourse of reductive myth. The book is thus itself, to the extent that it works, perhaps a new myth of deconstructive scientific discourse; as disseminative as Gillian Beer's reading of Charles Darwin[28] and Barthes's of Balzac in *S/Z*.

Later Delany texts return more forcefully to the sf vocation. *Nova* employs just as many mythic substructures in its use of Tarot and Grail, Kennedy's death and the Cold War, but does so within an explanatory frame – historical models of society, cybernetic reconstructions of work and subjectivity, the search for rare energy sources – consistent with sf's cognitively elaborated requirements. It is to these later texts that we must turn for a fuller understanding of Delany's trajectory, a history which remains at once idiosyncratic and curiously paradigmatic of mature sf as 'high' paraliterature at this pivotal moment when it veers toward and across postmodernism in just the kind of textual intersection of relativism and a more drastic uncertainty which the earlier novel prefigured.

10

SF AS A MODULAR CALCULUS

From the time that I became aware the Nevèrÿon tales would become a series – from the time I became aware of a certain dissatisfaction with the idea that a sequence of encounters with a set of socially central institutions was constitutive of the 'civilized' subject . . . and turned back to critique that notion with the idea that a more marginal institution could be equally constitutive . . . – I more or less thought of these tales as a Child's Garden of Semiotics.

(Samuel R. Delany)[1]

At the outset, I posed certain broad questions which this investigation might attempt to resolve. Are there specific textual strategies which constitute the writing and reading of sf? What are its generic components and how are they deployed? How are the notations of sf texts concretised by readers and how, in turn, do they construct their potential readers? How does sf resemble and differ from those forms of storytelling denoted by the word 'literature'? More: if science is arguably another form of discursive negotiation and construction, principally a kind of textuality, does this shed any light on sf's linguistic inventions and plays? Most ambitiously: can science fiction's own peculiar textuality help in bridging these two still isolated cultures?

We have been exploring in some detail one answer evolved within the *textus*, the web of Samuel Delany's fictional and theoretical writings in the last couple of decades. ('Text and *textus*?' asks Delany. Text is from the Latin for 'web'. These days books are printed on a 'web', a vast ribbon of paper. 'All the uses of the word "web", "weave", "net", "matrix" and more, by this circular "etymology", become entrance points into a *textus*, which is ordered from all language and language-functions, and upon which the text itself is embedded' (*Triton*, p. 333).) Beyond the play of unusual signifiers which index the virtual presence, and so construct or constitute the actual presence, of new signifieds articulated within new or renewed syntagms, Delany has recently focused on the cultural schemata or scripts which underlie or imbricate those inscribed discourses we 'read' through our competency in cultural coding. Delany's own fictive discourse has increasingly involved a paradoxical search for rich ('valid') heuristic *models* of this kind which are immediately subjected to ceaseless revision, inversion and deconstruction.

A MIRROR FOR OBSERVERS

The isomorphic or homological image of 'the real' within the frame of a mirror, and the metaphorical 'mirroring' of self in other, via projective empathy and identification, has been the traditional figure for any nearly adequate model of one phenomenon by another. A mirror image, of course, is never fully adequate, being always at least bilaterally reversed. Yet this very figuration has been thoroughly assailed in recent theory. Delany's most substantial fiction, four genre-shattering volumes of poststructuralist 'sword & sorcery', contains an epigraph from Rodolphe Gasché's *The Tain of the Mirror*,[2] a formidable study that hangs its critique of Derrida's philosophical novelties precisely on the image of the mirror. The first book in the 1,285-page sequence devotes many pages to an exposition, by a Neolithic wise-woman named Venn, of the logical and economic hazards of modular theory, using mirrors as the basis for her reflections. The entire *Nevèrÿon* tetralogy (to date) is a generous, self-subverting machine for modelling practically everything mundane and contentious in our contemporary epistemic and social order, including AIDS, semiotics, paraliteratures emphasising the object and, reflexively, Delany's own struggles to perfect such a craft.

The shorthand figure for this programme, introduced by Delany in his 1976 sf novel *Triton* and continued through other texts in a sort of serious running gag, is 'the modular calculus'. *Modular* here is simply the adjective from *model*. Kathleen L. Spencer, in an exceptionally deft preliminary survey of this beguiling notion, lays out the philosophical questions which precede its invention:

> how do we construct models? Especially, how does language function in the modelling process? How do the models adopted by individuals or cultures shape their perceptions and responses? How can we determine the relative coherence, accuracy, or appropriateness of competing models? To what extent can a model actually succeed in mastering the thing it models? All of these questions Delany has, as a writer of SF novels, raised in the context of yet another: in what ways can fiction model the real world?[3]

One principal way, for Delany, is by refusing to respect conventional limits between fiction and reflections on fiction. The modular calculus – literally, a rigorous technique of modelling or simulation – is advanced, exemplified, explored and undermined in a series of fictions, parodies and theoretical ruminations, 'Some Informal Remarks toward the Modular Calculus'.[4] It is itself a model of what the mechanism of science fiction might be *if* sf were truly the bridge between science and literature, a notional gadget for postulating the hidden works of a black box which might hide the fundamental physical laws of the universe, or the obscure heart of a suffering human being.

BLACK BOX AND FINAGLE FACTOR

'Modular calculus': the very sound, bearing connotations of 'modal calculus' and other mysterious arcana, captures the cartoon-strip pretentiousness of sf, where giving a crazy idea a fancy name is equivalent to lending it reality. Scuffing his toe, Delany confesses as much:

> [It] began as a science fictional notion that turns out to be somewhat related to the famous Finagle Factor (that illusory constant sought by all researchers, by which the wrong answer is adjusted to get the right one).[5]

Such wry candour does not last long. At once, Delany is expounding Quine's 'fitting' and 'guiding' grammars, systems of (emic, or empathetic) description and (etic, or detached) explanation respectively.

> The modular calculus is an [imaginary] algorithm or set of algorithms . . . that can be applied to any fitting grammar to adjust it into a guiding grammar. . . . In short, the problem of the modular calculus is: How do we know when we have a model of a situation; and how do we know what kind of model it is?
>
> (*Flight From Nevèrÿon*, pp. 376–7)

Rich descriptions, Delany states, approach functional or explanatory force. In fact, many do not. One thinks of alchemy versus chemistry in respect of their empirical and theoretical competence to operate on the external world, outside of a closed textual system. One thinks of psychoanalysis: compellingly ornate in its accounting procedures, arguably irrelevant at any interesting explanatory level to the actual 'black box' it seeks to model and manipulate.[6] Delany knows how implausible his 'modular calculus' is, admitting that probably 'such an algorithm is a total fantasy' (p. 376). Even so, in terms of sf at least, he insists on this question:

> Might there be an [algorithmic procedure] that would tell us how close or how far a given description is from explanation, or that would tell us, from a given description, what kind of explanation may eventually be possible from it, or where the description might be further enriched to achieve explanation. For a limited set of situations, such algorithms might be developed and generalized. (p. 377)

What is the *Nevèrÿon* sequence a model of, with its playful, blatantly fake-historical 'reconstructions' of Neolithic city life, sexual fetishism, revolt against slavery, ceaseless invention? Delany's answer would not offend a Jameson in search of historicism:

a model of late twentieth-century (mostly urban) America. . . .
What sort of relation does it bear to the thing modeled?
Rich, eristic, and contestatory (as *well* as documentary), I hope.

(ibid.)[7]

The sequence is an archive, then, which places itself under scrutiny. By the nature of the problem it can hardly expect to escape its epistemic bonds, but it may challenge them to the hilt (to conscript a figure apt to sword & sorcery), using as its cutting instrument the conceit of the modular calculus. A search of the greater archive which is Delany's *oeuvre* to date reveals, interestingly, that he has not always viewed the notion so blithely. In a somewhat rambling *assemblage* of journal notes published in *Foundation* in 1974–5, he declares with almost embarrassing fervour:

The mistake at *Tractatus* 2.261 is heartrending:

There must be something identical in a picture and what it depicts to enable the one to be a picture of the other at all.

If for *must be* and *identical* he had substituted *is obviously* and *similar* – and then taken up the monumental task of running these down to their propositional atomisation – he would have solved the problem of the modular calculus (i.e., *the* critical problem).[8]

Wittgenstein's error, in short, was to search for essential identity rather than reception-determined homology between 'sets of internal relations' (Delany, 1978a, p. 52) in systems which were marked solely, on Delany's proto-Saussurean structuralist understanding, by patterns of difference. But these structural similarities are *chosen* from an indefinite number of features by the observer. A model's validity is tested pragmatically not ontologically, by 'the use you are putting it *to* – the context you are putting it *into*'. Its validity *within* a context may depend on the model's internal structure, but whether it functions at all 'has to do with the structure *of* the context' (ibid., p. 57).

THE RUDDER OF LANGUAGE

A useful consequence of Delany's interdisciplinary interests, common to most sf writers and many sf readers though far less common, perhaps, in 'literary' circles, is his early realisation that cognitive science had already answered certain traditional philosophical puzzles. Empirical evidence points

to a revitalization of the concept of mental occurrences as brain processes. [. . . I]t seems as silly to say that the brain contains *no* model

of what the eye sees . . . as it is to say that the circuitry of a TV camera
. . . contains no model of what is in front of the image orthicon tube. . . .
We can not only locate ['mental events'], we can measure them, map
them . . . cut them out, and put them in backwards!

(ibid., p. 49)[9]

Such models might be in the head, and stabilised, as Delany would come to
stress, by language,[10] but they must be objective to be useful: they must be
self-critiquing (ibid., p. 68). When models are constructed in a marketplace
context of storytelling, especially the science fictional variety, that set of
contextual or reception constraints tends, despite writer's and reader's best
efforts, to stabilise aspects of the text which each might wish to criticise. If
sf is a kind of rough-and-ready approximation to a modular calculus (of the
object, perhaps, rather than of the subject or, better, of the subject inter-
actively constituted with the object), must the story it tells us about the hidden
innards and workings of the black box (whatever it is) inevitably 'reinforce
commonly accepted prejudices'? No, says Delany, but this

> is certainly an inherent tendency of the medium. To fight it, and triumph
> over it, I must specifically go into the world I have set up *far* more
> thoroughly . . . and treat it autonomously rather than as *merely* a model
> of a prejudiciary situation. I must explore it as an extensive, coherent
> reality – not as an intensive reflection of the real world where the most
> conservative ideas will drain all life out of the invention.
>
> (ibid., p. 41)

So Delany's search is for an order of formal representation which is neither
wholly arbitrary in its coding, like the digital pits burned into the surface of
a compact disc that are related to acoustic analog signals only via a complex
transduction, nor 'transparently' isomorphic. In the words of his imaginary
metalogician Ashima Slade, Mars-born and repeatedly sex-changed inventor
of the modular calculus,

> A modular description allows us reference routes back to the elements
> in the situation which is being modeled. A nonmodular description is
> nonmodular precisely because, complete or incomplete as it may be, it
> destroys those reference routes: it is, in effect, a cipher.
>
> The problem that still remains . . . is the generation of formal
> algorithms for distinguishing incoherent modular descriptive systems
> from coherent [versions].
>
> (Delany, 1976, p. 369)

WRITING IN PHASE SPACE

More than a decade later, Delany's ludic stipulations had a somewhat
different goal: a hyperspace or phase space of signification matrices capable

of modelling and permitting transcoding between all conceivable subject positions and interactions. (This is my figure, not Delany's, introduced in Chapter 2, above.) Frye's and Todorov's generic ambitions pale. Delany does not initially challenge the cultural parameters he attempts to graph, because he asserts that some version of this grid sustains '[a]ll novelistic narrative' (*Flight From Nevèrÿon*, p. 378). The chart

> must eventually specify every possible racial/social/age/gender/sexual type, all of which become ideally equal through their ideal accessibility. . . . Like the novel itself, this chart has nothing to do with the statistical prevalence of any one group in our society. . . . Next, we must consider a set of novelistic relations: Friendship; sexual love; enmity; economic antagonism; religious approval; etc. . . . Given any two characters, in any relation, that relation must be seen as having the potential to change into any other. (pp. 378–9)[11]

Placed against this vast virtual *combinatoire*, any given fiction reveals what it excludes. A random sampling of any culture's texts will provide a telling display in phase space of its ideological contours. But Delany proposes this thought-experiment under a more generous impulse than doctrinal self-criticism:

> This grid is what allows us to ask of any fiction: precisely what does it have to say in excess of its ideological reduction . . . and the subsequent revelation of vast and overdetermined elements? The deconstructionists have led off this set of new readings most energetically by asking of certain texts: 'What do they have to say that specifically undermines and subverts their own ideological array?'[12]

Wryly, Delany adds that 'we must remember that there are still going to be many texts for which we can expect the answer: "Not much".' In his 'K. Leslie Steiner' persona, Delany defines deconstruction thus: 'an analysis of possible (as opposed to impossible) meanings that subvert any illusions we have of becoming true masters over a given text',[13] a not wholly disseminative definition that attempts to sidestep well-founded strictures against deconstruction. Of course, possible/impossible, in this context, is itself a binary opposition which deconstructors would find a suitable case for treatment. 'Steiner' identifies a necessary auto-deconstruction of Delany's regnant narrative voice in the *Return to Nevèrÿon* sequence – 'benevolent, oppressive, insistent' (p. 304)[14] – between the Master's (Marxist) claim that history 'is intellectually negotiable' and can be changed for the better, and his contrary (Hegelian) 'lie' that history is fixed and normative. 'Steiner' comments:

> Because it always bears that double message, that voice has value only in a dialectical, if not dialogic, process. . . . But if we cannot silence the lie completely – for it is too intimately bound up with experience,

language, and desire – at least the writer can worry over how to articulate the truth of that voice; and can try to write up the lie for what it is.

The recourse here is always to form. (p. 302)

One of Delany's self-interrogative devices, used increasingly through *Return to Nevèrÿon*, is the delightful if fey running exchange between K. L. Steiner, a mathematician specialising in 'Naming, Listing, and Counting Theory'(a version, it seems, of the modular calculus),[15] and the gay but conservative archaeologist S. L. Kermit; like the initials of their names, their positions mirror each other in reverse. Putting forward every objection likely to occur to the sceptic, Kermit complains: 'even in terms of his own allegory, just look at what he's done.[. . . S]lowly and inexorably the Discourse of the Master displaces everyone else's . . . for all his marginal numbers, his Benjaminesque montage, or his Bakhtinian polylogue, or whatever, there's not a new – much less radical – thing *in* it. . . . "Allegoresis", my ass!'[16] Steiner's defence is that 'It's just fun – to sort of play with in your mind', and that perhaps Delany's allegory is of a feeling rather than of a political situation in this long AIDS-echoing 'Tale of Plagues and Carnivals' (*Flight from Nevèrÿon*, pp. 330, 333). Ultimately the burden is placed back with the reader, where Delany would claim it has always rested:

> And as far as the allegory, well . . . you have to read the textual shape as just the kind of conservative reification you do, but at the same time opposing it with a vigorous deconstruction.
>
> (ibid., p. 328)

This is also the task Delany charges his new readers with when they turn back to his early books. If these texts retain interest two decades on, he tells them,

> it is where, in terms of the old stories, they fight with themselves, where they come up against the contradictions, where they stall at some moment of metaphor or within some narrative aporia or allegorical ambiguity – where, as science fiction, the world of the story organizes itself in some way in which the fictive subject becomes, momentarily, elusively objective.[17]

And it is in precisely this self-reflexive distancing, I would argue, that at last we are sure how appropriate it is to read Delany's fictions as allegories of their own production and consumption.

CONCEPTUAL BREAKTHROUGH

This may be extended to all sf texts, even that huge majority 'in a commercially fixed form the writers themselves would be the first to admit was dead from the outset'.[18] It is a strategy which in turn allegorises the historically specific experience of industrial/post-industrial epistemic crisis. That experience – however clouded, resisted, impalpable to the 'common-sense' of a majority of subjects – is the defining characteristic of our century. At the expressly cognitive level, it is a function of what Peter Nicholls terms 'conceptual breakthrough', the very hallmark of sf:

> The quest for knowledge remains sf's central vision. . . . Of all the forms [it] takes in modern sf, by far the most important, in terms of both the quality and the quantity of the work that dramatizes it, is conceptual breakthrough. [Samuel Johnson's *Rasselas*] – which recognises that even though the new world-picture may be uglier than the old we need to know about it – captures exactly the accepting tone which was to permeate so much sf [. . . which] is pre-eminently the literature of the intellectually dissatisfied, the discontented, those who need to feel there must be more to life than this, and therein lies its maturity, which by a paradox can be seen as a perpetual adolescent yearning.[19]

Like the Elizabethans, we are notoriously at the centre of a change from one episteme to another, or so it is argued by observers as various as Foucault, Jameson and Prigogine. If this much is granted, none the less its details are hidden from us, by the very nature of the crisis. It is an affliction of our cognitive (I do not exclude ideological and affective) strategies. Delany draws a similar comparison with the native reception of Shakespeare's *Tempest*:

> [C]ontemporary play-goers who did not 'believe' in the roundness of the Earth . . . and had no feeling for the new distinctions between fantasy/magic/reality/science that were then being etched on the modern English-speaking consciousness [. . . would be] totally at sea. They would simply not be able to make the storm-tossed landing on that tropical island, nor read properly the emblems of what is real and what is not and the dialogue between them which are the structure, significance, and charm of the play. It is not that they would miss the surface plot: they would miss the sub-text which gives the surface plot its reason for being what it is.[20]

Without denying the real, the referent which kicks back, one can agree with Delany that fiction within today's played-out but persistent episteme 'begins as a response to an industrial phenomenon'. Mechanical and electronic reduplication, as semioticians have told us for decades, drenches the world in signs. Even for the classic bourgeois novelist

> to describe an object was to generate a web of commentary . . . on the politics, economics, and religion of both the material and the fictive world. . . .
> The entire visible surface of every urban landscape . . . as well as

ninety-nine per cent of the visible surface of every human being in it, is constituted of signs of specifically human actions [and histories], ordered in informative, syntactic relations. . . . Nature, or the study of nature, as soon as we turn to a book to help us pursue it, is absorbed in the implied discourse of human technology.

(Delany, 1987b, pp. 21–2)

Delany's complaint with modern canonical literature is its epistemic inertia. While the complaint is largely justified, of course this does not, by some automatic corollary, validate science fiction as the alternative of choice:

What makes modern fiction *so* uninteresting is that the causality and analysis implied . . . is demonstrably *not* the matrix . . . the writers themselves could possibly believe in. We are at a point in history where the basic models proposed by the objective discourse of sociology and psychology – even in their most vulgarized, cocktail party version – are more accurate and interesting than the basic models that underlie the most 'serious' novels.

(ibid., p. 34)[21]

That modular calculus instantiated in 'literature', in short, is giving inadequate answers. The fictive models it yields fail to project 'rich' or 'oppositional' shadows[22] over the signification spaces we inhabit like half-formed ghosts from Lobey's world of *The Einstein Intersection*, trapped in an epistemic labyrinth which lends our path shape even as it restricts, labels and even brutalises our possibilities. The question remains whether science fiction *does* offer more plenteous options,[23] or whether it is finally locked into the most miserable role available to any writing practice: narcotising the dissatisfied. Positioned somewhere between contested genre formulae and the postmodern, novels such as *Triton, Stars in My Pocket Like Grains of Sand* and the *Return to Nevèrÿon* sequence suggest that, however despicable by properly literary standards sf's tropes and concerns are bound to remain, it escapes the twin temptations, so rarely refused, of current 'serious' fiction: sensitive benediction of the quotidian, hieratic bliss of intertextual self-approval.

11

THE MULTIPLICITY OF WORLDS, OF OTHERS

[W]e all know science fiction provides action and adventure, as well as a look at visions of different worlds, different cultures, different values. But it is just that multiplicity of worlds, each careening in its particular orbit about the vast sweep of interstellar night, which may be the subtlest, most pervasive, and finally the most valuable thing in s-f. . . .

This experience of constant de-centered de-centeredness, each de-centering on a vaster and vaster scale, has a venerable name among people who talk about science fiction: 'the sense of wonder'. . . .

[T]he basic s-f construct, the worlds to come and the flights between them, suggest, by those de-centerings ways to *under*-cut that up/down thinking, ways to *over*-come it, ways to surprise it and to subvert it. . . .

(Samuel R. Delany)[1]

[General Information] on Kantor dwarfs any on any given world. To walk in the weak gravity by the great aluminum and ceramic banks in hot and cold storage is to walk past macro-encyclopedias – encyclo-pedias of encyclopedias! I recall my first time through, when I stood on a plane of scarlet glass under an array of floating light tubes and thought out: 'What is the exact human population of the universe?' and was informed, for answer: 'In a universe of c. six thousand two hundred inhabited worlds with human populations over two hundred and under five billion, "population" itself becomes a fuzzy-edged concept. . . .'

Broad, breezy, full of detours, underpasses, and overhangs, the hallways I walked back down to ground level through were an allegory of the informational complexities that Free-Kantor both was and was made for.

(Samuel R. Delany)[2]

I currently suspect that all revolutions involve . . . the abandonment of generalizations the force of which had previously been in some part that of tautologies.

(Thomas S. Kuhn)[3]

137

If what we deem rational thought is never access to an essential Real but always nothing better than manipulation of encrusted metaphors by rules which are themselves drawn from metaphor, these in turn can always be 'de-centred', 'inverted', and 'interrogated' (more metaphors, of course), without ever 'bringing us closer' to any central, upright or unquestionable truth.

But the exercise of iconoclasm is at least usually exhilarating, if only briefly. When culture teaches that important *doxa* are perennial truths, and marks that persistence by inscribing the truths on stone, it is bound to be refreshing to learn that virtue lies, rather, in smashing up the stone and scattering the words. When culture preaches drunken spontaneity, it is heartening to learn, by the same token, that value is located, rather, in stern adherence to sober regularity.

ART AS PLAY, ART AS REVELATION

Current reading practices totter at a metastable lip. Critical theory has been teaching free play, baroque hermeneutics, the primacy of reader over text. The 'underlying, fundamental' metaphor here derives from the simplification that a writer is a crude disciplinarian who employs brute authority to prevent any but a single monotonous game to be played with the linguistic toy set; or a miser who hides an item of value behind a lock with a single key.

An alternative view, perhaps returning to fashion as the century closes in typical apocalyptic mood, shows the artist as a privileged seer, recording with pain and exultation what is almost impossible of access for the rest of us, so that we might benefit at second hand by simulating in prompted imagination the artist's experience, including, perhaps most importantly, the experience of writing the very words we are reading.

Many other alternatives are feasible, of course, few of them as crude as these contrasted sketches. Yet these two, which look like 'binary opposites', are closely aligned. Delany's writing often veers between these two mirror surfaces. If his theories, worked through and through his fictive texts, urge deconstruction and the obliteration of auctorial centrality or regnancy, his tales are blatantly derived from the stuff of his biography, whether flagged as in *The Einstein Intersection* or available for the curious in interviews and memoirs, including the extraordinary semi-memoir *Heavenly Breakfast*, a non-sf metafictional 'essay' of sleazy bliss in the 'winter of love', 1967,[4] and his wily autobiography *The Motion of Light in Water*.[5]

So while Delany is a declared poststructuralist, his fiction is articulated about a semiotic programme which seems, at its limit, to merge with human-ist, albeit highly relativist, liberal pluralism. Even in his most strenuous efforts to attain the transgressive, to treat the human subject as an object of cultural manufacture, he seems to be writing his own life and his apologia for it from a position of extreme and admirable wilfulness.

By a necessary artistic irony, this dynamic has powered and shaped his most successful bid at radical world creation, *Stars in My Pocket Like Grains of Sand*, announced as the first part of a diptych; the long-delayed second part is to be *The Splendor and Misery of Bodies, of Cities*.[6] True to the Balzacian resonance of this second title, the published volume is dense with the detail and structure of quotidian life high and low – save that these lives are entirely imagined, and run their course in a galactic culture of many intelligent beings with all their tremendously, inexhaustibly multifarious lifeworlds. Delany here chooses the exact opposite of his method, as self-described, in his other masterpiece, *Dhalgren*:[7] *récit*, where the narrator's on-going subjectivity is paramount, rather than *foreground*, which deploys a kind of narrative empiricism.

> [O]nly those novels proportionately rich in *récit* (James, Proust, Joyce, Stendhal, Kafka, or Faulkner, for examples) are likely to be much commented on at length. Novels proportionately rich in foreground (Chandler [. . . etc.]) are experienced as more or less richly detailed slabs of experience itself. . . .
>
> *Dhalgren* is (as is most sf) practically all foreground – at any rate, the proportion of foreground to récit is high enough to assume a paucity of *serious* written analysis.[8]

Delany notes that a Robbe-Grillet can reduce foreground to the status of récit by use of impoverished language (Delany, 1987b, pp. 14–15). His own method in *Stars in My Pocket* reverses this strategy, deluging the reader with sensory and cognitive impressions of the alien and the ever more alien, while narrator or implied narrator endlessly explains, analyses, reflects, interprets, comments on the 'what was there', the 'what happened to it'.[9] The second paragraph enacts this method, at first sight extremely clumsily:

> His big-pored forehead wrinkled, his heavy lips opened (the flesh around his green, green eyes stayed exactly the same), the ideogram of incomprehension among whose radicals you could read ignorance's determinant past, information's present impossibility, speculation's denied future. (p. 3)

Is this foreground? Yes, for as well as the simple physical description, it far more importantly appropriates, and thus performs in typical sf fashion, the kind of notation that the character's culture employs. The implied reader is supposedly privy to it as well: 'you could read'. Or is it récit? Certainly it differs from the lush foregrounding for which Delany's youthful work was prized, and which opens a fragment published several years earlier, presumably a trial run at this universe:

> Bloody lace lazied on the bay.
> Pink clouds filigreed the sky.
> The great red sun, at the world's rim, worked its changes on the green

sea below her, the coppery east beyond her, the marbled rocks she climbed on.

Squinting, she turned to face it.[10]

Not that such effects are absent in *Stars in My Pocket*; far from it. A typical passage, instantly recognisable as Delany in his patented stylish-pulp voice, blends onomatopoeia and visual cues:

Water rilled, divided at the shallow carvings, closed over them, chattering, and rippled up the tall ones to the brown and green water line. Blue and white water spumed along the spill, to swirl the ramp foot across the hall before it fountained and fell, foaming. (p. 306)

ASSAILING DOGMA

Yet all this sensory massaging is at the service of a powerfully disruptive argument, a cognitive assault on late twentieth-century certitudes, or at least on what the text assumes by its activities are such smug prejudices. Of course, by another necessary paradox, Delany's readers can hardly be the bearers of such self-satisfied dogmatisms or they would recoil in horror from the tale. Instead, like the transgression-hungry adolescent readers of Heinlein's *Stranger in a Strange Land* two or three decades previously, we take these shocks with a certain eagerness if not complacency.

But on the face of it, Delany's *mise-en-scène* is a long way from the staid Connecticut infidelities of an Updike novel. One of his chief characters is, to begin with, the victim of radical brain mutilation, and then the sole survivor of a planetary holocaust. The other, a male homosexual human cathected to lovers with either savagely chewed fingernails or strong claws (depending on species), shares in extended-familial and sexual life with intelligent, six-limbed lizards. To portray the subject under such diegetic exigencies is thus first to expound the object. Delany's foregrounding is therefore everything. But to expound the object on such a radically disjunct scale is to bring forward the processes of exposition and hermeneutics. Delany's récit is therefore everything. . . .

The storyline, once its enamelled detail-work is peeled away, is scant indeed. In the novella-length third-person Prologue, 'A World Apart', an unnamed *marginalisé* is 'treated' by a bureaucratic medical-social Institute, in an operation which effectively severs his volition, and then sold as a slave to a series of cruelly heedless institutions (individual ownership being forbidden). Trained by one supervisor, he is wasted by others. With his fellow 'rats' – who have also undergone Radical Anxiety Termination – he spends years in appalling deprivation and squalor. Homosexual by inclination, he is illegally purchased by a woman who makes good his deficit with a glove-shaped neural device. In conjunction with the glove, his damaged brain permits him to tap into an information network at vastly accelerated baud

140

rates, so that he can 'read' entire volumes in half a second. Before he can turn this epiphanic redemption to much use, he is recaptured and returned, poignantly diminished, to servitude. Years later, while he delves in a refrigerated storage crypt, all other life on the planet Rhyonon is destroyed by a firestorm.

The body of the text and its Epilogue are narrated in past tense, by and large impersonating the informational limitations of diegetic time, by industrial diplomat$_1$ Marq Dyeth of the planet Velm. (The job/role subscripts are never explicated.) There, humans and trisexed dragon-like evelmi live harmoniously in the south but under great stress in the north. Marq's primary profession takes him to many worlds, where he functions as an expediter of trade, using his skills as semiotician and cultural translator. On one of these, Nepiy, he first hears of a survivor of that global holocaust known as Cultural Fugue (observed if not occasioned by a huge fleet of non-communicating aliens, the Xlv), a fate which has afflicted some 49 of the 6,200 worlds torn between allegiance to Family or Sygn factions, under the uneasy semiotic/informational hegemony of the Web.

A second motivational strand is introduced, though it is slow in developing, when Marq returns home to find the Thant family, from the distant world Zetzor, visiting Dyethshome, a multi-generational castle deeded to his seven-times grandparent Gylda Dyeth (adherent of the Sygn) by a former psychopathic ruler of the universe, Vondramach Okk (of the Family). The Thants return later in the novel, in a welter of cultural difference, confused signals and mutual anger. Like many readers of the book they disapprove of the Dyeth (pronounced 'Death') way of life, especially its utterly casual, often homosexual and generally interspecific sexuality, pilloried as 'bestiality' by the Thants.

Japril, a Web 'spider' or official, tells Marq the survivor's tale and name (Rat Korga); that his defect has been repaired by synaptic rings constructed for Okk, an early 'rat'; and that each is the other's 'perfect erotic object' to many decimal places (p. 179). The rest of the thirteen Monologues, collectively 'Visible and Invisible Persons Distributed in Space', largely recount Marq's passionate one-day relationship with Korga before alarmed Web functionaries realise that his presence (or the lovers' synergism) is about to precipitate Cultural Fugue on Velm. The Web permits Korga's removal, by the mysterious agent JoBonnot, to the latter's home world, Nepiy. Here the plot elements approach closure, for the Thant family have elected a Family alliance, removing to Nepiy, another world in risk of Cultural Fugue, as 'Family Focus' or prime exemplar: global royalty, in effect. Their furious rudeness to the Dyeths is manifested at a highly formal dinner, an affair grossly barbaric by our standards, where neither moiety grasps the intertext of the other. This discourtesy by the Thants is understood finally as grounded in fears of Web intervention in their ambitions. As the first volume ends, it is quite unclear whether their fear is justified. Marq has been brutally separated from Desire hypostatised, but his world has been spared Cultural Fugue, marked by the departure of a vast fleet of alien Xlv observers.

In short: boy loses world, boy meets boy, boy loses boy, boy saves world.

THE POSTMODERN INTERSECTION

While this is an unusual and somewhat megalomaniacal turn on the cliché, its simplicity cannot be denied. For all its prodigious and decorated exoticism, scamped almost entirely in my bald summary, Delany has written a novel as heavily concentrated on récit, on nuanced observation of social interaction and its meaning, as any by Jane Austen or Thomas Mann. By his own account, therefore, it is this book especially which should attract copious critical exegesis and attention. It is doubtful, however, whether his reasoning is portable across modal boundaries. To the trained taste of a canonical reader, its foregrounding of the invented alien, for all that one might read it as allegory, is simply *too much* (and of a bad thing, at that).

Immediately, of course, this notional objection from the site of privilege reminds one of Sobchack's reading of the Jamesonian postmodern, as a space at once flattened and inflated by excess scenography. In this respect, and others, *Stars in My Pocket* is a strikingly postmodernist science fiction text, a place where the tropes of the other intersect with the tropes of overlay and repetition, of pastiche and subversion by rhetorical overkill.

The other?[11] At a crux, Marq cites one of Vondramach Okk's idiographic yet 'participatory' – gapped – poems:

> Its title translates 'The Strange' . . . or maybe better, 'The Awkward.' But the word can also mean 'The Exotic', or simply 'Another Person' – or also 'Another System'. . . . 'The alien is always constructed of the familiar,' is as good a translation as any of 'The Alien''s opening half-line, though it lacks all music. (pp. 130, 143)

Daily life for Marq and his fellows is a non-stop tussle at the confusing boundaries of the alien and the familiar. No sign is without its ambiguity, its alternative decoding in another signification system which just *might* happen to be that in use as frame by one's interlocutor. Joyously non-bigoted, Marq's 'stream', his always adoptive 'family', go out of their way to offer visitors the gift of adopted ritual. Meeting the Thants, they chant the disturbing chorus which lends the volume its title:

> 'We're plotting to steal time itself from you,' declared Fibermich. 'We're going to spike it to the floor as it slips by. And just as you come over to see why it's so still, we'll pull it out from under you –'
> '– and send you spinning off around the galaxy's edge,' my sister Alyxander took it up, 'on your grandest adventure yet, Thad!'
> 'We're planning to pluck all the best stars out of the sky and stuff

them in our pockets,' I said, 'so that when we meet you once again and thrust our hands deep inside to hide our embarrassment, our fingertips will smart on them, as if they were desert grains, caught down in the seams, and we'll smile at you on your way to a glory that, for all our stellar thefts, we shall never be able to duplicate.' (p. 132)

This childlike doggerel captures the heightened (and to us, yes, embarrassing) tone of many exchanges between these future culture-bearers, most notably exemplified in the virtual arias where the spider Japril recites Korga's discovery, recuperation and disposition (pp. 149–78). And like much of the linguistic play in the novel, its provenance is at first uncertain. The reader takes it for Dyeth ritual, which is undeniably baroque, as the notorious feast at the book's climax instances (especially pp. 319–24). Later, one finds that the ritual's foot-scuffing deference-cum-braggadocio is reflected to its true source, the Thants' own ritual, with proleptic accuracy. A collectivity, they are hive-like, laughing in eerie unison, like machines (p. 117) or swaying leaves (p. 119). Yet they are also bitterly individuated within 'privacy clouds' (p. 311, though in this case it is a joint gambit), rapaciously hungry for esteem and paranoically projective of ill-will.

And the ritual hums with historical reverberations and inversions. Vondramach Okk, ambivalent patron of the Dyeths, literally stole stars in her rise to empire, and felt no trace of shame. Neither does Korga feel ashamed, denuded of that single world in which he was the least resident, when he prepares (the reader suspects, guessing at the sequel, as a literal avatar of Okk) to unleash a new conscienceless imperialism upon the universe. 'Now you *must* give me a world,' he declares. 'Or I may take ten, thirty, or a hundred' (p. 177).

WORLDS OUT OF WORDS

Unorthodox verbal formulae are the warp and woof of this text, suitably, given Delany's model of sf as, in Douglas Barbour's apothegm, 'worlds out of words'. The most audacious and challenging affront to the schemata we have been socially constructed to read as pre-eminently natural is the Web's gender convention. In its universal though always locally variable language Arachnia (pp. 73, 216–17), all conscious beings are 'women', whatever their gender or species, taking the pronouns 'she' and 'her' except when the entity referred to by an individual is an object of 'her' sexual excitement, when 'he' is appropriate.

The device goes beyond a simple assault on sedimented sexism in English and presumably most other contemporary languages, though it is that as well. Retaining 'he' for either male, female or neuter objects of lust is an implicit signal that natives of this macro-culture are urged by the very forms of language into declaring publicly those states of personal, intimate desire which our culture treats as private and protected. It is possible, though, that this Arachnian usage is normative but not necessarily statistically normal in a universe of such extreme diversity: Rat Korga's world, as sexually repressive as ours, retains the archaic forms. Thus, my précis above is unfaithful to the text, for Marq and Korga are 'he' only to each other, 'she' for the purposes of most other people, except when they are cruising a 'run', a culvert set aside for random sexual adventures and/or aesthetic admiration of the statuary housed there.[12]

The surface of the book is littered with teasing word games, mostly less disturbing than this one but many requiring a *tour de force* of attention in their construction and decipherment. Evelmi have twelve taste parameters where humans have five (p. 310), and several tongues apiece. Beings lick and taste each other constantly on Velm, and suck stones or bark of diverting consistency and flavour. These many tongues become the information channel of choice for images, though visual figures are not absent, and capable of separate utterance in a display emblematic of Lacan's decentred self. Then again, the selves projected are hardly ever internally inconsistent, and hence figure each evelm, to the twentieth-century reader, only as a sort of one-woman version of Donald Duck's nephews.

The alien is built up by warping or diverting the familiar. The alien is indeed made to become the familiar, and the familiar alien. Thus we begin to internalise the codes of Dyethshome, eventually finding the Middle American crudities of the Thants unpleasant and ignoble.

Partly this is a sleight: the evelmi are too lovably a blend of large lolloping dogs, sweet-natured children, natural wonders, and all-round nice, wise folks. We see no ill-tempered evelmi, and when the local population of Morgre turns into a traditional menacing crowd it is only its size and monomania which causes distress. These humans and lizards are not mean people, though they can be thoughtless. It is hard to believe in such universal benevolence, though we have reason to attribute it to the south's mixed-species upbringing and 'bureaucratic anarchy' (pp. 113, 184) which ensures that citizens move often, changing jobs$_2$ and taking their fair share (one gathers) in homework$_3$.

NORMAN ROCKWELL ON MARS

Delany draws on sf mega-text and non-generic intertexts alike in structuring his effects. Entering his vast home 'through immense silver petals, blooming around me in the black wall, turning red' (p. 188), Marq passes two of his elders taking their ease:

Large Maxa (my mother the biogeneticist$_1$, evelm) sat on her porch, where she usually does these days, blinking about the hall with quiet, gilded eyes, her gorgeous wings folded about herself, their polychrome membranes rustling in the draught from the high grate to the south court. Egri (my mother the industrial diplomat$_1$, retired, human) squatted beside Max, forearms above her knees, her toenails slightly yellow, her biceps sinewy, her long hair – slightly yellow – thinning over her freckled scalp. A childhood memory of the two of them, engaged in endless discussions in three languages about the complexities of the world and interworld information field, its signifying ramifications, its semiotic specifications. Now they just sit together, keeping each other company, looking up at the balcony platforms across the hall, down through the transparent stretches of flooring at the hall courts below, out at the rest of us. (p. 189)

The Gothic overtones are no more lost on Marq than on us. 'Lurking there in the entrance hall – which is the way evelmi from Maxa's part of the world sit around in their own home caves – they've always struck me as probably a little daunting to most visitors' (ibid.). Quite: these are a pair of gargoyles from a thirteenth-century cathedral . . . chatting, like Umberto Eco's monks of the same period, on the niceties of semiotics. Simultaneously they are a couple of codgers from a Norman Rockwell *Saturday Evening Post* cover, perhaps as rendered Martian and macabre, in the midst of their poignant nostalgia, by Ray Bradbury, on their small-town stoop in the cool of evening. And they are sf's scientific elite, naturalised into retirement. And lares and penates, beneficent at the superstitious gate. And St George and the Dragon, on the same side at last. And so on, in a rich skein of reference and connotation which in the 'realist' register exceeds any 'mundane' linguistic web by orders of magnitude, as advertised.

At another level of scrutiny, Delany's text is everywhere braced by, and intaglioed over with, explicit science fictional structures and iconic citations. The title itself echoes Brian Aldiss's 1960 short-story collection *Galaxies like Grains of Sand*. 'The door deliquesced' (p. 244) is a rather swaggering play on Heinlein's paradigmatic 'The door dilated', discussed above. 'The blue crystal, behind us now, began to foam; the foam rose, climbing at the jambs faster than in the middle and darkening, and shutting out light as the door's semi-crystals effloresced' (ibid.). This is absurd as technology; it might be decorative special-effects, however, for one of the book's principal cognitive shocks – whose slow fore-tremors build as we try to correlate place and movement – is that an indeterminate amount of the 'excess scenography' displayed is fraudulent, generated by brain-tricking 'cassettes'.

This is finally brought to our attention on pages 339–41, where George Thant turns off Marq's gorgeous open-air sleeping platform and reveals a rundown 3-metre-square metal box. It is an interesting tactic, for Delany (mis)uses our familiarity with sf mega-text decoding conventions to trick us into supposing that 'limen-plates' teleport people to distant locations, when in fact they are merely local entrances into detailed holographic fake environments. With a moral jolt one asks: does this mean that Korga, the only person in the world unable to access information sources by direct neural connection, moves through a savagely denuded homescape, one more overlooked item of psychic and social dispossession?

Many more of these citations are third-order sf reworkings from the larger mega-text of Western culture. Rat Korga is a holy fool on the Parsifal model. His first egregious mistake comes from his incapacity to ask questions,[13] and his ruin at the hands of society is prelude to his transfiguration and triumph. Gully Foyle, hero of Alfred Bester's *Tiger! Tiger!*, is the transcendental figure of this trope, and his propulsive *bête noire* 'Vorga' is echoed in Korga's name (though this name is withheld from us until as late as p. 149). Surely his other name, 'Rat', puns on the tragic lab mouse in Daniel Keyes's poignant classic of the retard Charlie, who is graced by medicine's knife first with ordinary intelligence, then genius, only to see it drain away.[14] His surgically fitted mirror-eyes (pp. 156–7) are pure cyberpunk, while his lanky body reminds one of the Mule, the damaged superman who nearly undoes Hari Seldon's Web-like schemes in Asimov's *Foundation* sequence. Certainly he resembles the passive but hypersexual Valentine Michael Smith from Heinlein's *Stranger in a Strange Land*, whose Martian adoptive parents ate their dead, as Mike's followers partake of his flesh in a cannibalistic Eucharist. Marq's own tribe eat 'long-pig', a cloned synthetic meat derived from human flesh, though the notion of consuming anything which once walked around is nauseating to them (pp. 155–6).[15] In a darkly hilarious passage, Korga, subject of a growing storm of numinous rumour, is 'sampled' in the street by a butcher eager to grow a memorial culture:

> Si'id released the trigger. Somewhere from within Rat's shoulder a microneedle withdrew. The blades came away from the flesh, leaving three little reddish lines, one of which spilled one, and another, then a third scarlet drop down Rat's arm.
>
> 'Oh, thank you,' Si'id exclaimed. 'Yes, a beautiful sample. We will savor the complexities of your flesh for years to come, and it will lend its subtleties to myriad complex meals. . . .' (p. 303)

SELF-REFERENCE

Delany's idiolect, too, dines upon its own flesh. Perhaps the most minatory figure – multivocal symbol, icon, archetype – is *the great red sun* announced in his paradigmatic sf sentence (discussed in Chapter 5, pp. 66–7), where it is twinned with the distant blue star. It draws his questers into its Moloch fire, its renewing furnace. At the close of *Stars in My Pocket* Marq passes through the vast alchemic mystery of Aurigea's purple winds, watching with his fellow cruise passengers the stilled simulation of its swelling red and black dawn orb, a dawn which rises not overhead but *from left to right*. Behind this largest star in the galaxy is its other self, Aurigea as titular symbol of *Empire Star*. Its surreal other looms like a thermonuclear detonation above the trashed postmodern city of Bellona in *Dhalgren*. Its imploding other, source of blindness and insight, is entered by Lorq von Ray, grasping inconceivable riches at the cost of universal upheaval, in *Nova*.

'Perhaps the greatest generosity of my universe,' cries grieving Marq, of his peculiar sexual fixation, 'is that in so much it's congruent with the worlds of others' (p. 370). He might easily be speaking of Delany's intra- and intertextual transcodings of the tropes of science, psychoanalysis of several schools, and mythology, with those of the high cultural universe of literary discourse which largely excludes writing like his from its evaluative compass.

A less propitious play at reference beyond the text's self-constituting perimeters recalls the deplorable pun in *Nova*, where the doubled artist-figures are Katin and Mouse, in a cat-and-mouse game with mythic destiny.[16] When one finds Rat Korga 'hunting' dragons in the desert, the fond reader of Cordwainer Smith cannot fail to recall, though to no purpose I can discern, his germinal tale 'The Game of Rat and Dragon' (Smith, 1955). Within Delany's self-generated intertext, of course, Rat is a homonym of Mouse, the rough-voiced street kid from *Nova*. His neurological injury reflects Prince Red's in the same novel, where cyborg telefactor 'studs' equate with the GI knowledge enhancements in this universe. The 'black widows' and 'spiders' of the Web remind us of other Spiders and webs, perhaps especially that ambiguous Judas-figure Spider who is a Dragon-Lord in *The Einstein Intersection*, as well as the webbing which Babel-17 permits Rydra Wong to break and re-weave through her linguistic insight into an isomorphism between its physical structure and its vocalic representation:[17]

> not 'webbing', but rather a three particle vowel differential, each particle of which defined one stress of the three-way tie, so that the weakest points in the mesh were identified when the total sound of the differential reached its lowest point. By breaking the threads at these points, she realized, the whole web would unravel.
>
> (*Babel-17*, p. 99)

Webs, nets and texts have long been a favourite Delany trope, figuring economic and other power relations throughout *Nova* –

> imagine, a great web that spreads across the galaxy, as far as man. That's the matrix in which history happens today. . . . Each individual is a junction in that net, and the strands between are the cultural, the economic, the psychological threads that hold individual to individual. Any historical event is like a ripple in the net.
>
> (*Nova*, p. 203)

– theorised as the *textus*, in so many words, in Appendix A to *Triton* (cited above at the start of Chapter 10), and in *Stars in My Pocket* elaborated to the point of tedium. This image of interrelated data as a network makes the entire book an allegory of information-as-weaving, as this chapter's second epigraph foreshadows.

Delany introduces a countervailing figure which in *Stars in My Pocket* does not quite attain specificity: the flower. His second chapter, in fact, is 'The Flower and the Web'. The blooms in question are certainly Baudelairean flowers of evil, associated with the mendacious JoBonnot, who is probably an assassin and by her own admission an impostor (p. 294). She dresses in complex garments reminiscent of the 'bloody crenna' tattooed all about the body of the declared psychotic sadist, Clym, who might be her associate.[18] Later she wears a 'body mask' with a 'petular collar' (p. 293) among people who tend to go naked.

Masks are another Delany ensign, of course, here invoked from the very first page, when Rat's people wear complex web-like masks called 'faces' (p. 37). Culture and Nature are deliberately and provocatively confounded: the network or web is surely a primary figure of civilisation, of the contrived, the inorganic. Yet, raised to the level of universal semiosis, it symbolises everything 'organic' in the interchanges of consciousness. The blooms are here made of plastic or ink, and signify death and deprivation. One recalls the dragon-killing flowers of *The Einstein Intersection*, its hunted rat, its bloody fishheads:

> At a sudden shrieking I whirled: half a dozen wailing cats hurled themselves about my feet and fled after a brown rat. Chills snarled the nerves along my vertebrae. I looked back at the water: six flowers – roses – floated from beneath the bridge, crawling over the oil. . . .
>
> I walked through the waterfront fish market where the silver fish had their gills pulled out and looped over their jaws so that each head was crowned with a bloody flower.
>
> (*The Einstein Intersection*, pp. 8, 128)

THE ANTINOMIES OF SPACETIME

Behind the many images of nets is the great shadow of the conflict heralded throughout the text and never quite confronted: the Family versus the Sygn,

> the Family trying to establish the dream of a classic past, as pictured on a world that may never even have existed [mythic 'Earth'] in order to achieve cultural stability . . . the Sygn committed to the living interaction and difference between each woman and each world from which the right stability and play may flower, in a universe where both information and misinformation are constantly suspect. (p. 88)

This is a dichotomy more subtle and disturbing than Lo Hawk's '. . . must preserve', and La Dire's '. . . must change'. If the Family are something like the dynastic fantasy of much sf, parodied and brandished in the same moment

148

by Frank Herbert in his *Dune* saga, the Sygn are a kind of poststructuralist religion. Their insignia or floating signifier is the 'cyhnk', described variously (what else?) but often having a form readable as unity-in-diversity: it is at once a sign, an ankh, the *synch*ronic and, not impossibly, the kitchen sink.

The thrust of Delany's *oeuvre* identifies itself strongly and unequivocally with the Sygn. This partisanship tends to defeat the sense one suspects the book strives to attain, of chaotic equilibrium between the two. On death, for instance, an evelm philosopher distils Sygn doctrine as 'Live life moment by moment as intensely as possible, even to the moment of one's dying' – and, one suspects, whether or not your desires transgress accepted boundaries. By contrast, the Family's structuralist maxim is 'Concentrate only on what is truly eternal – time, space, or whatever hypermedium they are inscribed in – and ignore all the illusory trivialities presented by the accident of the senses, unto birth and death itself' (p. 139). Perhaps these positions could be crudely identified (but I shall qualify this shortly) with emphasis on the diachronic versus the synchronic, spontaneous anarchy versus studious Platonism.

While Delany's texts seem always to lean toward advocacy of the former, it is a demonstration of his own principled inconsistency that in an earlier novel he presented a sect called the Sygn who eschewed speech, writing, publicity and sex, engaged in 'self-mortification and mutilation . . . and two of the leading-lady gurus – as well as one of the gentlemen – had their brains publicly burned out' (*Triton*, p. 15).[19] If this is a foretaste of Vondramach's elective RAT surgery, driven by her desire for a kind of Rasputin sanctity, the irony is her highly profitable adherence to Family formulaic rigidity and hierarchic domination rather than *Stars*-style Sygn generosity, self-confidence, mutual support, intensely communicative turbulence. . . .

I wrote 'crudely identified' above because Delany's *textus* is a web of aporia, a poststructuralist construct where every statement contains its opposite and its opposite's *Aufhebung* (to borrow Hegel's dialectical term for 'surpassing' or 'depassing' an original condition by first negating it, and then negating its negation). The Sygn, Marq tells us,

> is concerned with preserving the local history of local spaces. . . . [O]ne of the Sygn's most widely spread tenets (and, like everything else in the Sygn dogma, it, too, no matter how wide, does not obtain everywhere) is that history is what is outside, in both time and space, the current moment of home. And without history, there is no home. (p. 104)

Like existentialists, to become free we must 'assume' or deliberately embrace the history that determines us (ibid.). The cyhnk's variable form embodies this aporetic doctrine, and is contained within its own equally aporetic hermeneutics:

> On some worlds, apparently, it's a trunk with just two branches. On others . . . it had five branches, each of which was a regular helix. And

on some . . . it is simply a cluster of a hundred and eleven twisting spokes; then, on others, it's only a single bar with a jewel at each end [and so on]. . . .

[O]n many worlds the cyhnk signifies, as it does on Velm, a difference between one part of itself and another. [. . . Elsewhere] it signified the difference between one cyhnk and another, the difference between the myriad kinds of cyhnks that exist on myriad worlds, the difference between the myriad dogmas, each one different for each different part of each different world [etc.]. (pp. 134–5)

This equivocation attains an intellectually audacious and dizzy pitch in Marq's citation of his mother Egri's account of industrial diplomatic practice, a form of semiotic policing:

There is only one right thing to say in any crisis situation, as there is only one trunk to a cyhnk; yet there are more ways to say it than there are branches leading away from the trunk to the bright and scattered gems of truth. When we were older, she announced: If you can list for me everything wrong with that very seductive and profoundly wrong-headed statement, you are ready to deal with diplomacy₁ as the art, rather than as the science, that it is. (p. 317)

'Multiplexity' is a useful term introduced in *Empire Star*, where statements or perceptions, in rising order of elaboration, are simplex, complex or multiplex. Like all Delany's fiction, *Stars in My Pocket* is a multiplex enactment of civilisation and its contexts, contents, discontents and contentments. Like the myths of *The Einstein Intersection*, the multifarious semiotic structures which weave the textus of this 6,000-world culture must be assumed in an act of will, so that their provisionality, fuzziness and overdetermination can never be mistaken for essence, crisp definition and univocity. The alternative is to have them invest the individual and the micro-culture like a demon, or a dynastic imperative. For all that, Delany's ostensibly de-centred subjects are not blurred into fuzzy undecidability in their piercingly felt relations with each another. Marq's desolation when Rat Korga is taken away from him is as traumatic and affecting as Korga's earlier lobotomy of the will:[20]

'It's like the switches in my head that allow the proper emotions to come through to let me function have been shorted closed or else jammed and smashed that way, so that I believe I *can* function, yes, but without nuance or color to what I perceive or do. . . .

'Desire isn't appeased by its object, Japril, only irritated into something more than desire that can join with the stars to inform the chaotic heavens with sense. . . . You've stolen – you've practically destroyed – my home. . . .

'In a single gesture you've turned me into the most ordinary of human creatures and at once left me an obsessive, pleasureless eccentric, trapped in a set of habits which no longer have reason because they no longer lead to reward. . . .' (pp. 367, 370–1)

Yet this Lacanian account of desire (as absence endlessly pursued) does not, I think, support a poststructural anti-humanism. Rat Korga's heart-breaking condition is precisely to lack a self. In this he is like The Butcher in *Babel-17*, whose subjectivity is almost obliterated by its construction in an artifical language lacking reflexive shifters ('you', 'I'), terms that alter their point of reference depending on *who is speaking*. Rat's redemption lies initially in neurological and cultural repair, but the unfinished form of the diptych urges us to look for fulfilment if not closure in his return to Marq. A hooked lure curves out from the textual surface before us. When Marq is offered a recording of interview with Japril's briefing, he declines: 'And I began rueful years of regretting my idiocy' (p. 182). 'Rueful' suggests a less than happy passage in the sequel, but not a tragic one.

The fundamental enabling device of this universe is the General Information system, brooding like a semiotic oracle over the cultures which employ it and those which refuse its service. It is modest in its fuzzy omniscience, always out of date, ever ready to chide any user who supposes its answers possess hard edges. The Web, who command it, do not scruple to interdict data in the interests of stability, even at the price of judicious assassinations (p. 95). Yet its presence makes everyone, potentially, an expert system, within Wittgensteinian limits, in any discipline:

'What can be talked of clearly, General Info can teach you in under three-tenths of a second.' (That's the time for neural firing throughout a cubic-third-of-a-centimeter of brain material. . . .) 'The rest one must mumble about. . . .' (p. 160)

This recalls the mantra-mumbling Poor Children of the Avestal Light and Changing Secret Name (*Triton*, p. 2), first cousins to the neo-Thomist (from the inventor of Catastrophe Theory, René Tom, not Aquinas) Rampant Order of Dumb Beasts, rump of the Sygn. . . . Reviving Korga, the spiders 'gazed, regazed, reprobed, and reread among the synaptic nerve-patterns' possibilities of meaning. (They unpack, like any text, not always with what has been packed into them)' (p. 160).

And even though Web brain technology permits total simulacra of the dying, as Marq's founding ancestor Gylda Dyeth is simulated within a 'synapse casting' (p. 115), Delany insists on a poststructural and quantum-cum-chaos theoretic uncertainty in 'reading' such synaptic texts:

She was a book, she was a text, she was a set of signs, some present, some absent, to be interpreted. . . . She was a hermeneutic enterprise I could not bear, who mocked me by the miming of a desire stronger than mine to withdraw from the encounter. 'No, don't go yet, Marq.' (pp. 345–6)

A book (a self, a simulacrum) which catches one's sleeve and bids one tarry: the very image of postmodern frustration, tedium, hunger for whatever lies beyond formula and pattern, even if it is only repetition estranged into the unbearable. That is the possibility implicit in all science fiction, Modern or postmodern, a kind of textuality that renders personality into object and is then held (then reconstituted, in whatever small or large degree) by that object's pitiless delphic gaze. That is Delany's text, too.

12

THE AUTUMNAL CITY

What I have done here is told you a story, a fiction, several fictions in fact. I've given them a more or less systematic presentation, held together by certain ~~themes~~ . . . which is to say that they will serve us only if we realize they are too simple: too many things have been left out, too many questions remain, not enough history and socially stabilizing institutions have been examined . . .

. . . to dissolve the introductory problem, to search out a common vocabulary among the debates' discussants, to pinpoint common ideas or presuppositions they share, to locate common centers for argument, or to describe the general paradigm of language-as-model-for-all-meaning-processes that much of the dialogue has taken place under, might well be construed . . . as an aspect of a totalizing urge, a will to knowledge-as-power, a desire for mastery. . . .

(Samuel R. Delany)[1]

I am too weak to write much. But . . . I have come to

to wound the autumnal city.
    So howled out for the world to give him a name.
    The in-dark answered with wind.

(Samuel R. Delany)[2]

The hazard awaiting any belated scholarly or critical attention to a marginalised mode is that its texts will be treated only as symptoms of something else. This is the risk, admittedly, which Marxist, psychoanalytic, feminist and other oppositional criticisms always run even with the texts of literature and the fine arts. It is especially marked with a paraliterary mode such as sf which explicitly and in advance addresses a large part of its energies to schemata.

Sf, as we have seen, is rarely about the realities of science. Still, in fictive narratives ranging from the gaudiest outer space adventures to the loftiest 'technologically constituted space, in which language reaches toward the lyric and death changes its status',[3] it undoubtedly emblematises the investigative, sceptical, objectifying aspects of science, in preference to the incorporative, subject-centred tonalities of most canonical literature.

So it is easiest, if any attempt is made to recover sf's texts for serious study, to read them as allegories from a self-aggrandising position as hermeneuticist or diagnostician. No doubt this is why the most provocative of recent sf criticism has tended to emerge from the generosity of post-structuralism towards popular culture. While I have doubts about decon-struction's rather imperial claims,[4] I can appreciate why Delany expresses a certain proselytising zeal for both its attempts at philosophical rigour and its ludic *jouissance*:

> The usual situation of the sf reader, confronted with criticism in general, is to discover, after whatever initial period of critical enthus-iasm the critic claims for the genre, only the genre's lacks. In the post-structuralist mode of critical discourse, however, there is a good chance for us to forge a dialogue in which to speak with both passion and precision about our strengths.[5]

This is a passionate and precise declaration in keeping with, for example, current feminist projections of poststructural critique that recognise the merits of speaking from a grounded position. Delany's embrace of decon-structive poststructuralism also has strategic merit, as he is the first to admit:

> [T]he traditional thematic critical stance of the SF academic critic has been (if I may be forgiven such a crude characterization) to shout, 'Look! Look! We're literature too!' . . . I know that when I have discussed science fiction and its marginal status, how it has used its marginal status as a position from which to criticize the world, how it has organized itself differently from literature in everything from its material practices of publication and printing to the semantic con-ventions that govern the reading of the sentences that make up its texts, and when I have suggested sf has a philosophical worth and an esthetic beauty that can be valorized by intensive analysis, among critics with more recent allegiances I've often felt that I am being heard. . . . When I talk with thematic critics, however, frequently their response is: 'But surely you too want science fiction to be literature . . . ?' To which my answer is (surprising as some still find it) I don't and never have.
> I don't even want literature to be literature.[6]

THE OBJECT OF SCIENCE FICTION

In short, Delany is calling in this moment of critique for closer attention to the object of discussion (to twist the trope I have been using to discriminate sf from literature), rather than the subject of science fiction. That object is a series of texts constituted out of signifiers with unusual properties linked in syntagms of unorthodox structure, standing in an unprecedented fictive relation to the cultural surround which frames them and which they influence.

Traditional thematic analysis, even the kind which points to sf's iconography, risks reducing its texts to unproblematic meditations on, or diversionary exploitations of, such themata as 'New Worlds', 'The Alien', 'Technology', 'Time', 'Space', and 'Utopia/Dystopia'. All of these, for Delany,

> can here and now be abandoned to the archaeology of our criticism. And as a longer-term strategy, I propose that what is deeply needed in our field is people to read science fiction carefully, synchronically with the historical and social occurrences (both inside and outside the sf field) around its composition, who are willing to discuss with precision, creativity, and critical inventiveness what they have read.[7]

If innovatory forms have the potential to intrude into and destabilise the dynamic equilibrium which is the vast vibrating web of information linking and constituting the subjects – the human people – in our enormously object-oriented civilisation, to be the reorganising noise of culture,[8] they certainly deserve no less than this whole-hearted measure of attention.

Delany's suggestion carries the usual risk of a criticism of commitment. Like Leavis's muscular, ethical readings in the mid-century, schools of eulogistic and denunciatory fashion that form around such key poststructuralist figures as Foucault and Derrida can all too easily press their own ideological quirks under the guise of either play or a rigour that depasses conventional rationality.

'. . . Must change'. . . .

'. . . Must preserve'.

A DEFINITION OF SF

Positioned like science fiction itself on a meta-stable lip of uncertainty, we may contemplate with some sense of always-already-ruptured closure a somewhat complicated definition of sf:

> *Sf is that species of storytelling native to a culture undergoing the epistemic changes implicated in the rise and supersession of technical-industrial modes of production, distribution, consumption and disposal. It is marked by (i) metaphoric strategies and metonymic tactics, (ii) the foregrounding of icons and interpretative schemata from a collectively constituted generic 'mega-text' and the concomitant de-emphasis of 'fine writing' and characterisation, and (iii) certain priorities more often found in scientific and postmodern texts than in literary models: specifically, attention to the object in preference to the subject.*[9]

Let us break that down into its components. Sf is a species of storytelling marked by:

- metaphoric strategies, for it constructs its narrative maps not from the schemata of the commonplace but out of endlessly inventive and open-ended analogies, catachreses, paradigm-elisions, puns, conceits; out of dream echoes or deformations and satirical distortions of the quotidian, and scientific or pseudoscientific diagrams of the inaccessible: the new signifiers of sf's novel paradigm sets;
- metonymic tactics, for its outrageous inventions tend to mimic the mimetic, to copy the realistic modes of representation, to link the signifiers it invents or appropriates into syntagmatic strings whose forms perform and formulate new formulae of narrative topology: structures of connection and disconnection which track like paths the trajectories and pathos of sentences until now incapable of utterance;
- the foregrounding of icons and interpretative schemata from a generic 'mega-text', for sf is explicitly a communal narrative form, escaping synchronic definition as each moment passes into the next because that is the diachronic shape of our meta-stable culture: fuelled and bodied forth by the images and *praxis*, for good or ill, of consumerist technological society;
- the concomitant de-emphasis of 'fine writing', which is the insignia and medium of a socially restricted paradigm set deployed through recognised and canonised syntagmata, tropics of discourse, which sf escapes at the very instant it fails to meet tests of literary credential;
- the backgrounding of subjectivity, which is the hallmark of a kind of writing valorising the given in its exquisite nuance, whether or not this attention equates superficially with endorsement of the subjectivities portrayed; for if the loss of fine register in constituting imaginary subjects is historically a frailty shared with other wish-fulfilling entertainment media, sf's turn away from character (as literature understands it) is made inevitable by its alternative focus on an alienated *mise-en-scène*;
- communicative priorities more often found in scientific and postmodern texts than in literary models, so that the algorithmic, the blatantly schematic, the communal, the epistemic, the spatial, the unknown are given priority over the individuated, the comfortingly quotidian, the known;
- attention to the object in preference to the subject, where 'object', under the scrutiny to which we have subjected discursive sites, is no unimpeachable essential Real yet retains a genuine externality, a power to shock equal to Dr Johnson's stone striking back at his shoe; and where 'subject', if not quite de-centred, is labile, socially miscible, cognitively multiplex.

All of these factors, taken together, constitute a kind of narrative native to a culture undergoing the epistemic changes implicated in the rise and supersession of technical-industrial modes of production, distribution, consumption and disposal; a world of culture which has virtually replaced nature, remade it, and stands at the edge of destroying it.

SF AND THE RENOVATED NOVEL

For all that, it is not inauthentic to claim that sf retains singular merit. For sf's semantic hyperspace – its armoury of tropes and narrative devices, its extensive mega-text – is positioned at a fruitful angle to the 'sequence of discoveries' Milan Kundera has traced as marking the European novel's evolution.[10] At the invention of the novel, Don Quixote sets forth into a world as strange, in its way, as any extraterrestrial locale, yet his principal findings are those poststructuralist tenets, the internally riven self and the 'wisdom of uncertainty' (Kundera, 1988, p. 7). Diderot's *Jacques le Fataliste* exists 'in a time without beginning or end, in a space without frontiers' (ibid., p. 8) – not unlike the denuded, totipotent landscapes of space opera. With Balzac, time rides the track-bound steam locomotive of History through a world remade by social institutions: 'the police, the law, the world of money and crime, the army, the State' (ibid.) – the richly elaborated site drawn to our attention in Delany's late texts. With Flaubert, the 'lost infinity of the outside world is replaced by the infinity of the soul' (ibid.), or more precisely of the daydream – a move familiar in postmodern sf, from Ballard to Greg Bear's virtual realities. Thereafter, for the European novel, Tolstoy and Joyce, Broch, Musil and Hasek surge toward the black hole of Kafka's K. Such steps can never be taken by a commercial form like sf, I think, though Lem's more austere and blackly funny tales approach its destination. History now, for Kundera, is 'impersonal, uncontrollable, incalculable, incomprehensible – and it is inescapable' (ibid., p. 11).

This seems pretty final. Does Kundera therefore despair, adding his signature to those decreeing the death of the novel? Not at all. He espies missed opportunities, unheard appeals to partake in the cultivation of fictions bypassed by that earlier steam train. Even in view of the marketplace victories of fat feckless pastoral fantasies and gore-obsessed horror, and of latter-day 'hard sf', it seems to me that Kundera's bill of four candidates for a renovated novel fits sf most wonderfully. They are the appeals of *play*, *dream*, *thought* and *time* (ibid., pp. 15–16).

Unlike the canon of contemporary fiction, sf is well-placed to answer these appeals, which almost constitute a summary of the crimes its best works are held to be guilty of. Sf is not serious, it is recreational, it toys with the known laws of time, place, mind and causality: it *plays*. True, sf's is by no means the sense of adult play Kundera had in mind, yet perhaps it is not altogether distant from it either.

Sf denies the absolute claims of the wide-awake world that *is*, the apparently hard-edged world which its audacious fictions, in common with high critical theory, bid to unmask as social construct. Like surrealism, sf from Van Vogt to Swanwick borrows from *dream* and imagination in deconstructing and recasting the known.

Beyond the artful transcription of dream, sf is undoubtedly a writing steeped in the will to *thought*, steeped in cognition, however ineptly it manages the task.

And, *pace* Jameson (who, you'll recall, sees sf as pre-eminently a spatial genre), it soars beyond the limits of History, reaching for that perspective given us by deep evolutionary *time* and the sounding depths of cosmological duration. The time of sf can be the century after this or the one next door but it is also the time of cosmogonic myth, written anew in all the playful, dreaming voices of men and women thinking as hard as they can about a universe endlessly, beautifully, excitingly open.

STRANGE ATTRACTORS

If sf is even now largely a formula fiction devoted to frightening its readers with images of unknown terrors, and beguiling them with other no less puerile images of power and knowledge, that is a measure of our compliance with the energies which bend us aside from our joint and individual determinations in every moment when we fail to take charge of them to make our own ends.

And it is perhaps a reflection of a larger pathology in the will to critique. I mean Theory's (theories') incapacity to relate the signifier to the referent without lurching into, on the one hand, some disabling worship of the text – certainly the risk Delany constantly runs, for all his avowed stress upon the object – or, on the other hand, an uncritical empiricism. Science fiction has no special role at this level. But in its own distinct discursive emphases, sf may be able to offer what neither literature nor science can provide from within their authorised and authorising bastions. Perhaps it can tell us with some precision, to our cognitive and our aesthetic benefit, *what works us* within our turn-of-the-twenty-first-century dreams of reason and unreason. Permit me to advance this conjecture in a metaphor I once filched from the mathematics of chaos:

> Like the mathematical point forming random order ineluctably within the envelope of the Strange Attractor, like a ghost of the unborn, from Chaos, sf blows its warm breath on the pane which divides us from tomorrow and our own deep awareness, and in its dews and condensations shows us patterns we scribble there, absent-minded children, all unknowing.[11]

NOTES

INTRODUCTION

1 The term/concept *episteme* is usually associated with Michel Foucault, and has been subjected to considerable critical surveillance and punishment. The semioticians Greimas and Courtes give two alternative definitions; they see Foucault's as 'a connotative meta-semiotics'. Their primary usage, close to my own, designates 'the hierarchical organisation of several semiotic systems. This organisation, located at the level of deep semiotic structures, can generate, by means of a combinatory principle and of selective rules of incompatibility, the set of manifestations (either realised or potential) included in these systems within a given culture' (Greimas and Courtes, 1982, p. 105).

2 Suvin (1979).

3 See Eco (1976) and his important discussion of the rival worth of two models in Chapter 2, 'Dictionary vs. Encyclopedia', in *Semiotics and the Philosophy of Language* (1984).

4 Theroux (1986). Considerable critical difference has been expressed about the worth of this novel. George Turner, for example, favours its deviations from exhausted sf traditions (1988, p. 23). Thomas M. Disch finds it 'dull, ill-written, misconceived, nakedly exploitative – and a botch even at that unworthy task' (1989, pp. 10–11).

5 The appeal of such 'supplementation' is evident in the enormous success of *Omni* (selling nearly ten times as many copies as the average sf magazine, and as many as an sf paperback bestseller), where the popularised science, 'personalised' and consumer-oriented, far outweighs the fiction, which is frequently rather vapid (perhaps because any employment of arcane and specialised sf tropes must there be restricted, as it is in most movie and television sf, to function within the limitations of an untrained mass readership).

6 Though it turns out, in what might be regarded as an institutional invariance-under-transformation, that the bulk of sf fails most of these new comparisons also. Such popular culture criticism tends to find sf insufficiently relativist, deeply conservative even where it might appear to be satirically anarchic, and so forth.

7 See, for example, Gilbert and Mulkay (1984), and Collins and Pinch (1982).

8 See, for example, the kinds of rebukes offered by Patrick Parrinder in *The Failure of Theory* (1987). Professor Parrinder has also written interestingly on sf.

9 An early demonstration of this was John Berger's television series *Ways of Seeing* (BBC), and its book recension (Penguin, 1972).

10 Robinson (1992), p. 69.

11 Grosz (1990), pp. 147–74.

159

12 Lloyd (1984), p. 109.

13 A representative reading 'against pluralism' is Hal Foster's, in *Recodings* (1985). Pluralism 'grants a kind of equivalence: art of many sorts is made to seem more or less equal – equally (un)important. Art becomes an arena not of dialectical dialogue but of vested interests, of licensed sects. . . . The result is an eccentricity that leads, in arts as in politics, to a new conformity: pluralism as an institution' (p. 15).

14 Compare Sandra Harding's exploration of distinctively feminist 'ways of knowing' in *Whose Science? Whose Knowledge?* (1991); specifically, the epistemological investigation *passim*, grounded in what she calls 'feminist standpoint theory', which tries to construct knowledge from the perspective of women's lives' (p. vii).

15 There are many useful introductory books expounding the ideas of these theorists. One of the most interesting is Harland (1987).

1 NEW WORLD, NEW TEXTS

1 Michel Serres, *Les Cinq Sens* (1985), p. 371, trans. Paulson, in his *The Noise of Culture* (1988), p. 51. By 'supposing', Paulson glosses, Serres denotes an interest not 'in copying science or in judging it but in placing science in the position of the subject of his discourse'. Clearly Serres is not referring to sf; just as clearly, his essay at transcoding the exact and the human sciences is precisely pertinent.

2 Delany, *Babel-17* (1987a; 1966 edn), p. 88.

3 Although 'sci fi' is usually held to have been coined by fan enthusiast Forrest J. Ackerman, the community of readers and practitioners generally eschews the term; Brian Aldiss, in *Billion Year Spree*, notes: 'Only would-be trendies use sci-fi' (1975, p. 10). More placatory is the recent concession by Arthur C. Clarke: 'Perhaps it is time to call a truce; at least sci-fi has the advantage of being instantly understandable to everyone' (1989, p. 11). Lately, Greg Bear tells me, the provenance has been traced back to Robert Heinlein, who also coined 'speculative fiction' (subsequently appropriated by the left-anarchist, experimental 'New Wave', doubtless to Heinlein's displeasure). Personally, I continue to detest and denounce 'sci fi', with its 30 or more years of connotative barnacles: tawdriness, illogicality and, above all, schlock know-nothing carelessness.

4 A narratological term, defined and discussed in detail in Chapter 5 below, borrowed usefully by Christine Brooke-Rose in her analysis of fantastic literatures (1981).

5 The authoritative *Anatomy of Wonder* (2nd edition, Barron, 1981; there was a third in 1987) categorised 'The Modern Period' as '1938–1980', that is, as everything since John W. Campbell set his editorial stamp on ASF (*Astounding Science Fiction* magazine). This is a broader denotation than some would permit. In the glossary to his survey 'Paradise Charted', in *TriQuarterly*, no. 49 (Fall 1980) Algis Budrys offered these more circumscribed definitions: *Modern science fiction*: 'Specifically, stories in the style of ASF 1938–1950. Derives from references in the 1946 anthology, *Adventures in Time and Space* [ed. Raymond J. Healy and J. Francis McComas], which segregated such stories from all other sorts of [science fiction]. In current critical writing, sometimes "'Modern' science fiction".' *Post-modern science fiction*: Sf 'from 1950 to 1960, as typified by work published in *Galaxy* magazine 1950 and later. . . ' *Contemporary science fiction*: 'purely a description, without limitation except by chronology' (all citations, Budrys, 1980, p. 74).

6 This includes, in translation, important work by Soviet and East European writers

(Stanislaw Lem especially), who have not been altogether without influence on their Western colleagues – whose influence in turn is clearly marked in their own work. Scant Asian sf (let alone African, if any) is available outside visual-media varieties from, especially, Japan, but (like most Western cinematic sf) these have little direct salience to the production and reception of sophisticated print-medium sf. The scholar and sf editor David Hartwell states: 'There is not yet a really identifiable third world SF. The underdeveloped countries have not responded to the technologically optimistic appeal of SF, perhaps because that visionary future filled with mechanical wonders seems so far beyond their present resources' (Hartwell, 1989, p. xvi). Sf is not only, or even perhaps most importantly, optimistic about science-driven technology, but this assessment remains plausible.

7 A titular example is Professor James Gunn's annotated anthology *The Road to Science Fiction: From Gilgamesh to Wells* (1977), though Gunn disclaims attempts to conscript, as sf, texts prior to the early nineteenth century. 'My point in including the earlier works was to [show] that SF evolved out of previous human impulses when the time was right, as contrasted to the viewpoint that SF was born spontaneously out of the Industrial and Scientific Revolutions' (private communication).

8 Prime exemplar is Robert Heinlein's 'Future History' *oeuvre*, charted in *Astounding* in May 1941 and later revised, which offered a detailed chronology from the 1960s to 2140 (later 2600, and beyond); Heinlein attempted to integrate a sociological account of change with technical speculations: moving roadways, solar energy, space travel, etc.

9 Cf. Bruno Bettelheim's Freudian case in *The Uses of Enchantment* (1976).

10 Aldiss (1975).

11 Aldiss (1985b), p. 115.

12 Introduction to Asimov *et al.* (1983), p. 10.

13 Campbell (1952).

14 Campbell's slapdash writing might be noted in passing: 'filled with a touch of' is quite typical.

15 'Vault of the Beast', by A. E. van Vogt, in Campbell (1952), p. 60.

16 Peter Nicholls *et al.* (eds), *The Encyclopedia of Science Fiction* (1979). The revised second edition is edited jointly by John Clute and Peter Nicholls, contributing editor Brian Stableford (1993). The revised entry 'Definitions of Sf' reduces these citations to (by my count) 11 definitions, several with subsidiary refinements. In 1993, Nicholls concludes, 'There is really no good reason to expect that a workable definition of sf will ever be established. None has been, so far. In practice, there is much consensus about what sf looks like in its centre; it is only at the fringes that most of the fights take place' (p. 314).

17 Cited ibid. (1979 edn), p. 658.

18 Wordsworth (1952), p. 342.

19 DeLillo (1983).

20 Suvin (1983).

21 Hugo Gernsback's originary ostensive definition pointed to the stories of Jules Verne, H. G. Wells and Edgar Allan Poe (see next paragraph). Poe's importance might no longer seem so crucial, until he is seen abruptly as a figure for the New Wave stylistic revolution which remade Campbellian sf in the 1960s (and which in turn might claim Campbell himself, writing as 'Don A. Stuart' in the late 1930s, as its moody forerunner). James Gunn's discussions of the first two exemplify the standard estimate of their importance: Verne is 'The Indispensable Frenchman' (Gunn, 1977, p. 253), Wells 'The Father of Modern Science Fiction' (ibid. p. 380).

22 A portmanteau naming which did not last, except in some fans' preference for the abbreviation 'stf'.

23 Cited in Nicholls *et al.* (1979), p. 159.

24 In the form of 'thought experiments'.

25 Cited in Nicholls *et al.* (1979), p. 159.

26 Disch (1978), p. 142.

27 '[A]lthough we rarely notice it, we are all the time engaged in constructing hypotheses about the meaning of the text. . . . The text itself is really no more than a series of "cues" to the reader. . . . The work is full of "indeterminacies", elements which depend for their effect upon the reader's interpretation, and which can be interpreted in a number of different, perhaps mutually conflicting ways. . . . The literary work itself exists merely as what the Polish theorist Roman Ingarden calls a set of "schemata", or general directions, which the reader must actualise' (Eagleton, 1983, pp. 76–7).

28 Aldiss (1988). 'Green Mouth' is Sheila, the successful fantasy-sf series writer wife of Clement Winter, the novel's principal focaliser. 'Affectionately called Dragonlady by SF fans,' according to Gunn (1988, p. 289), Anne McCaffrey has written *Dragonflight* (1968), *Dragonquest* (1971), *The White Dragon* (1978), *Dragonsong* (1976), *Dragonsinger* (1977), *Dragondrums* (1979), and, stretching credulity to the limit, *Moreta: Dragonlady of Pern* (1983). Another woman writer from fandom, Julian May has written the open-ended 'Saga of the Pliocene Exile', starting with *The Many-Colored Land* (1983).

29 Jameson (1981), p. 185.

30 A perception sometimes flaunted wilfully by genre proponents. An advertisement for its own wares on the back page of *The Magazine of Fantasy and Science Fiction (F&SF)* in May, 1963, for example, offers a sidebar of citations from such notables as Clifton Fadiman and Louis Armstrong. The musician finds that *F&SF* 'appeals to me because in it one finds refuge and release from everyday life. We are all little children at heart and find comfort in a dream world, and these episodes in the magazine encourage our building castles in space.'

31 Robert Silverberg, 'The Making of a Science-Fiction Writer', in Silverberg (1988), p. 3.

32 Disch (1980), pp. 77, 79. The knowing sf reader detects at once the flaying of that sf nova of the 1970s, John Varley, whose much-liked story 'The Persistence of Vision' (*F&SF*, March 1978) sanctifies the paranormal and epiphanic fellowship of a tribe of congenitally deaf, dumb and blind victims of medical disaster; this in turn reprises Theodore Sturgeon's equally well-loved *gestalt* superbeing comprised of cripples physical, psychological and moral in *More Than Human* (1953).

33 See Derrida (1976), pp. 153–7. For a dissenting view on this logic of the supplement, compare the late Geoffrey Thurley, in his *Counter-Modernism in Current Critical Theory* (1983): 'The things supplemented by Derrida are so amorphous or aggregative that they can be neither supplemented nor complemented' (see especially pp. 252–3).

34 Delany, Appendix B, *Flight from Nevèrÿon* (1985c, p. 358; ellipses mine): '[F]or Barthes, semiology was "the labor that collects the impurity of language, the wastes of linguistics, the immediate corruption of any message: nothing less than the desires . . . of which active language is made." This idea of semiology as the excess, the leftover, the supplement of linguistics brings us round to Jacques Derrida's logic of the supplement, without which semiology and, indeed, poststructuralism in general would be hugely impoverished.' The monistic moralism grounding this figure is very odd.

35 This assertion skips all too lightly over such gigantic monuments of modernism and postmodernism as Kafka's and Borges's fables, and the Latin-American-

influenced strands of magic realism; for all that, it seems to me clearly more valid than otherwise, and not merely in a statistical sense.

36 These publishers' puffs are all from a 1989 advance order list.
37 Anderson (1991), p. 69.
38 Often Poul Anderson's work is very much better than merely workmanlike, as in his novel *Midsummer Tempest* (1974), a technical *tour de force*.
39 Farmer (1982), p. 15. This slim (and presumably hastily written) nightmarish vision (of the Hell which *precedes* earthly life) is a sort of sketch of the naturalistic theodicy subsequently elaborated in Farmer's Riverworld series.
40 Crowley (1988), p. 5.
41 Ryman (1989), p. 388.
42 Eileen Gunn points out that 'Patel is a Pakistani name and carries with it . . . a host of associations turned inside out: *My Beautiful Laundrette* twisted through the fifth dimension' (1992, pp. 1, 10). To me, Rolfa is closer to a stoned Rasta.
43 Jameson (1991), p. 191.
44 Dowling, *Rynosseros* (1990); *Blue Tyson* (1992); *Twilight Beach* (1993).
45 Foyster (1987), p. 5.
46 Cited by Foyster (1989), from the *New York Times Book Review*, 16 April 1989.
47 Stableford (1979), p. 3.
48 Hartwell (1985), p. 3.
49 Panshin and Panshin (1989).
50 It should be noted that Australia, nevertheless, has hosted two world (that is, American-oriented) conventions and holds its own annual national convention, as well as numerous smaller occasional 'cons'.
51 It is absolutely appropriate that the founder of scientology was a 'Golden Age' formula sf writer of some narrative power. See Russell Miller's *Bare-Faced Messiah* (1988). This impulse in readers and writers is devastatingly deconstructed in Fritz Leiber's classic 'Poor Superman' (1951).

2 GENERIC ENGINEERING

1 Clute (1975), in Clute (1988), pp. 116–17.
2 Richard Ohmann, 'Where Did Mass Culture Come From?', in Ohmann (1987), pp. 138–9.
3 Cioffi (1982), pp. 19, 23.
4 Davies (1992), p. 500.
5 Wolfe (1979).
6 The reference is to John Cawelti's influential *Adventure, Mystery, and Romance* (1976).
7 Levin (1980) (The 1st Eaton Conference on Science Fiction and Fantasy Literature, 1979, at University of California Riverside), pp. 20–1.
8 Suvin (1979).
9 Benford (1988, 1990). This sequence takes place in the far future of another sequence begun with *In the Ocean of Night* (1977), set in our near future, thus providing a linking bridge to the quotidian which is absent in 'Nightfall' (so that, by this standard though hardly by any other, Asimov's much earlier story is the more sophisticated).
10 An example of the latter is Jack Womack's *Ambient* (1988). Womack turns the Greenhouse-ruined future into a chainsaw circus; Manhattan is more inhumanly gruesome than Lebanon, Iran or El Salvador. The decoration, though, is lush. Damaged by anti-radiation drugs, the Ambients are a vital sub-class of freaks;

their fans pay doctors to remove limbs or breasts, implant nails in their scalps. They speak, by a kind of cultural compensation, a delicious Elizabethan argot.

11 Van Vogt (1951). The book is clearly the source of the movie *Alien*. 'Fix-up' is Van Vogt's own useful coinage for such an assemblage or novelisation.

12 Bear (1987).

13 Bear (1986).

14 Zindell (1989).

15 The cognitive scientist Howard Gardner has analysed the persistence in the thinking of even trained students of erroneous 'schemata' or 'stereotypes' established in early childhood, in his *The Unschooled Mind* (1991). The major culprit is schooled learning by drill rather than for supple understanding. Citing New Zealand educator Roger Osborne, Gardner lists three kinds of physics used by students: 'gut dynamics', learned prior to language; 'lay dynamics', 'conveyed by nonspecialist adults . . . as well as by the electronic media and the books in his milieu', and 'physicist's dynamics', based on Newtonian (and often counter-intuitive) abstractions (p. 227). Outside quite artificial examination (or, later, professional) settings, an uneasy blend of the first two kinds seems to serve as the default for most intuitions nearly all of us have about the world we inhabit. Sf is a frequent source of lay dynamics: children 'learn about weightless astronauts, they can talk about force fields and time warps, and they appear knowledgeable at a linguistic level about the world of science. In fact, however, this knowledge is superficial, not rooted in experience, and of little practical use' (ibid.). Perhaps, though, the pleasure sf provides from its simulacrum of canonical dynamics – so delightful, compared with the grey drone of rote-learned data and algorithms – offsets the errors it supports.

16 In, for example, Franklin (1980), p. vii.

17 Russ (1976), p. 12.

18 Scholes (1975).

19 'The first scholarly meeting devoted to science fiction was held in New York in December 1958 [in an MLA Conference entitled "The Significance of Science-Fiction", chaired by Dr Thomas D. Clareson].' In October 1970, the Science Fiction Research Association held its first business meeting. But an MLA-linked periodical, *Extrapolation*, has appeared from December 1959. *Science-Fiction Studies*, established by Dale Mullen and Darko Suvin, appeared in 1973, calling for, *inter alia*, '"An opening on the various methodologies of *contemporary literary theory* – genre morphology, narrative semiotics, Freudian and Marxist criticism"' (quotes from Lerner, 1985, pp. 90, 96).

20 Todorov (1975). Although his approach is very usefully critiqued by Christine Brooke-Rose (1981, pp. 55–71), his 'basic division' is generalised by her 'as an extremely useful working hypothesis'. His analysis is even more central to Rosemary Jackson's treatment in *Fantasy: The Literature of Subversion* (1981) while anathema to Stanislaw Lem (who pilloried it in 'Todorov's Fantastic Theory of Literature', in *Microworlds*, 1985, pp. 209–32).

21 Cited in Brooke-Rose (1981), p. 66.

22 Rabkin (1976), p. 147.

23 Rabkin's study is notable for sensitive readings of such canonical sf texts as Clarke's *Childhood's End* (1961) and Sturgeon's *More Than Human* (1953), in which the latter is seen as more ordered and less fantastic than the former, hence a 'better' work of pure sf, even if less popular. I am not convinced, however: Clarke's novel, which Rabkin reads as invoking the non-scientific impulse of traditional Christian religion (the descent of Grace), seems to me exemplary also of major paradigm crisis. Its paranormal interventions and revelations reveal aporia in reductive science, but hardly foreclose on the possibility of an expanded

science (such as the Guardians use under the auspices of the transcendental Overmind) or even a science of the Overmind itself, which might be to our physics (say) as quantum theory is to Aristotelianism.

24 Suvin (1979), p. 20.
25 One might map these against Todorov's (forbidden) poetic and allegorical readings of the fantastic; sf which seems extrapolative is often an airy sculpture of signifiers, while the analogical (often 'comic inferno' satirical) is a sort of lay sociopolitical allegory. Again, then, Suvin's model of sf requires what Todorov disallows in the fantastic.
26 Brooke-Rose (1981), p. 77; her italics. She makes the telling point later that Suvin 'having established [these] criteria and his distinction between extrapolative and analogical models, forgets them in his subsequent chapters which discuss utopias, Wells, Verne, Russian SF and Capek, without in any way linking his analyses to his typology. Nor *a fortiori* does he link this typology with language or questions of narration' (ibid., p. 82). It is probably true that Suvin's signal contribution was the adaptation of Russian formalist theories to sf's especially cognitive character.
27 Jameson cites Suvin's *Metamorphoses* in his 'Progress Versus Utopia' (Jameson, 1982a, p. 158), describing it as 'a pioneering theoretical and structural analysis of the genre to which I owe a great deal'.
28 Clute (1992), p. 13; the following citations are from the same page.
29 Renault (1980), p. 115.
30 Suvin (1979), p. 84.
31 Eagleton (1983), pp. 101–2.
32 A clear introduction to these distinctions is given in Hawkes (1977), pp. 77–9.
33 Delany (1978a), pp. 255–6; my italics.
34 Which he states (1978a, p. 260) 'may now be called [he means "deemed"] "*sous rature*"'.

3 GENRE OR MODE?

1   Freadman (1987), pp. 120–1.
2   Hernadi (1972), p. 4.
3   Karl Popper, *The Logic of Scientific Discovery*, cited ibid., p. 4.
4   Culler (1988), p. 225.
5   Fokkema (1984); Scholes (1982).
6   Parrinder (1980), p. xviii.
7   Usefully summarised ibid., p. 44.
8   Parrinder here summarises from Angenot's *Le roman populaire* (1975).
9   The term 'mega-textual' is not used by Angenot.
10 Jameson (1987a), p. 242.
11 Cited in Nicholls *et al.* (1979), p. 160.
12 *The Pale Shadow of Science* (1985b), p. 110. It appears in this form on p. 25 of *Trillion Year Spree* (1986), but no acknowledgement of Ms Jackson's influence is given there (or anywhere in the volume).
13 Suitably enough, since another of his definitions of sf is 'Hubris clobbered by nemesis': this *bon mot*, Aldiss notes, quoting it, 'has found its way into a modern dictionary of quotations' (Brian Aldiss, with David Wingrove, 1986, p. 26.)
14 Jackson (1981), p. 7.
15 Jameson (1975c), cited ibid., p. 7.
16 Jameson (1981), p. 9.
17 Gunn (n.d.; post-1985), p. 3.

18 Part of the symposium 'Change, SF, and Marxism: Open or Closed Universes',
   reprinted from Mullen and Suvin (1976), pp. 275–6.
19 I mean especially his 'Postmodernism, or The Cultural Logic of Late Capitalism'
   (1984), pp. 53–92.
20 E.g. Jameson (1975b), pp. 221–30; (1982a), pp. 147–58; and his fidelity to the
   impulse of Ernst Bloch's hopeful utopianism.
21 A narratological mechanism employed in many discussions; early instances are
   Chapter 4 of *The Political Unconscious* (1981), and 'Generic Discontinuities in
   SF: Brian Aldiss's *Starship*' (1973). A brief summary of this important concept
   is in his paper on Le Guin, cited above, in which he shows that her *The
   Dispossessed* is 'constructed from a heterogeneous group of narrative modes
   artfully superposed and intertwined, thereby constituting a virtual anthology of
   narrative strands of different kinds' (1975b, p. 221); the effect is a strengthening
   of the text by its introduction of *collage* (see the Aldiss analysis, 1973, p. 65), the
   very principle, as subsequent work was to show, of the emerging postmodern
   programme in literature proper.
22 See especially his *tour de force* semiotic analysis of Philip K. Dick's apparently
   anarchic texts in 'After Armageddon: Character Systems in *Dr Bloodmoney*'
   (Jameson, 1975, pp. 31–42).
23 Jameson provided the Foreword to the English translation of Jean-François
   Lyotard, *The Postmodern Condition: A Report on Knowledge* (1984).
24 Nicholls (1978b); my compressed citation is from pp. 180–3.
25 Samuel R. Delany, '*Dichtung und* Science Fiction', in Delany (1984), p. 182.

4 THE USES OF OTHERNESS

1 William Atheling, Jr, 'A Question of Content', in Atheling (1973), pp. 138–9.
2 Kessel (1991), pp. 250–1. As well as being a stylish and prize-winning sf writer,
   Kessel is a professor of literature at North Carolina State University.
3 Culler (1983), p. 24.
4 From J. Willett (ed.), *Brecht on Theatre* (London, 1964), cited in Eagleton
   (1976), p. 13.
5 Derrida (1982), p. 76.
6 Comprising *Titan* (1979), *Wizard* (1980a), and *Demon* (1984).
7 Robinson (1984), p. x.
8 Broderick, Introduction to *Strange Attractors* (1985), p. 11.
9 Graff (1979), pp. 74–5, 99–100.
10 Suvin (1983), p. 419.
11 Le Guin (1989), p. vii.
12 In Asimov (1983).
13 A discussion of recent developments in the field is my *The Lotto Effect*
   (Broderick, 1992).
14 Davies and Gribbin (1991).
15 See, for example, Dennis Overbye's wonderful *Lonely Hearts of the Cosmos –
   The Story of the Scientific Quest for the Secret of the Universe* (1991). Overbye
   paints Hawking in 1963, at 21: 'Wagner blared from the record player. Science
   fiction books lay about' (p. 85). Also see Kitty Ferguson, *Stephen Hawking –
   Quest for a Theory of Everything* (1992), and Michael White and John Gribbin,
   Stephen Hawking. A Life in Science (1992), a book that constitutes a kind of
   parodic refutation of the Two Cultures hypothesis; the sections due to White, a
   musician and scriptwriter, are so ineptly written that Gribbin's plain style gleams
   by contrast. White's passage on Hawking's parents is a special treat: 'It was there

that the vivacious and friendly Isobel, mildly amused at the position she had found herself in but with sights set on a more meaningful future, first met the tall, shy young researcher fresh back from exciting adventures in exotic climes' (p. 6). And I don't think I have ever before read a book where an author wrote unblushingly 'Little did he know . . .' (p. 104). White confirms Hawking's appetite for sf (p. 48).

16 See, e.g., Paul Davies's account in *Other Worlds: Space, Superspace and the Quantum Universe* (1980), and more recent volumes. The history of quantum superposition is sketched in Abraham Pais's magisterial *Niels Bohr's Times, in Physics, Philosophy, and Polity* (1991).

17 'The Price of Survival', in Asimov (1987), p. 69.

18 Lefanu (1988), p. 5.

19 A poignant comment on the conditions under which most of these novelists function is found in Lefanu's note of thanks to a fellow writer who 'generously funded a full week of childcare', allowing her to take time off to plan the study (1988, p. 1).

20 An argument advanced compellingly by David Lodge in *The Modes of Modern Writing* (1981).

21 Delany (1978a), pp. 31 ff.

22 Brooke-Rose (1981).

23 Hamon (1973), cited ibid., p. 85.

24 Maddox (1992), p. 31.

25 Perhaps 'hypertext' would describe it better if the term had not been appropriated by software designers.

26 Wolfe (1979).

27 Sobchack (1987), p. 66.

28 I draw these examples from Sobchack's discussion of these films and others in her chapter on sf iconography.

29 See Marie Maclean's useful discussion (1984, pp. 166–73), influenced by Marc Angenot's 'The Absent Paradigm' (*Science Fiction Studies*, vol. 6, pp. 9–19).

30 Culler (1988), p. 101.

31 Amis called him 'a kind of science-fiction poet laureate of the countryside' (1963, p. 62), a countryside stocked with grouchy but loyal robots, talking dogs, paranormal powers around the cosmic village pump. . . .

32 Jablokov (1992), p. 17.

5 READING THE EPISTEME

1 'Shadows', in *The Jewel-Hinged Jaw* (Delany, 1978a), pp. 74–7; interestingly, this material is repeated as Appendix A of Delany, *Triton: An Ambiguous Heterotopia* (1976), pp. 332–6.

2 See, for biographical details, 'Shadows' in Delany (1978a); 'The Necessity of Tomorrows' in Delany (1984), p. 25–35; Weedman (1982); McEvoy (1984); and for his early years, his remarkably candid memoir *The Motion of Light in Water* (1990).

3 The only major contemporary American sf writers he has not studied are Philip K. Dick and Gene Wolfe, though curiously, for such an internationalist and polyglot, he has not paid much attention either to such pre-eminent non-American sf writers as J. G. Ballard, Brian Aldiss and Stanislaw Lem.

4 *The Jewel-Hinged Jaw: Notes of* [*sic*; presumably 'on'] *the Language of Science Fiction* (1978a), pp. 21–37.

5 Parrinder (1979a), pp. 337–41.

6 Delany (1978a), p. 21.

7 It is interesting, therefore, in a writer whose recent sf and fantasy, as well as his criticism, are rich with citations to various poststructural luminaries that Delany never references Roman Ingarden, Wolfgang Iser or Hans Robert Jauss; nor, as far as I can tell, do Jürgen Habermas or any of the Frankfurt School seem to have played much part in the development of his aesthetic.

8 In Hay (1970), p. 134.

9 My usage, not Delany's, and drawn from Wolfgang Iser, in, for example, *The Act of Reading* (1978).

10 This is not true for me nor for that considerable proportion of the reading population who are not adept at, or perhaps even neurologically capable of, vivid visual 'inner imaging' in the waking state. I suspect that this difference largely underlies a hidden segregation, within educated populations, of those who read fiction and poetry for pleasure from those who prefer literal imagery in the form of cinema, television or other graphic arts. Because texts are massively over-determined it is possible, however, for the 'image blind' to concretize them by other means, and even write sentences by imitation that evoke pictures in the heads of others. I am always flabbergasted when people praise my own fiction for its 'vivid, visual imagination'; it's all word-juggling to me – and words are rhythmic, musical, idea-rich, wonderful things even without pictures.

11 Langford (1989), p. 7.

12 Even without appealing to the deep structures surmised by transformational grammars to underlie and sustain the meaning of linear word strings like Delany's example, one might note this caution from Wilden's *System and Structure*: 'Bronowski . . . points out that "the normal unit of animal communication, even among primates, is a whole message", and Bruner emphasizes McNeill's argument that the child's first semantic system is a holophrastic "sentence dictionary" in which words correspond to complete sentences' (1984, p. 173).

13 That exemplar and several others more recent ground Kathleen L. Spencer's useful '"The Red Sun is High, the Blue Low"' (1983), pp. 35 ff. Spencer is a devoted and insightful critic of Delany; we shall return to her readings. In this paper, however, she makes interesting errors in applying the idea of signifiers with absent paradigms. Citing Delany's favourite example, from Heinlein's 1942 *Beyond This Horizon* ('The door dilated', which Spencer incorrectly gives as 'The door irised', ibid., p. 40), she goes beyond the text's internal coding to speculate that this structure 'implies something about the physiology of the creatures for whom such doors were originally designed: its roundness suggests that they, too, will be more nearly round than human beings' (ibid.). The novel has neither aliens nor robots of this kind; my guess is that the trope is a sort of conceptual back-formation from spaceship airlocks. It signifies difference *simpliciter*, brilliantly.

14 Reprinted in Delany (1984), p. 217.

15 Barbour (1979), p. 7.

16 Not all commentators share in this esteem. The invaluable John Clute (who blithely confesses that his critique is somewhat self-reflexive) is scathing about 'the clotted preciosity of his prose . . . its uneasy condescension and agglutinative gumminess' (1988 , p. 39); 'beyond the word-deaf gaucheries of the style, beyond the self-congratulatory garish foregrounding of the auctorial voice with all its morose cheeriness and duckpond aggro – lay a sense that when I *did* think I understood the terms and assumptions shaping a paragraph, by dint of a lot of deconstruction work, what I was left with was a kind of shambles strewn with disqualified data and beheaded arguments' (p. 40). Clute documents some of this claim by reference to historical and literary howlers in Delany's appreciation (in *Jewel-Hinged Jaw*) of Disch and Zelazny. Damon Knight too has questioned

Delany's scholarship: 'Is Delany's [historical] assertion as loony as it sounds? Indeed it is; both the problem and Delany's solution of it are entirely the product of his brilliant and ethereal imagination' (Knight, 1982, p. 27).

17 As one of the principals of the Dragon Press, Hartwell was agentive in publishing the first three of Delany's volumes of theory and criticism. As adviser to various US publishers, he has been instrumental in seeing recent controversial Delany fiction into print, as well as Delany's important autobiography, *The Motion of Light in Water*. Hartwell has been a medieval scholar and holds a PhD from Columbia.
18 Cf. Nabokov's discussion in *Lectures on Literature* (1980), pp. 258–60.
19 Tallis (1988), pp. 29–30.
20 Which is to say, knowingly: always-already as readers armed with sf codes learned from previous encounters with the mega-text.
21 'Some Presumptuous Approaches to Science Fiction', in Delany (1984), p. 49.
22 'I am in no way suggesting that SF writers are historically free of their times in any way that allows them to be ideally critical, ideologically neutral, or "scientifically" objective' ('Reflections on Historical Models', ibid., p. 241).
23 However, Delany argues much later that 'the notion of narrative texts expressive of the Zeitgeist is a specifically literary model – a model that has its certain use when applied to a sociologically dense, comparatively mimetic narrative . . . (i.e., the 19th Century novel), but which is clearly inadequate for a sociologically thin, comparatively non-mimetic narrative (i.e., post-1937 science fiction)' (ibid., p. 241).
24 Delany (1987c), p. 10.
25 In Delany (1984), pp. 165–96; the allusion is to Goethe's autobiographical *Aus meinem Leben, Dichtung und Wahrheit* (1811–22): 'Writing/Poetry and Truth'. It is a mark of Delany's singularity among sf writers that such intertextual jests are within his reach.
26 'Science Fiction and Literature', in Delany (1984), p. 100.
27 Paulson (1988), p. 52.
28 Jameson (1988a), p. 16.

6 DREAMS OF REASON AND UNREASON

1 McCrone (1993), p. 1.
2 Le Guin, 'Some Thoughts on Narrative' (1980), in Le Guin (1989), pp. 44–5.
3 Card (1986).
4 Card (1985).
5 This explanation for an interstellar, interspecies war, in terms of what we might dub *Weltbild* incompatibility, is similar to that devised by Joe Haldeman for his sequence of stories compiled as *The Forever War* (1974), an explicit reply to the manifest destiny militarism of much of Robert Heinlein's sf.
6 What is more, in this book, as in its predecessors, the artificial intelligence, in its puissance and disseminated location, is closer to the divine than to the human. That trope is developed even further in the third volume of the Speaker sequence, *Xenocide* (Card, 1991).
7 Mann (1982).
8 Nabokov (1980), p. 288. His sentence begins 'All art is in a sense symbolic, but . . .'
9 I am thinking especially, of course, of Paul de Man's *Allegories of Reading* (1979). De Man's allegories, admittedly, are far from 'stale', though this plea might not have soothed Nabokov.
10 Bettelheim (1976).

11 The Hugo is awarded at the annual World Science Fiction Convention, usually hosted in the USA but regularly held in other countries; only members are eligible to vote, though not all do so. *The New Encyclopedia of Science Fiction*, ed. James Gunn, states: 'Because of its broad electorate the Hugo Award represents the most significant sampling of reader popularity' (1988, p. 32). The Locus Poll is conducted via the semi-professional 'newszine' *Locus*; the *New Encyclopedia* states that 'Consistently more votes are recorded in the Locus Poll than for any other award; in 1986 the votes totaled over 1000 (more than the totals for the Hugo and Nebula awards combined. For this reason if for no other [it] can claim to be most authoritative' (p. 33).

12 Barron (1987). This useful volume includes historical surveys of the field, discussions of foreign-language sf in German, French, Russian, Italian, Japanese and Chinese, and a battery of research aids and annotated bibliographies.

13 Magill (1979). A large collection (500 essays each of 2,000 words) of readings of exemplary sf works, by 133 contributors.

14 Pringle (1985). Pringle is former editor of *Foundation*, the journal of the scholarly British Science Fiction Foundation, and author of several monographs on leading sf writers (such as his *Earth is the Alien Planet: J. G. Ballard's Four-Dimensional Nightmare*, 1979).

15 Burgess (1984).

16 Blish and Knight (1967). I am not being abusive in so describing the politics: Blish and Knight note, 'It will surprise some readers, and perhaps horrify a few, that the economic system we settled upon for our Utopia is a form of the corporate state, or what was once called fascism. We were interested in the fact that this kind of economic system has actually never been tried. (Mussolini's version was a clumsy and indifferent fake[. . .])' (p. 10).

17 'SF Alternatives' by John Goodchild Publishers, Wendover, UK, in 1984. Each volume is illuminatingly introduced by Wingrove, though his scholarship is by no means all one might expect; see below, note 43.

18 Zelazny (1968; first published 1966), or its 1965 Nebula-winning novella recension 'He Who Shapes', in Zelazny (1980).

19 Zelazny (1983).

20 Bester (1980).

21 Bester (1981).

22 Gibson (1984).

23 Gibson (1986b).

24 Gibson (1988).

25 'Cyberpunk is dead,' begins an article by Neil Easterbrook, 'The Arc of Our Destruction: Reversal and Erasure in Cyberpunk', *Science Fiction Studies* (1992). In the same issue, John Fekete concludes: 'Long live cyberpunk' (p. 403). Larry McCaffery's collection of fiction and essays, *Storming the Reality Studio* (1991), is an expanded version of a special double issue he edited of the *Mississippi Review* (47/48, 1988). Donna J. Haraway canvasses some of the same virtual ground in *Simians, Cyborgs, and Women* (1991).

26 Ross, 'Cyberpunk in Boystown', in Ross (1991), p. 152.

27 Compare the stories collected in John Varley's books *In the Hall of the Martian Kings* (Varley, 1978b), *The Barbie Murders* (1980b), *Blue Champagne* (1986), and the unsatisfactory but influential novel which Pringle lists, *The Ophiuchi Hotline* (Varley, 1978a).

28 Swanwick (1988).

29 Swanwick (1992).

30 Varley (1992).

31 Williams (1992).

32 Turner (1985), p. 19.
33 Blackford (1985), pp. 18–20.
34 Turner (1985), p. 19.
35 Since Gibson coined the term, 'cyberspace' has become the term preferred by computer specialists developing just these realms. See the dense, fertile presentations in Benedikt (1991).
36 This of course is a version of the celebrated Turing test for artificial intelligence, and in the Gibson universe the most menacing authorities are the Turing cops.
37 Nixon (1992).
38 I am thinking of Stone's masterful novels of marginal American life, *A Hall of Mirrors* (1966), *Dog Soldiers* (1974), and especially *A Flag for Sunrise* (1981). Gibson has confirmed his debt to Stone, in an interview in *Foundation* (1986c).
39 Lem, 'Philip K. Dick – a Visionary Among the Charlatans', in Lem (1985), pp. 106–35.
40 Jameson (1984).
41 This segment is from Gibson's short story 'Burning Chrome', reprinted in the collection *Burning Chrome* (Gibson, 1986a), p. 181.
42 Amis (1963), p. 115.
43 Pohl and Kornbluth (1984). Wingrove's edition has the co-author's name incorrectly on the cover: Frederik Pohl and C. M. Kornbluth, not 'Frederick'; and it was first serialised as 'Gravy Planet', not 'Gravy Train' (first page of unnumbered introduction).
44 Aldiss (1984).
45 Federman (1982).
46 My own cat, a black, one-eyed and very woolly Persian, now sadly deceased, was named Darko Suvin.
47 Jones (1986); Thomas (1981).

7 THE STARS MY DISSERTATION

1 Aldiss (1977), p. 9.
2 Aldiss (1975), p. 3.
3 Weiner (1993), p. 21.
4 Jaynes (1976).
5 This remains true even when we see that the 'boys' own' quality of such passages is hardly accidental. 'Throughout all three volumes,' John Clute notes, 'BWA pays homage to various high moments of pulp sf, rewriting several classic action climaxes into a dark idiom that befits Helliconia' ('Aldiss, Brian W.', in Clute and Nicholls, 1993, p. 12). Much more is lost than is gained in this gambit.
6 Aldiss (1976), p. 59.
7 Aldiss, 'Magic and Bare Boards', in Aldiss and Harrison (1976), p. 189.
8 Aldiss in *The Metaphysical Review*, no. 3, ed. Bruce Gillespie (May 1985), p. 41.
9 Myers (1956), Introduction, unnumbered p. ii.
10 Jameson (1973), pp. 67–8.
11 Jameson (1985), pp. 84. Jameson here also responded to an earlier version of some of these remarks: 'I quite disagree with Broderick, however, as I found volume I . . . the most interesting, and II . . . more of a let-down' (pp. 83–4).
12 Jameson (1971), p. 309.
13 Fallaci (1981).
14 For a well-documented experimental account of canonical work in this area,

culminating in the discovery of the *W* and *Z* particles which mediate the weak nuclear force, see Sutton (1984).

15 Jameson (1988b) vol. I, p. 183.

8 MAKING UP WORLDS

1 McHale (1987), pp. 9, 10, 59. Ruthlessly following this rather striking if glib poetics, McHale is obliged to declare merely modernist Delany's *Triton*, a text at once generically scandalous and paradigmatic of the cognitively estranged, which further obliges him to find the no less paradigmatically postmodern *Dhalgren* a perfect exemplar of sf. While *Dhalgren*'s status as an sf text can be defended, it is less evident that one would put it forward – when works such as Bester's *Tiger! Tiger!* and Gregory Benford's *Timescape* are available – as the very model of a modern major science fiction text.

2 Jameson (1984), pp. 53–92.

3 Jameson poses (if only on an empirical basis) that 'our psychic experience, our cultural languages, are today dominated by categories of space rather than by categories of time', typical of 'the great high-modernist thematics of time and temporality' (ibid.).

4 The citation is from p. 75, where one of Jameson's preposterous bids is offered with a straight face: 'This new mode of relationship through difference may sometimes be an achieved new and original way of thinking and perceiving; more often it takes the form of an impossible imperative to achieve that new mutation in what can perhaps no longer be called consciousness' (ibid.). His instance of this regenerate state is multi-screen 'de-centred' video performance art.

5 The reference is to Mandel's *Late Capitalism* (1975) (Jameson, 1984, p. 78).

6 Which 'might better be termed multinational capital' (Jameson, 1984, p. 78), an account which failed to deal with Soviet technology, though perhaps forecasting the post-glasnost free market revival of a decade later.

7 A charming intersection of the fictive and the analytic arises in Jameson's discussion of his paradigm of the postmodern, the Bonaventure Hotel, with its bafflingly uncoded hyperspaces for a new hyper-crowd (ibid., p. 81): 'one would want . . . to stress the way in which the glass skin repels the city outside; a repulsion for which we have analogies in those reflector sunglasses which . . . achieve a certain aggressivity towards and power over the Other' (p. 81). Just such glasses are the chosen emblem of cyberpunk; Bruce Sterling's gathering of representative Movement stories is entitled *Mirrorshades* (1986). This 'uncanny' similarity has also been noticed by N. Katherine Hayles, in *Chaos Bound* (1990), pp. 275–8, where she also draws the by now standard comparison between Gibson's cyberspace and Baudrillard's hyperreality (p. 275).

8 Having forecast the move, I was smugly gratified to see him take this step.

9 Robinson (1990).

10 Robinson (1992), p. 299.

11 Greenland (1983), p. 190.

12 Which Jameson has announced as 'the world space of multinational capital', though I am inclined to see it as the world space of the cognitive and technological episteme grounded in, and in many ways brutally constrained by, the prevailing orders of power.

13 I would rather broaden this to 'late industrial civilisation' (I see no evidence that it is impossible in the non-capitalist nations, for example) though I understand Jameson's polemical reasons for denying this generalising move.

14 Jameson (1975b), pp. 222–3.

15 Jameson (1987b), pp. 44–59.
16 Ibid., p. 51.
17 Jameson (1991), p. 419.
18 Jameson (1984), p. 76–7.
19 Dick (1984).
20 The quotation that follows is from Dick (1984), p. 40. Interestingly, this passage is cited independently, though for the same purpose, by David Lehman, in his assault on poststructuralist theory, *Signs of the Times* (1991), pp. 100–2. Lehman adds astutely: 'Ragle's peculiar occupation [forecasting patterns in a daily newspaper contest, actually a coded protocol for precognising Lunar rocket attacks on Earth] makes him a kind of allegorical representation of the sci-fi [sic] writer, of Dick himself' (p. 101). Jameson situates Dick's novel interestingly, though only in passing, in his *Postmodernism* (1991), pp. 279–86.
21 Jameson (1982a), p. 157. He draws here upon the Soviet brothers Strugatski's *Roadside Picnic* (1977).
22 Sobchack (1987).
23 Clute (1988), p. 119. His analysis of the 1950s schlock sf classic *Them!* deserves to be read in detail.
24 Sobchack (1987), p. 229.
25 Jameson (1984), p. 64.
26 Sobchack (1987), p. 282; her italics.
27 In Foucault (1983), p. 32, 'resemblance' is a relation of subordination to an original, while 'similitude' 'develops in series that have neither beginning nor end', are transitive or reversible, and 'propagate themselves from small differences among small differences'.
28 Ebert (1980), pp. 93, 96.
29 This is not the tautology it seems: I mean the varieties of innovative fiction which McHale (1987) groups quite illuminatingly into such categories as 'tropological worlds', 'styled worlds', 'worlds of discourse'; the kinds of writing associated paradigmatically with Donald Barthelme or (in a different register) Australian writer Gerald Murnane.
30 I develop a poststructural version of this model at some length in my doctoral dissertation, 'Frozen Music' (1990), which attempts a transcoding between the discourses of the sciences and the humanities.

9 ALLOGRAPHY AND ALLEGORY

1 Ebert (1980), pp. 91–5.
2 This term is a play on Terry Dowling's useful critical coinage, 'xenography': 'the art of devising and exploring exotic and alien societies in a very distant future period when humankind has spread far from our own planetary system' (Dowling, 1980, p. 131). Not every critic will be pleased with the emphasis I place on this notion; Fredric Jameson noted recently, 'it seems worth observing in passing that Otherness is a very dangerous concept, one we are well off without; but fortunately, in literature and culture, it has also become a very tedious one. Ridley Scott's *Alien* may still get away with it (but then, for science fiction, all of Lem's work . . . can be read as an argument against the use of such a category even there)' (1991, p. 290). One would have thought that much of Lem's most potent work, especially *Solaris* and *His Master's Voice*, demonstrated precisely the opposite: that 'the other', no matter how culturally constructed it might be in any given case (even in the limit of an alien or artificial consciousness), can remain unappeasably opaque and problematic. Then again, Jameson is here objecting to

the Gothic desire to project Otherness as *evil*; sf tends to make the Other a site of endless multivocal play.

3 Significantly, a chapter epigraph in *The Einstein Intersection* (Delany, 1981b, p. 49) is from Sartre's *Saint Genet*: 'Experience reveals to him in every object, in every event, the presence of *something else*.'

4 Delany's own title, reinstated in an omnibus edition from Bantam (Delany, 1986) of his Nebula-winning fiction but not replacing its single-volume recension, is Yeats' 'A Fabulous, Formless Darkness' (cited in a closing epigraph, p. 137).

5 'There was a rash of hermaphrodites the year I was born, which doctors thought I might be. Somehow I doubt it' (1981b, pp. 1–2). Is it reductive or overly hermeneutic to see in Lobey's mouth-work (not to mention hand and footwork) on his 'blade' some impress of Delany's prodigious predilection (notated in some detail in *The Motion of Light on Water*, Delany, 1990) for another forbidden marker of difference in males, fellatio?

6 Maxwell (1984).

7 This apotheosis reminds one of Clarke's *Childhood's End* ([1954], 1961), Simak's *City* (1952), and more recently of the nano-world quantum-state consciousnesses in Greg Bear's *Blood Music* (1985) and the disappearance of all humans from the world in Vernor Vinge's *Marooned In Real Time* (1986), following the technological Singularity, the point at which accelerating vectors of power/knowledge reached the asymptote.

8 *Sic*. Possibly this ought to read: 'one another'.

9 Friza-Eurydice is murdered on the next page; her dying shriek is 'the only sound I ever heard her make other than laughter'.

10 Presumably he means 'my implications'.

11 Epigraph from the US poet John Ciardi (Delany, 1981b), p. 58.

12 Presumably she means 'the previous' or 'the last', though that implies a temporal linearity which conceivably could be alien to these deceptively familiar aliens. It is interesting to compare this dictum with Aldiss's refrain on enantiodromia in the *Helliconia* sequence, discussed above in Chapter 7.

13 An alternative, 'naturalistic' reading may not be possible, but hints suggest we should try to make one (adding to the multivocal diversity). Lobey as Theseus slays a Minotaur in a detailed scene (*The Einstein Intersection*, pp. 19–32, in a volume only 147 pages long). PHAEDRA, the computer in the radiation-intense 'source-cave' (the 'Psychic Harmony and Entangled Deranged Response Associations' device (p. 33), an improvement over the dyslexic original [1967 edn, p. 35]), speaks to him here and later (on p. 140 she says, 'Mother is in charge of everything down here. . . . Seek somewhere outside the frame of the mirror –'), which just might be fantasy, as Kid Death's manifestations (except the last, where Spider whips him to death) might be illusions: 'Yes, I may just have been talking to myself,' Lobey remarks (p. 33). There are no empirical consequences of these paranormal effects; might Friza then have died at the Minotaur's rather large hands? (Probably not; the beast is very noisy. But its arrival and dispatch at that early juncture then remains quite inexplicable, except as a myth screw-tightener.)

14 Lobey identifies Spider as Judas Iscariot, Minos and Pat Garrett; Spider declares that 'If the Dove is Jean Harlow I'm Paul Burn' (ibid., p. 127). He means Paul Bern, Harlow's movie-executive husband, a suicide. In fact, Lobey is the true Judas, having told Pistol (p. 107) that Green-eye is with the herders. Spider signed the death decree (p. 132), making him Pilate. Perhaps this signifies corruption of the mythic record, like the garbled tales of the Beatles (e.g. p. 12).

15 All citations ibid., p. 124.

16 Except when Green-eye rebukes Lobey for giving up and dying, making it

necessary to resurrect him (or perhaps Lobey brings himself back to life; it is left unclear) (ibid., pp. 96–7).

17 At the end of the previous section I mentioned sf's use (at its best) of 'the subjectivity of character' to access the objective. Peter S. Alterman (1977) makes a similar point: Delany's 'methodology implies a rigid adherence to the concrete, the sensual, the "realistic" world on the one hand, and to the mythic, metaphoric elements of language on the other. . . . Delany's novels display an intense sense of being in touch with the physical world. . . . The prose attempts to capture the multiplicity of the real moment, not so much by applying a literary code, but by presenting a sense of the multiplicity of experience within the prose. . . . The order of realism rests uneasily on the chaotic subjectivism of the perceiving narrator' (pp. 29, 33). This is theoretically muddled, however: the benefit Delany offers is *a multiplicity of codes*, constructing his texts by interactions across Jameson's 'generic discontinuities'. Alterman really knows this: 'Delany's prose is an amalgam of elements, the precise visual rendering of images with a conscious use of metonymy to create a language of experience' (p. 31). (Presumably he means 'verbal rendering of visual images'.)

18 Delany had little objective cause to embrace such a message, of course. His previous book, *Babel-17*, had won the Nebula award for best sf novel of the year; *The Einstein Intersection* was itself fated to win another (for precisely the 'poetic' explosions of style and subject which were his generic infractions), reflecting Delany's popularity among his peers. Still, it is interesting that his (mocking?) dedication in this book is to Don Wollheim, the text editor who had cut his work to fit a paperback format (and removed or lost an entire chapter in this one!), and Jack Gaughan, whose tasteless cover illustration was pilloried by Judith Merril as 'a lurid red demon-thing' (Books column, *F&SF*, November, 1967).

19 Delany (1981c), pp. 13–14.

20 Delany, *Babel-17* (1987a; 1966 edn), pp. 17–18.

21 Barthes (1974), p. 41.

22 Delany (1981a), p. 386; Delany's ellipses.

23 A convenient summary of Lacan's theories as applied to literature is Chapter 5 of Eagleton (1983).

24 Although Rydra does momentarily lose speech while locked into a dyadic merging of identity with the Butcher, as both are 'written' into this state by Babel-17, a computer code-cum-language which lacks any signifier for the speaking subject: '"The lack of an 'I' precludes any self-critical process. In fact it cuts out any awareness of the symbolic process at all – which is the way we distinguish between reality and our expression of reality. . . . And the lack of an 'I' blinds you to the fact that though it's a highly useful way to look at things, it isn't the only way"' (Delany, 1987a, p. 190.)

25 This is well expressed by Emerson Littlefield in 'The Mythologies of Race and Science in Samuel Delany's *The Einstein Intersection* and *Nova*'(1982, pp. 240–1): 'In the Goedelian universe of infinite possibility, every occasion needs its own ordering principles; the universe is not chaotic but constantly shifting, and people need to change, too, in order to keep up. The Einsteinian universe, by contrast, was regular everywhere. . . . Paradoxically, Kid Death, too, is "different", but he is also a psychological anachronism; he fits by temperament into the Einsteinian world because he depends on that knowledge and order, that pattern of ancient scientific myth. . . . The universe, in short, is different, and the Kid, fighting the universe, warping his difference, wanting the past (and so playing cowboy), does not fit in.'

26 Parrinder (1980), pp. 23–5.

27 Aldiss and Wingrove, *Trillion Year Spree* (1986), correctly disdain Zelazny's

'reduction of a complex and powerful myth to a comic book formula with technological trimmings' (p. 473), a complaint which can be squared for his endless 'Amber' sequence of Grail entertainments (has someone wittily called them 'Westons'?) valorised with scholarly ingenuity but scant critical distance by Carl Yoke, in *Roger Zelazny* (1979), pp. 80–91.
28 Beer (1983).

10 SF AS A MODULAR CALCULUS

1 Delany, 'Appendix B: Closures and Openings', in *Flight from Nevèrÿon* (1985c), p. 357.
2 Delany, 'The Tale of Rumor and Desire', in *The Bridge of Lost Desire* (1987d), p. 138.
3 Spencer (n.d.; pre-1985), p. 2. Notably, Spencer offers an account of Delany's late work as allegory of reading drawn explicitly from De Man.
4 These comprise: as Part One, the entire novel *Triton* (1976), and Part Two, its Appendix, p. 344; Part Three is the playful Appendix to *Tales of Nevèrÿon* (1979b), p. 247; Part Four is the entire novel *Neveryóna, or the Tale of Signs and Cities* (1983b), though not its Appendices; Part Four is 'Appendix A: The Tale of Plagues and Carnivals' (a complex meditation on the AIDS plague and how to write about it), pp. 173–353 of *Flight from Nevèrÿon* (1985c). It does not include the 'Appendix: Return . . . A Preface', by 'K. Leslie Steiner', a Delany *alter ego*, which concludes the latest (last?) volume, *The Bridge of Lost Desire* (1987d), p. 297; this offers some useful if immodest hints on how to read 'Delany's mega-fantasy, . . . a fascinating fiction of ideas, a narrative hall of mirrors, an intricate argument about power, sexuality, and narration itself' (ibid., p. 302). Certain other Appendices in these books, as Delany remarks in Appendix B of the third volume (pp. 381–2) are, suitably, of undecidable status (like those very remarks).
5 Delany (1985c), p. 375.
6 Delany disagrees: 'The Nevèrÿon series takes place at the edge of the shadow of the late French psychiatrist Jacques Lacan', though he objects to an essentialising tendency in Freud. In 'vulgar Freudianism', he notes, 'metonymies are interpreted as metaphors for their originary terms and situations. The valid Freudian enterprise is rather to discern the several social and psychological systems (clearly distinguishing which is which) by which metonymies exfoliate.[. . . I]t is precisely within social sedimentation that these battles must be fought' (ibid., pp. 359, 361, 365).
7 I doubt that Delany really sees his work as 'eristic' – that is, aimed at rhetorical victory rather than truth – although that is a fashionable way to construe the relativist ascendancy in his favoured theories.
8 Section 25, 'Shadows', in Delany (1978a), pp. 51–2.
9 Delany cites his own observation of Vikki Sperling's mapping of a salamander retina image from its visual tectum; personal encounter with the scientifically mediated real had changed Delany's philosophical signifieds in a drastic fashion.
10 Delany (1985c), p. 362: 'Language is first and foremost a *stabilizer* of behavior, thought, and feeling, of human responses and reactions. . . . Its aid in intellectual analysis and communication are (one) secondary and (two) wholly entailed. . . . When the world is projected through the hierarchical oppositions available to the sensory and sensual body . . . it produces a spectacularly unstable text.'
11 This notional chart brings to mind the useful questions which underlie a complex fiction, as Delany understood when he was only 17: how does each character react alone or in a group by reference to such crucial commonplaces as food, sleep,

money and social status (see 'Characters', in 1978a, p. 158). His own sf is notable for dramatising character within a full matrix of social factors.

12 This and the following citation from Delany (1985c), p. 380.

13 Delany (1987d), p. 302.

14 John Clute, as noted previously, is less kind to late Delany's typical narrative presence, while Patrick Neilsen Hayden, in Gunn's *New Encyclopedia of Science Fiction*, calls the auctorial voice 'authoritative, good-humored (even fey), and ornate' (1988, p. 124).

15 Described (somewhat hazily) in the Appendix to *Tales of Nevèrÿon* (1979b), pp. 256–8: its 'third level order', nicknamed 'language', is 'a non-commutative substitution matrix', which is a set of rules 'that allows unidirectional substitutions of listable subsets of a collection of names'; 'these rules will sometimes make complete loops of substitution. Such a loop will be called, by N/L/C/ theoreticians, a "discourse"' (p. 257). Applying it to the uninterpretable 'Missolonghi Codex', 'Steiner has been able to offer a number of highly probable (and in some cases highly imaginative) revisions of existing translations based on the theoretical mechanics of various discursive loopings' (p. 258). This sounds like an unholy cross between information theory decipherment and 'nothing outside the text' deconstruction.

16 Delany (1985c), pp. 326, 327, 333.

17 Delany (1986), pp. 406–7.

18 Delany (1987b), p. 11. This long, pivotal meditation was written in 1975 for a fanzine which failed before publication. It remains extraordinarily interesting, especially its abstemious remarks toward a reading of *Dhalgren* (Delany, 1975).

19 Nicholls (1979), pp. 134–6.

20 Delany (1987b), pp. 17–18.

21 His examples are Norman Mailer and Joyce Carol Oates.

22 I play here on Delany's dictum: 'Science fiction is a way of casting a language shadow over coherent areas of imaginative space that would otherwise be largely inaccessible' ('Shadows', in Delany, 1978a, p. 118).

23 *Stars in My Pocket* (Delany, 1985a), as we shall see, is above all a rigorous (and wistful) review, on thematic, dramatistic and linguistic-textual levels, of the cultural *and* individual need for, and the endlessly inevitable failure to find, just such a calculus.

11 THE MULTIPLICITY OF WORLDS, OF OTHERS

1 Delany, Introduction to his comic book *Empire: A Visual Novel* (1978b), illustrated by Howard V. Chaykin, unpaginated.

2 Delany (1985a), pp. 73, 77–8. His non-bracketed ellipses.

3 Kuhn (1970), Postscript, pp. 183–4.

4 Delany (1979a). Even more abundant evidence for autobiographical sources (and differences) is his memoir *The Motion of Light in Water* (1990), which gives a detailed account of his encounter with Ron Helstrom, a heterosexual prawn-fisherman who had attended beauty school briefly (!), hardly without relevance to the naming of Bron Helstrom, the disturbed heterosexual protagonist of *Triton* who changes sex without notable improvement (1990, p. 288), and an extensive account of the 'triple' relationship between Delany, his wife Marilyn Hacker, and Bob Folsom (did Bob gnaw his nails? no: p. 260), alluded to in many three-way bonds from *Empire Star* and *Babel-17* to *Dhalgren*'s Kidd, Lanya and Denny (where DEnnyLANYa can be no accident either). *Motion* is rich in such humus: cf. young Chip Delany and the frightening chicken with Rydra's semiotic/

telepathic terror of a baby bird gorging itself on a worm (ibid., pp. 198–200; 1987a, pp. 22–3).

5 Delany (1990).

6 See the Writer's Note fronting *Stars in my Pocket Like Grains of Sand* (1985a). Page references to this volume will henceforth appear in parentheses in the text.

7 Delany (1975).

8 Delany (1987b), pp. 14–15.

9 Delany's account of 'referential' foregrounding, ibid., p. 14.

10 Delany, 'Omegahelm', in *Distant Stars* (1981c), p. 265.

11 As Delany might put it; a common quirk in his writing is this rhetorical question, a device for soliciting (or mimicking) the reader's complicity in the text's forward movement.

12 Despite his care in setting up this formalism, Delany seems to nod on p. 173, where the Web official Japril refers to Korga first by 'his', then (correctly) as 'her'; this occurs again on pp. 366–7: 'she/his', so perhaps something about Japril's status is being signalled. Noticing this apparent error draws one's attention to the general painstaking avoidance of pronouns, which has the curious effect of depersonalising the subjects, not just obliterating sexist distinctions ('the voice', 'those big fingers', etc., p. 173).

13 I am thinking of the frightening scene at the hot polar desert (itself a simple reversal symptomatic of the value-inverting method used throughout) where he walks almost to his death into the wasteland because 'the man who told him was new and pointed in the wrong direction' (p. 8).

14 Keyes, *Flowers For Algernon* (1987). It is perhaps relevatory of sf's generic strabismus that this latest paperback, in the prestigious Gollancz Classic imprint, is blurbed simultaneously by David Pringle as 'A narrative *tour-de-force*, very moving, beautiful,' all of which is apt; and by *Books and Bookmen* as 'A novel to thrill and chill', while the *Guardian* finds that 'For quick-paced storytelling, this one would be hard to beat'; for a crass eye to a surmised vulgarian main chance, these last two really would be hard to beat.

15 In another intertextual connotation, we recall that it was this infraction of 'civilised decency' which brought Lilo-Alexandr-Calypso undone (she marketed cloned human tissue as 'Bananameat') in John Varley's *The Ophiuchi Hotline*, 1978a, pp. 7–8. A 'Class-II read-rating' report of the heinous deed ended with these stirring words: 'Eat death, gene-trasher! The Hole waits!' (ibid., p. 8). Delany's protagonist is more liberal.

16 I am not against puns in their place, which is virtually everywhere, as a glance at my novel *The Dreaming Dragons* (Broderick, 1980) will confirm, but I was relieved that I missed this pun until I read George Edgar Slusser's *The Delany Intersection. Samuel R. Delany Considered as a Writer of Semi-Precious Words* (1977), p. 60. Slusser's own title is a truly dreadful pun on Delany's Hugo-winning novella 'Time Considered as a Helix of Semi-Precious Stones'; Slusser thinks he is being complimentary. He also draws attention to a possible link between Dhalgren as 'Gren-dhal', and 'the man-fish monster' of the title *Triton* (Slusser, 1977, pp. 62–3).

17 This is just the kind of motivated iconicity, incidentally, which Saussureans like Delany usually prefer to discount.

18 'Sporting spikey [*sic*] leaves, the stem of the crenna went under his jaw, down his neck, and disappeared beneath the black collar' (p. 90). Recalling the shoulder-inserted dragon in *Babel-17* (a kind of three-dimensional tattooing) is the 'multifanged beast's head ornament[ing] the ham of his thumb' (ibid.).

19 Ashima Slade, inventor of the modular calculus, ended her/his days in a Sygn co-op (p. 355).

20 Rat is told: 'Maybe thirty brain cells will die. . . . Maybe six thousand synapses will be shorted open and left that way. Maybe another thousand will be permanently closed' (p. 4). This measure also closes off the neurological pathways whereby one accesses the vast encyclopaedia – the mega-text – of the General Information system. An excellent account of the consequences, especially Delany's bravura scene where Korga absorbs at superhuman speed a small library of books, is Russell Blackford's 'Debased and Lascivious?' (1986), pp. 8–21, which offers a reading that emphasises many of the rich features of *Stars in My Pocket* perforce ignored, for reasons of space, in my own treatment.

12 THE AUTUMNAL CITY

1 Delany (1989a). The first section of the citation is the incomplete paragraph which ends the series; the second section is the opening passage; in both cases, unbracketed ellipses are Delany's. The Joycean 'riverrun' re-entrant structure appears to imply that every useful reading is a rereading; during these repeated passes the always-unstable 'meaning' is further de- and re-constructed. ~~Themes~~ is *sous rature*.

2 Delany (1975), pp. 879, 1. As in the previous epigraph, this citation is the 'riverrun' close and opening of the text. While the passages seem to weld at the common word 'to', it should be noted that the one is in first person, the other in third. In conversation with me (October 1981), Mr Delany pointed out that the combined sentence might imply an awakening of consciousness: 'I have come to, to wound . . .'.

3 Delany (1989a) Part 3, p. 10. See also his reflections at the Whitney Museum on the new technology of the body: 'The Future of the Body – and Science Fiction and Technology'(1992), pp. 1–5.

4 Science fiction scholarship has had no trouble absorbing this method. A typical essay, Veronica Hollinger's 'Deconstructing the Time Machine' (1987), inevitably finds that Wells's '*The Time Machine* accomplishes its own ironic deconstruction of Victorian scientific positivism, couched in the very language of the system which it sets out to undermine' (p. 201). Derrida, we are reminded, 'offers the "play" of *différance* as the (non)principle of reality' (p. 206). This is, of course, (non)sense. It is not only too easy; it encourages such extreme errors as her account of relativity: that 'Time has no reality outside of our interpretations' (p. 208)! Actually, relativity is founded in the invariance of the space-time interval for all frames of references.

5 Delany (1989a), Part 2, p. 18.

6 Delany (1989a), Part 1, p. 10.

7 Delany (1989a), Part 3, p. 10.

8 See Paulson (1988).

9 Delany has lately declared the futility of such attempts at definition (in 1989a, Part 3, no. 8, p. 9): 'We are not defining our object of inquiry here because it is not an object; it is a vast and sprawling debate, a great and often exciting dialogue', etc. But sf *is* an object, therefore: of the debate, the dialogue, etc. . . .

10 Kundera, 'The Depreciated Legacy of Cervantes', in *The Art of the Novel* (1988), p. 6.

11 Broderick, editor's introduction in *Strange Attractors* (1985), p. 13.

BIBLIOGRAPHY

Aldiss, Brian W. (1968) *Report on Probability A.*, London: Faber & Faber.

Aldiss, Brian W. (1975) *Billion Year Spree: The True History of Science Fiction* [Weidenfeld & Nicolson, 1973], London: Corgi.

Aldiss, Brian W. (ed.) (1976) *Galactic Empires*, vol. 1, New York: Avon Books.

Aldiss, Brian W. (1977) *Last Orders*, London: Jonathan Cape.

Aldiss, Brian W. (1978) *Enemies of the System*, London: Jonathan Cape.

Aldiss, Brian W. (1980) *Moreau's Other Island*, London: Jonathan Cape.

Aldiss, Brian W. (1982) *Helliconia Spring*, London: Jonathan Cape.

Aldiss, Brian W. (1983) *Helliconia Summer*, London: Jonathan Cape.

Aldiss, Brian W. (1984) *Hothouse* [1962], Wendover: Goodchild.

Aldiss, Brian W. (1985a) *Helliconia Winter*, London: Jonathan Cape.

Aldiss, Brian W. (1985b) *The Pale Shadow of Science. Recent Essays*, Seattle: Serconia Press.

Aldiss, Brian W. (1988) *Forgotten Life*, London: Gollancz.

Aldiss, Brian W. (1989) *Galaxies like Grains of Sand* [1960], London: VGSF.

Aldiss, Brian W. and Harry Harrison (eds) (1976) *Hell's Cartographers* [Weidenfeld & Nicolson, 1975], London: Orbit.

Aldiss, Brian W. with David Wingrove (1986) *Trillion Year Spree* (revised edn of *Billion Year Spree*), London: Gollancz.

Alterman, Peter S. (1977) 'The Surreal Translations of Samuel R. Delany', *Science Fiction Studies*, vol. 4, March, pp. 25–34.

Amis, Kingsley (1963) *New Maps of Hell* [Gollancz, 1961], London: Four Square.

Amis, Kingsley (ed.) (1981) *The Golden Age of Science Fiction*, London: Gollancz.

Anderson, Poul (1974) *Brain Wave* [1954], New York: Ballantine.

Anderson, Poul (1975) *Midsummer Tempest* [1974], London: Orbit.

Anderson, Poul (1991) *The Shield of Time* [1990], New York: Tor.

Asimov, Isaac (1941) 'Nightfall', in *Astounding* (New York), September.

Asimov, Isaac (1964) *The Foundation Trilogy*, London: Panther.

Asimov, Isaac (1983) *Asimov on Science Fiction*, London: Granada.

Asimov, Isaac, (1987) *The Roving Mind* [1983], Oxford: Oxford University Press.

Asimov, Isaac, Charles G. Waugh and Martin Greenberg (eds) (1983) *Isaac Asimov Presents the Best Science Fiction of the 19th Century*, London: Gollancz.

Atheling Jr, William [James Blish] (1970) *More Issues at Hand. Critical Studies in Contemporary Science Fiction*, Chicago: Advent.

Atheling Jr, William [James Blish] (1973) *The Issue at Hand. Studies in Contemporary Magazine Science Fiction* [1964], 2nd edn, Chicago: Advent.

Barbour, Douglas.(1979) *Worlds Out of Words: The SF Novels of Samuel R. Delany*, Frome, Somerset: Bran's Head Books.

Barnes, Barry (1974) *Scientific Knowledge and Sociological Theory*, London: Routledge & Kegan Paul.

Barron, Neil (ed.) (1987) *Anatomy of Wonder: A Critical Guide to Science Fiction*, 3rd edn, New Providence, NJ: R. R. Bowker.

Barth, John (1982) *Sabbatical*, New York: Putnam.

Barthes, Roland (1974) *S/Z*, New York: Hill & Wang.

Bazerman, Charles (1988) *Shaping Written Knowledge. The Genre and Activity of the Experimental Article in Science*, Madison: University of Wisconsin Press.

Bear, Greg (1986) *Blood Music* [1985], London: Gollancz.

Bear, Greg (1987) *The Forge of God*, London: Gollancz.

Beer, Gillian (1983) *Darwin's Plots. Evolutionary Narrative in Darwin, George Eliot, and Nineteenth-Century Fiction*, London: Routledge & Kegan Paul.

Benedikt, Michael (ed.) (1991) *Cyberspace: First Steps*, Cambridge, Mass: MIT Press.

Benford, Gregory (1978) *In the Ocean of Night* [1977], London: Futura.

Benford, Gregory (1980) *Timescape*, New York: Pocket Books.

Benford, Gregory (1988) *Great Sky River* [1987], London: VGSF.

Benford, Gregory (1990) *Tides of Light* [1989], London: VGSF.

Bennett, Tony (1987) 'Texts in History: the Determination of Readings and their texts', in Derek Attridge, Geoffrey Bennington and Robert Yound (eds), *Post-structuralism and the Question of History*, Cambridge: Cambridge University Press.

Berger, John (1972) *Ways of Seeing*, Harmondsworth: Penguin.

Bester, Alfred (1967) *Tiger! Tiger!* [1955], Harmondsworth: Penguin.

Bester, Alfred (1980) *Golem-100*, London and New York: Simon & Schuster.

Bester, Alfred (1981) *The Deceivers*, London and New York: Wallaby/Simon & Schuster.

Bettelheim, Bruno (1976) *The Uses of Enchantment: The Meaning and Importance of Fairy Tales*, London: Thames & Hudson.

Blackford, Russell (1985) 'Mirrors of the Future City: William Gibson's "Neuromancer"', *Science Fiction*, vol. 7, no. 1.

Blackford, Russell (1986) 'Debased and Lascivious?', *Australian Science Fiction Review*, 2nd series, vol. 1, no. 4, September, pp. 8–21.

Blish, James (1970) *Cities in Flight*, New York: Avon.

Blish, James and Norman Knight (1967) *A Torrent of Faces*, New York: Ace Science Fiction Special.

Broderick, Damien (1980) *The Dreaming Dragons*, New York: Pocket Books.

Broderick, Damien (ed.) (1985) *Strange Attractors: Original Australian Speculative Fiction*, Sydney: Hale & Iremonger.

Broderick, Damien (1990) 'Frozen Music', PhD thesis, Deakin University, Victoria, Australia.

Broderick, Damien (1992) *The Lotto Effect: Towards a Technology of the Paranormal*, Hudson: Hawthorn.

Brooke-Rose, Christine (1981) *A Rhetoric of the Unreal. Studies in Narrative and Structure, especially of the Fantastic*, Cambridge: Cambridge University Press.

Budrys, Algis (1977) *Michaelmas*, London: Gollancz.

Budrys, Algis (1980) 'Paradise Charted', *TriQuarterly*, no. 49, Fall.

Budrys, Algis (1984) 'Can Speculative-Fiction Writers and Scholars Do Each Other Good?', *Extrapolation*, vol. 25, no. 4, pp. 306–13.

Burgess, Anthony (1984) *Ninety-Nine Novels: the Best in English since 1939*, London: Allison & Busby.

Campbell, John W. (ed.) (1952) *The Astounding Science Fiction Anthology*, London and New York: Simon & Schuster.

Card, Orson Scott (1985) *Ender's Game*, London: Century.

Card, Orson Scott (1986) *Speaker for the Dead*, London: Arrow Books.

Card, Orson Scott (1991) *Xenocide*, London: Legend.

Carter, Paul A. (1977) *The Creation of Tomorrow: Fifty Years of Magazine Science Fiction*, New York: Columbia University Press.

Cawelti, John (1976) *Adventure, Mystery, and Romance. Formula Stories as Art and Popular Culture*, Chicago: University of Chicago Press.

Christopher, John (1956) *The Death of Grass*, London: Michael Joseph.

Cioffi, Frank (1982) *Formula Fiction? An Anatomy of American Science Fiction, 1930–1940*, New York: Greenwood Press.

Clareson, Thomas D. (ed.) (1972) *SF: The Other Side of Realism. Essays on Modern Fantasy and Science Fiction*, Ohio: Bowling Green University Press.

Clarke, Arthur C. (1961) *Childhood's End* [1954], London: Pan.

Clarke, Arthur C. (1965) *The City and the Stars* [1956], London: Corgi.

Clarke, Arthur C. (1989) *Astounding Days: A Science-Fictional Autobiography*, London: Gollancz.

Clarke, I. F. (1979) *The Pattern of Expectation. 1644–2001*, London: Jonathan Cape

Clute, John (1975) 'Trope Exposure', *New Worlds Quarterly*, vol. 9.

Clute, John (1988) *Strokes. Essays and Reviews 1966–1986*, Seattle: Serconia Press.

Clute, John (1992) review of *Universe 2*, *New York Review of Science Fiction*, no. 45, May.

Clute, John and Peter Nicholls (eds) (1993) *The Encyclopedia of Science Fiction*, revised edn, London: Orbit.

Collins, H. M. and T. J. Pinch (1982) *Frames of Meaning*, London: Routledge & Kegan Paul.

Costello, Peter (1978) *Jules Verne: Inventor of Science Fiction*, London: Hodder & Stoughton.

Crispin, Edmund (1955) *Best SF: Science Fiction Stories*, London: Faber & Faber.

Crowley, John (1988) *Aegypt* [1987], London: VGSF.

Csicsery-Ronay, Jr, Istvan (1985) 'The Book is the Alien: On Certain and Uncertain Readings of Lem's *Solaris*', *Science Fiction Studies*, vol. 12, pp. 6–21.

Culler, Jonathan (1975) *Structuralist Poetics: Structuralism, Linguistics, and the Study of Literature*, Ithaca, NY: Cornell University Press.

Culler, Jonathan (1981) *The Pursuit of Signs: Semiotics, Literature, Deconstruction*, Ithaca, NY: Cornell University Press.

Culler, Jonathan (1982) *On Deconstruction: Theory and Criticism after Structuralism*, Ithaca, NY: Cornell University Press.

Culler, Jonathan (1983) *Barthes*, London: Fontana.

Culler, Jonathan (1988) *Framing the Sign. Criticism and its Institutions*, Oxford: Blackwell.

Davies, Paul (1980) *Other Worlds: Space, Superspace and the Quantum Universe*, London: Dent.

Davies, Paul (ed.) (1992) *The New Physics*, Cambridge: Cambridge University Press.

Davies, Paul and John Gribbin (1991) *The Matter Myth – towards 21st Century Science*, London and New York: Viking.

De Lauretis, Teresa, Andreas Huyssen and Kathleen Woodward (eds) (1980) *The Technological Imagination: Theories and Fictions*, Madison, Wisconsin: Coda Press.

De Man, Paul (1979) *Allegories of Reading. Figural Language in Rousseau, Nietzsche, Rilke, and Proust*, New Haven: Yale University Press.

Del Rey, Lester (1980) *The World of Science Fiction: 1926–1976. The History of a Subculture*, New York and London: Garland Publishing, Inc.

Delany, Samuel R. (1966) *Empire Star*, New York: Ace.

Delany, Samuel R. (1968) *Nova*, London: Gollancz.

Delany, Samuel R. (1969) letter in John Foyster (ed.) *exploding madonna*, no. 5, January, pp. 1–10.

Delany, Samuel R. (1971) *Driftglass*, London: Signet.

Delany, Samuel R. (1975) *Dhalgren*, New York: Bantam.

Delany, Samuel R. (1976) *Triton: An Ambiguous Heterotopia*, New York: Bantam.

Delany, Samuel R. (1978a) *The Jewel-Hinged Jaw: Notes of [sic] the Language of Science Fiction* [1977], New York: Berkely Windhover.

Delany, Samuel R. (1978b) *Empire: A Visual Novel*, illustrated by Howard V. Chaykin, New York: Berkley Windhover.

Delany, Samuel R. (1979a) *Heavenly Breakfast. An Essay on the Winter of Love*, New York: Bantam.

Delany, Samuel R. (1979b) *Tales of Nevèrÿon*, New York: Bantam.

Delany, Samuel R. (1980) *The Tides of Lust* [1973], Manchester: Savoy Books.

Delany, Samuel R. (1981a) *The Fall of the Towers* [Ace Books, 1965], New York: Bantam.

Delany, Samuel R. (1981b) *The Einstein Intersection* [Ace, 1967; corrected Gollancz, 1968], repr. New York: Bantam.

Delany, Samuel R. (1981c) 'Of Doubts and Dreams', introduction to *Distant Stars*, New York: Bantam.

Delany, Samuel R. (1983a) '"Who Is John Brunner ... ?"', in *Constellation Programme Book*, Baltimore, pp. 27–32.

Delany, Samuel R. (1983b) *Neveryóna or the Tale of Signs and Cities*, New York: Bantam.

Delany, Samuel R. (1984) *Starboard Wine. More Notes on the Language of Science Fiction*, Pleasantville, NY: Dragon Press.

Delany, Samuel R. (1985a) *Stars in My Pocket Like Grains of Sand* [1984], New York: Bantam Spectra.

Delany, Samuel R. (1985b) 'In the Once Upon a Time City', *Locus*, February, pp. 21, 23.

Delany, Samuel R. (1985c) *Flight From Nevèrÿon*, New York: Bantam.

Delany, Samuel R. (1986)'Forward to an Afterword', in *The Complete Nebula Award-Winning Fiction*, New York: Bantam Spectra.

Delany, Samuel R. (1987) *The Bridge of Lost Desire*, New York: Arbor House.

Delany, Samuel R. (1987a) *Babel-17* [Ace Books, 1966], London: Gollancz.

Delany, Samuel R. (1987b) 'Of Sex, Objects, Signs, Systems, Sales, SF, and Other Things', *Australian Science Fiction Review*, 2nd series, vol. 2, no. 2, March.

Delany, Samuel R. (1987c) interviewed by Sinda Gregory and Larry McCaffery, 'The Semiology of Silence', *Science Fiction Studies*, vol.14, July, pp. 134–64.

Delany, Samuel R. (1989a) 'Neither the Beginning, Nor the End of Structuralism, Post-Structuralism, Semiotics, or Deconstruction for SF Readers: An Introduction', Parts 1–3', *New York Review of Science Fiction*, nos 6–8, February–April.

Delany, Samuel R. (1989b) *The Straits of Messina*, Seattle: Serconia Press.

Delany, Samuel R. (1990) *The Motion of Light in Water. Sex and Science Fiction Writing in the East Village, 1957–1965* [Arbor House, 1988]; expanded edn, London: Paladin.

Delany, Samuel R. (1992a) 'Zelazny/Varley/Gibson – and Quality', Parts I and II, *New York Review of Science Fiction*, nos 48 and 49, August and September.

Delany, Samuel R. (1992b) 'The Future of the Body – and Science Fiction and Technology', *New York Review of Science Fiction*, no. 51, November.

DeLillo, Don (1983) *White Noise*, London: Picador.

BIBLIOGRAPHY

Derrida, Jacques (1976) *Of Grammatology* [1967], trans. Gayatri Chakravorty Spivak, Baltimore, Maryland: Johns Hopkins University Press.

Derrida, Jacques (1981) *Dissemination* [1972], trans. Barbara Johnson, Chicago: University of Chicago Press.

Derrida, Jacques (1982) 'Choreographies', *Diacritics*, vol. 12, no. 2.

Dick, Philip K. (1984) *Time out of Joint* [1959], Harmondsworth: Penguin.

Disch, Thomas M. (1978) 'The Embarrassments of Science Fiction', in Peter Nicholls (ed.) *Explorations of the Marvellous* [1976], London: Fontana.

Disch, Thomas M. (1989) *SF Commentary*, no. 67, January, pp. 10–11.

Disch, Tom (1980) 'On Science Fiction', *TriQuarterly*, no. 49, Fall.

Dowling, Terry (1980) 'Jack Vance's "General Culture" Novels: A Synoptic Survey', in Tim Underwood and Chuck Miller (eds) *Jack Vance* (Writers of the 21st Century series), New York: Taplinger.

Dowling, Terry (1990) *Rynosseros*, Adelaide: Aphelion.

Dowling, Terry (1992) *Blue Tyson*, Adelaide: Aphelion.

Dowling, Terry (1993) *Twilight Beach*, Adelaide: Aphelion.

Eagleton, Terry (1976) *Marxism and Literary Criticism*, London: Methuen.

Eagleton, Terry (1983) *Literary Theory: An Introduction*, Oxford: Blackwell.

Easterbrook, Neil (1992) 'The Arc of Our Destruction: Reversal and Erasure in Cyberpunk', *Science Fiction Studies*, vol. 19, no. 58 (Part 3), pp. 378–94.

Ebert, Teresa L. (1980) 'The Convergence of Postmodern Innovative Fiction and Science Fiction: An Encounter with Samuel R. Delany's Technotopia', *Poetics Today*, vol.1, no. 4, pp. 91–104.

Eco, Umberto (1976) *A Theory of Semiotics*, Bloomington: Indiana University Press.

Eco, Umberto (1979) *The Role of the Reader: Explorations in the Semiotics of Texts*, Bloomington: Indiana University Press.

Eco, Umberto (1984) *Semiotics and the Philosophy of Language*, London: Macmillan.

Fabb, Nigel, Derek Attridge, Alan Durant and Colin MacCabe (1987) *The Linguistics of Writing. Arguments between Language and Literature*, Manchester: Manchester University Press.

Fallaci, Oriana (1981) *A Man*, London: Bodley Head.

Farmer, Philip Jose (1981) *The Unreasoning Mask*, New York: Putnam.

Farmer, Philip Jose (1982) *Inside Outside* [1964], London: Corgi.

Federman, Raymond (1982) *The Twofold Vibration*, Brighton: Harvester Press.

Ferguson, Kitty (1992) *Stephen Hawking – Quest for a Theory of Everything*, New York: Bantam.

Fiedler, Leslie (1983) 'The Criticism of Science Fiction', in G. E. Slusser, Eric S. Rabkin and Robert Scholes (eds.) *Coordinates. Placing Science Fiction and Fantasy*, Carbondale: Southern Illinois University Press.

Fitting, Peter (1983) 'Reality as an Ideological Construct: A Reading of Five Novels by Philip K. Dick', *Science Fiction Studies*, vol. 10, July, pp. 219–36.

Fodor, J. A. (1975) *The Language of Thought*, New York: Crowell.

Fodor, J. A. (1983) *The Modularity of Mind*, Cambridge, Mass.: MIT Press.

Fokkema, Douwe W. (1984) *Literary History, Modernism, and Postmodernism* (Harvard University Erasmus Lectures, Spring 1983), Amsterdam and Philadelphia: John Benjamins.

Foster, Hal (1985) *Recodings. Art, Spectacle, Cultural Politics*, Port Townsend, Washington: Bay Press.

Foucault, Michel (1983) *This Is Not A Pipe*, Berkeley: University of California Press.

Foyster, John (ed.) (1969) *exploding madonna*, no. 5, Jan.: *Special Samuel R. Delany Issue*; includes long letter by Delany, pp. 1–10; editorial comments, pp. 10–11a.

Foyster, John (1987) 'Our Collective Ways', *Australian Science Fiction Review*, 2nd Series, January.

Foyster, John (1989) 'The Role of the Science Fiction Reader: Cyberpunk and the Kids in Costume', *Australian Science Fiction Review*, 2nd series, June.

Franklin, H. Bruce (1980) *Robert A. Heinlein: America as Science Fiction*, Oxford: Oxford University Press.

Freadman, Anne (1985) 'Taking Things Literally (Sins of My Old Age)', *Southern Review*, no. 18, July.

Freadman, Anne (1987) 'Anyone for Tennis?', in Iad Reid (ed.) *The Place of Genre in Learning: Current Debates*, Typereader Publications no. 1, Centre for Studies in Literary Education, Deakin University, Victoria, Australia.

Freedman, Carl (1987) 'Science Fiction and Critical Theory', *Science Fiction Studies*, vol. 14, pp. 180–99.

Frye, Northrop (1973) *Anatomy of Criticism. Four Essays* [1957], Princeton, NJ: Princeton University Press.

Gardner, Howard (1991) *The Unschooled Mind. How Children Think and how Schools should Teach*, New York: Basic Books.

Gasche, Rodolphe (1986) *The Tain of the Mirror: Derrida and the Philosophy of Reflection*, Cambridge, Mass.: Harvard University Press.

Gerrold, David (1988) *When HARLIE was One* [1972], New York: Ballantine.

Gibson, William (1984) *Neuromancer*, London: Gollancz.

Gibson, William (1986a) *Burning Chrome*, London: Gollancz.

Gibson, William (1986b) *Count Zero*, London: Gollancz.

Gibson, William (1986c) 'A Nod to the Apocalypse: An Interview with William Gibson', by Colin Greenland, Foundation, no. 36 (Summer), pp. 5–9.

Gibson, William (1988) *Mona Lisa Overdrive*, London: Gollancz.

Gilbert, G. Nigel and Michael Mulkay (1984) *Opening Pandora's Box: A Sociological Analysis of Scientists' Discourse*, Cambridge: Cambridge University Press.

Graff, Gerald (1979) *Literature Against Itself*, Chicago: University of Chicago Press.

Greenland, Colin (1983) *The Entropy Exhibition: Michael Moorcock and the British 'New Wave' in Science Fiction*, London: Routledge & Kegan Paul.

Greimas A. J. and J. Courtes (1982) *Semiotics and Language. An Analytical Dictionary* [1979], Bloomington: Indiana University Press.

Grobman, Monica K. and Neil R. Grobman (1982) 'Myth, Cultural Differences, and Conflicting Worldviews in New Wave Science Fiction', *Extrapolation*, vol. 23, no. 4, pp. 377–84.

Grosz, Elizabeth (1990) 'Philosophy', in Sneja Gunew (ed.) *Feminist Knowledge: Critique and Construct*, London: Routledge.

Gunn, Eileen (1992) 'There's No Place Like Home', *New York Review of Science Fiction*, no. 51 (November), pp. 1, 10–11.

Gunn, James (1977) *The Road to Science Fiction: From Gilgamesh to Wells*, New York: Mentor Books.

Gunn, James (1982) *Isaac Asimov: The Foundations of Science Fiction*, Oxford: Oxford University Press.

Gunn, James (n.d.; post-1985) 'Toward a Definition of Science Fiction', typescript, University of Kansas.

Gunn, James (ed.) (1988) *The New Encyclopedia of Science Fiction*, London and New York: Viking.

Haldeman, Joe (1974) *The Forever War*, New York: St Martin's Press.

Hamon, Philippe (1973) 'Un discours contrait', *Poétique*, no. 16 [*Le discours réaliste*], pp. 411–45.

Haraway, Donna J. (1991) *Simians, Cyborgs, and Women: the Reinvention of Nature*, New York: Routledge.

Hardesty, William H, III (1980) 'Semiotics, Space Opera and *Babel-17, Mosaic*, no. 13, pp. 63–9.

Harding, Sandra (1991) *Whose Science? Whose Knowledge? Thinking from Women's Lives*, Milton Keynes: Open University Press.

Harland, Richard (1987) *Superstructuralism: The Philosophy of Structuralism and Post-Structuralism*, London: Methuen.

Hartwell, David G (1985) *Age of Wonders. Exploring the World of Science Fiction* [1984], New York: McGraw-Hill.

Hartwell, David G (ed.) (1989) 'Introduction', in *The World Treasury of Science Fiction*, New York: Little, Brown.

Hawkes, Terence (1977) *Structuralism and Semiotics*, London: Methuen.

Hay, George (ed.) (1970) *The Disappearing Future*, London: Panther.

Hayden, Patrick Nielsen (1983) *Inscape 2*, incorporating *Diffraction*, September, ed. Donald G. Keller.

Hayles, N. Katherine (1990) *Chaos Bound. Orderly Disorder in Contemporary Literature and Science*, Ithaca, NY: Cornell University Press.

Healy, Raymond J. and J. Francis McComas (1946) *Adventures in Time and Space*, New York: Random House.

Heinlein, Robert A. (1966a) *Beyond This Horizon* [1942], London: Sidgwick & Jackson.

Heinlein, Robert A. (1966b) *The Moon is a Harsh Mistress*, New York: Putman.

Heinlein, Robert A. (1970) *Have Spacesuit, Will Travel* [1958], London: Gollancz.

Heinlein, Robert A. (1971) *Stranger in a Strange Land* [1961], New York: Berkley.

Hernadi, Paul (1972) *Beyond Genre. New Directions in Literary Classification*, Ithaca, NY: Cornell University Press.

Hollinger, Veronica (1987) 'Deconstructing the Time Machine', *Science Fiction Studies*, vol. 14, pp. 201–221.

Holub, Robert C. (1984) *Reception Theory: A Critical Introduction*, London: Methuen.

Hutcheon, Linda (1984) *Narcissistic Narrative: The Metafictional Paradox* [1980], London: Methuen.

Ikin, Van (ed.) (1985) 'The Prognosis for SF', *Science Fiction* 20, vol. 7, no. 2.

Iser, Wolfgang (1978) *The Act of Reading*, Baltimore: Johns Hopkins University Press.

Jablokov, Alexander (1992) review, *New York Review of Science Fiction*, no. 49 (September), pp. 17–18.

Jackson, Rosemary (1981) *Fantasy: the Literature of Subversion*, London: Methuen.

Jameson, Fredric (1971) *Marxism and Form: Twentieth-century Dialectical Theories of Literature*, Princeton, NJ: Princeton University Press.

Jameson, Fredric (1972) *The Prison-House of Language: A Critical Account of Structuralism and Russian Formalism*, Princeton, NJ: Princeton University Press.

Jameson, Fredric (1973) 'Generic Discontinuities in SF: Brian Aldiss' *Starship*', *Science Fiction Studies*, vol. 1, pp. 57–68.

Jameson, Fredric (1975a) 'After Armageddon: Character Systems in *Dr Bloodmoney*', *Science Fiction Studies*, vol. 2, pp. 31–42.

Jameson, Fredric (1975b) 'World Reduction in Le Guin: The Emergence of Utopian Narrative', *Science Fiction Studies*, vol. 2, pp. 221–30.

Jameson, Fredric (1975c) 'Magical Narratives: Romance as Genre', *New Literary History*, Autumn, in Jameson (1981), pp. 103–50.

Jameson, Fredric (1981) *The Political Unconscious. Narrative as a Socially Symbolic Act*, London: Methuen.

Jameson, Fredric (1982a) 'Progress versus Utopia; or, Can We Imagine the Future?', *Science Fiction Studies*, vol. 9, pp. 147–58.

Jameson, Fredric (1982b) 'Towards a New Awareness of Genre', *Science Fiction Studies*, vol.9, pp. 322–4.

Jameson, Fredric (1984) 'Postmodernism, or The Cultural Logic of Late Capitalism', *New Left Review*, vol. 146, pp. 53–92.

Jameson, Fredric (1985) letter to Bruce Gillespie (ed.) *The Metaphysical Review*, no. 5/6, October.

Jameson, Fredric (1987a) 'Shifting Contexts of Science-Fiction Theory', *Science Fiction Studies*, vol.14, pp. 241–7.

Jameson, Fredric (1987b) 'Science Fiction as a Spatial Genre: Generic Discontinuities and the Problem of Figuration in Vonda McIntyre's *The Exile Waiting*', *Science Fiction Studies*, vol. 14, pp. 44–59.

Jameson, Fredric (1987c) 'Postmodernism and the Video-text', in Fabb *et al.*, *The Linguistics of Writing* (1987), above.

Jameson, Fredric (1988a) 'Metacommentary' [1971], in Jameson *The Ideologies of Theory* (1988b).

Jameson, Fredric (1988b) *The Ideologies of Theory. Essays 1971–1986. Vol. 1: Situations of Theory* and *Vol. 2: Syntax of History*, Minneapolis: University of Minnesota Press.

Jameson, Fredric (1991) *Postmodernism, or The Cultural Logic of Late Capitalism*, Durham, NC: Duke University Press/Verso.

Jaynes, Julian (1976) *The Origin of Consciousness in the Breakdown of the Bicameral Mind*, Boston: Houghton Miflin.

Jones, Rod (1986) *Julia Paradise*, Melbourne: McPhee Gribble/Penguin.

Keller, Donald G. (ed.) (1983) *Inscape*, no. 2, incorporating *Diffraction*, September. Includes interviews with Samuel R. Delany by Christopher Casper, Robert Morales, Pat Califia; 1981 Noreascon discussion of *Dhalgren*; of *Tides of Lust* by Camilla Decarnin; of *The American Shore*, by Donald G. Keller; of *Neveryóna*, by Ron Drummond; of *Nova* by Doug Barbour; letter from Delany.

Kessel, John (1991) 'Invaders' [*Fantasy & Science Fiction*, October 1990] in Gardner Dozois (ed.), *Best New SF 5*, London: Robinson Publishing.

Ketterer, David (1974) *New Worlds for Old: The Apocalyptic Imagination, Science Fiction and American Literature*, Bloomington: Indiana University Press.

Keyes, Daniel (1987) *Flowers for Algernon* [1959, 1966], London: Gollancz.

Klein, Gérard (1977) 'Discontent in American Science Fiction', *Science Fiction Studies*, vol. 4, pp. 3–13.

Knight, Damon (1967) *In Search of Wonder. Essays on Modern Science Fiction*, 2nd edn, Chicago: Advent.

Knight, Damon (1982) 'Reflections on "Reflections of SF Criticism"', *Science Fiction Studies*, vol.9, pp. 26–7; followed by a reply from Delany, pp. 27–8.

Knight, Damon (1988) 'Four in One' [*Galaxy*, February 1953] in Silverberg (1988), pp. 35–59.

Knorr-Cetina, Karin D. (1982) *The Manufacture of Knowledge. An Essay on the Constructivist and Contextual Nature of Science*, Oxford: Pergamon.

Kuhn, Thomas S. (1970) *The Structure of Scientific Revolutions*, 2nd edn (enlarged), Chicago: University of Chicago Press.

Kundera, Milan (1988) *The Art of the Novel*, London: Faber & Faber.

Langford, David (1989) 'Wisdom of the Ancients', *Australian Science Fiction Review*, 2nd series, vol. 4, no. 3, June.

Le Guin, Ursula (1969) *The Left Hand of Darkness*, New York: Ace Special.

Le Guin, Ursula (1982) *The Language of the Night. Essays on Fantasy and Science Fiction* [1979], ed. Susan Wood, New York: Berkley.

Le Guin, Ursula (1989) *Dancing at the Edge of the World. Thoughts on Words, Women, Places*, London: Gollancz.

Lefanu, Sarah (1988) *In the Chinks of the World Machine: Feminism & Science Fiction*, London: The Women's Press.

Lehman, David (1991) *Signs of the Times: Deconstruction and the Fall of Paul de Man*, New York: Poseidon Press.

Lem, Stanislaw (1985) *Microworlds. Writings on Science Fiction and Fantasy*, ed. Franz Rottensteiner, London: Secker & Warburg.

Lerner, Frederick Andrew (1985) *Modern Science Fiction and the American Literary Community*, Metuchen, NJ: The Scarecrow Press.

Levin, Harry (1980) 'Science and Fiction', in Slusser *et al.*, *Bridges to Science Fiction*, below.

Levine, George (ed.) (1987) *One Culture. Essays in Science and Literature*, Madison: University of Wisconsin Press.

Levine, George (1988) *Darwin and the Novelists. Patterns of Science in Victorian Fiction*, Cambridge: Harvard University Press.

Littlefield, Emerson (1982) 'The Mythologies of Race and Science in Samuel Delany's *The Einstein Intersection* and *Nova*', *Extrapolation*, vol. 23, no. 3.

Livingston, Paisley (1988) *Literary Knowledge. Humanistic Inquiry and the Philosophy of Science*, Ithaca, NY: Cornell University Press.

Lloyd, Genevieve (1984) *The Man of Reason. 'Male' and 'Female' in Western Philosophy*, London: Methuen.

Lodge, David (1977) *The Modes of Modern Writing: Metaphor, Metonymy and the Typology of Modern Literature*, London: Arnold.

Lodge, David (1981) *Working with Structuralism: Essays and Reviews on 19th and 20th Century Literature*, London: Routledge & Kegan Paul.

Lowentrout, Peter (1988) 'The "Metamorphoses" of Darko Suvin: Final Synthesis or Dogged Antithesis?', *Foundation*, no. 42, Spring, pp. 37–45.

Lyotard, Jean-François (1984) *The Postmodern Condition: A Report on Knowledge*, Manchester: Manchester University Press.

McCaffery, Larry (ed.) (1991) *Storming the Reality Studio: A Casebook of Cyberpunk and Postmodern Science Fiction*, Durham, NC: Duke University Press.

McCrone, John (1993) *The Myth of Irrationality: The Science of the Mind from Plato to 'Star Trek'*, London: Macmillan.

McEvoy, Seth (1984) *Samuel Delany*, New York: Frederick Ungar.

McHale, Brian (1987) *Postmodernist Fiction*, London: Methuen.

McIntyre, Vonda (1975) *The Exile Waiting*, Greenwich, Conn.: Fawcett.

Maclean, Marie (1984) 'Metamorphoses of the Signifier in "Unnatural" Languages', *Science Fiction Studies*, vol. 11, pp. 166–73.

Maddox, Tom (1992) *Halo* [1991], London: Legend.

Magill, Frank N. (ed.) (1979) *Survey of Science Fiction Literature*, Englewood Cliffs, NJ: Salem Press.

Mandel, Ernest (1975) *Late Capitalism*, London: New Left Books.

Mann, Phillip (1982) *The Eye of the Queen*, London: Gollancz.

Maxwell, Nicholas (1984) *From Knowledge to Wisdom: A Revolution in the Aims and Methods of Science*, Oxford: Blackwell.

May, Julian (1983) *The Many-Colored Land*, London: Fontana.

Mellor, Anne K. (1987) '*Frankenstein*: A Feminist Critique of Science', in George Levine, *One Culture*, above.

Merril, Judith (1967) Books column, *The Magazine of Fantasy and Science Fiction*, November.

Miller, David (guest ed.) (1986) Special science fiction number of *Modern Fiction Studies*, vol. 31, no. 1, Spring.

Miller, Russell (1988) *Bare-Faced Messiah*, London: Sphere.

Miller, Walter M. Jr (1975) *A Canticle for Leibowitz* [1960], London: Corgi.

Mullen, R. D. and Darko Suvin (eds) (1976) *Science Fiction Studies*, New York: Gregg Press.

Murphy, Patrick D. (1987) 'Dialogics and Didacticism: John Brunner's Narrative Blending', *Science Fiction Studies*, vol. 14, pp. 21–32.

Myers, L. H. (1956) *The Near and the Far* [1943], London: Reprint Society.

Nabokov, Vladimir (1980) *Lectures on Literature*, San Diego, Calif: Harcourt Brace Jovanovich.

Nicholls, Peter (ed.) (1978a) *Explorations of the Marvellous*, London: Fontana [first published as *Science Fiction at Large*, Gollancz, 1976].

Nicholls, Peter, (1978b) 'The Monsters and the Critics', in Nicholls' *Explorations of the Marvellous* (1978a).

Nicholls, Peter (1979) 'Conceptual Breakthrough', in Nicholls *et al.* (1979).

Nicholls, Peter *et al.* (eds) (1979) *The Encyclopedia of Science Fiction*, Granada, 1979; revised edition, Clute and Nicholls (1993).

Niven, Larry and Jerry Pournelle (1982) *Oath of Fealty* [1981], London: Macdonald.

Nixon, Nicola (1992) 'Cyberpunk: Preparing the Ground for Revolution or Keeping the Boys Satisfied?', *Science Fiction Studies*, vol. 19, no. 57, Part 2, pp. 219–35.

Ohmann, Richard (1987) *Politics of Letters*, Middletown, Conn.: Wesleyan University Press.

O'Reilly, Timothy (1981) *Frank Herbert*, New York: Frederick Ungar.

Overbye, Dennis (1991) *Lonely Hearts of the Cosmos – The Story of the Scientific Quest for the Secret of the Universe*, London: HarperCollins.

Pais, Abraham (1991) *Niels Bohr's Times, in Physics, Philosophy and Polity*, Oxford: Clarendon Press.

Panshin, Alexei (1968) *Heinlein in Dimension*, Chicago: Advent.

Panshin, Alexei and Cory Panshin (1989) *The World Beyond the Hill. Science Fiction and the Quest for Transcendence*, Los Angeles: Jeremy P. Tarcher.

Parrinder, Patrick (1979a) 'Delany Inspects the Word-Beast' (review of *The Jewel-Hinged Jaw* and *The American Shore*) *Science Fiction Studies*, vol. 6, no. 19.

Parrinder, Patrick (ed.) (1979b) *Science Fiction. A Critical Guide*, London: Longman.

Parrinder, Patrick (1980) *Science Fiction. Its Criticism and Teaching*, London: Methuen.

Parrinder, Patrick (1987) *The Failure of Theory. Essays on Criticism and Contemporary Fiction*, Brighton: Harvester Press.

Paulson, William R. (1988) *The Noise of Culture. Literary Texts in a World of Information*, Ithaca, NJ: Cornell University Press.

Peplow, Michael W. and Robert S. Bravard (1980) *Samuel R. Delany: a Primary and Secondary Bibliography, 1962–1979*, Boston: G. K. Hall.

Pohl, Frederik (1978) *The Way the Future Was*, New York: Del Rey.

Pohl, Frederik and C. M. Kornbluth (1984) *The Space Merchants* [1953], Wendover: Goodchild.

Pratt, Mary Louise (1977) *Toward a Speech Act Theory of Literary Discourse*, Bloomington: Indiana University Press.

Prigogine, Ilya and Isabelle Stengers (1984) *Order out of Chaos: Man's New Dialogue with Nature*, London: Heinemann.

Pringle, David (1979) *Alien Planet: J. G. Ballard's Four-Dimensional Nightmare*, San Bernardino, Calif.: Borgo Press.

Pringle, David (1985) *Science Fiction: the 100 Best Novels*, New York: Carroll & Graf.

Rabkin, Eric S. (1976) *The Fantastic in Literature*, Princeton, NJ: Princeton University Press.

Rabkin, Eric S. (1982) 'The Rhetoric of Science in Fiction', in Staicar's *Critical Encounters II* (1982), pp. 23–43.

Reilly, Robert (ed.) (1985) *The Transcendent Adventure. Studies of Religion in Science Fiction/Fantasy*, New York: Greenwood Press.

Renault, Gregory (1980) 'Science Fiction as Cognitive Estrangement: Darko Suvin and the Marxist Critique of Mass Culture', *Discourse*, no. 2, pp. 113–41.

Renault, Gregory (1983) 'Speculative Porn: Aesthetic Form in Samuel R. Delany's *The Tides of Lust, Extrapolation*, vol. 24, no. 2, Summer, pp. 116–29.

Riley, Dick (ed.) (1978) *Critical Encounters: Writers and Themes in Science Fiction*, New York: Frederick Ungar.

Rimmon-Kenan, Shlomith (1983) *Narrative Fiction: Contemporary Poetics*, London: Methuen.

Robinson, Kim Stanley (1984) *The Science Fiction of Philip K. Dick*, Ann Arbor, Mich: UMI Research Press.

Robinson, Kim Stanley (1990) *Pacific Edge*, London: Unwin Hyman.

Robinson, Kim Stanley (1992) *Red Mars*, London: HarperCollins.

Ross, Andrew (1991) *Strange Weather. Culture, Science, and Technology in the Age of Limits*, London: Verso.

Russ, Joanna (1976) 'Towards an Aesthetic of Science Fiction' [1975], from *Science Fiction Studies*, repr. in R. D. Mullen and Darko Suvin, *Science Fiction Studies*, New York: Gregg Press.

Ryman, Geoff (1989) *The Child Garden*, London: Unwin Hyman.

Scholes, Robert (1974) *Structuralism in Literature. An Introduction*, New Haven, Conn.: Yale University Press.

Scholes, Robert (1975) *Structural Fabulation: An Essay on Fiction of the Future*, Indiana: Notre Dame University Press.

Scholes, Robert (1979) *Fabulation and Metafiction*, Urbana: University of Illinois Press.

Scholes, Robert (1982) *Semiotics and Interpretation*, New Haven, Conn.: Yale University Press.

Scholes, Robert (1985) *Textual Power: Literary Theory and the Teaching of English*, New Haven, Conn.: Yale University Press.

Schulz, H.-J. (1987) 'Science Fiction and Ideology: Some Problems of Approach', *Science Fiction Studies*, vol. 14, pp. 165–79.

Schweitzer, Darrell (1976) *SF Voices*, Timore, Maryland: T-K Graphics.

Sebeok, Thomas A. (1974) *Structure and Texture*, The Hague: Mouton.

Sebeok, Thomas A. (1986) *I Think I am a Verb: More Contributions to the Doctrine of Signs*, New York: Plenum.

Serres, Michel (1982) *Hermes. Literature, Science, Philosophy*, ed. Josué V. Harari and David F. Bell, Baltimore, Maryland: Johns Hopkins University Press.

Serres, Michel (1985) *Les Cinq Sens*, Paris: Grasset.

Shinn, Thelma J. (1986) *Worlds Within Women. Myth and Mythmaking in Fantastic Literature by Women*, New York: Greenwood Press.

Silverberg, Robert (ed.) (1988) *Robert Silverberg's Worlds of Wonder*, London: Gollancz.

Simak, Clifford D. (1964) *Way Station* [1963], New York: Macfadden-Bartell.

Simak, Clifford D. (1988) *City* [1952], London: Methuen.

Slusser, George (1977) *The Delany Intersection. Samuel Delany Considered as a Writer of Semi-Precious Words*, San Bernardino, Calif.: Borgo Press.

Slusser, George E., George R. Guffey and Mark Rose (eds) (1980) *Bridges to Science Fiction*, Carbondale: Southern Illinois University Press/Feffer & Simons.

Slusser, George E., Eric S. Rabkin and Robert Scholes (eds) (1983) *Coordinates. Placing Science Fiction and Fantasy*, Carbondale: Southern Illinois University Press.

Smith, Cordwainer (1955) 'The Game of Rat and Dragon', *Galaxy*; reprinted in Smith, *You Will Never Be the Same*, New York: Berkley, 1963, pp. 93–109.

Snow, C. P. (1964) 'The Two Cultures: A Second Look', in *The Two Cultures and A Second Look. An Expanded Version of The Two Cultures and the Scientific Revolution*, Cambridge: Cambridge University Press.

Sobchack, Vivian (1987) *Screening Space. The American Science Fiction Film* [1980], 2nd enlarged edition, New York: Ungar.

Sontag, Susan (1967) 'The Imagination of Disaster' [1965], *Commentary*, no. 40 (4), pp. 42–8; in Sontag, *Against Interpretation*, London: Eyre & Spottiswoode, pp. 209–25.

Sontag, Susan (1972) 'Against Interpretation' [1964, *Evergreen Review*], in David Lodge (ed.) *20th Century Literary Criticism*, London: Longman.

Spencer, Kathleen L. (1983) '"The Red Sun is High, the Blue Low": Towards a Stylistic Description of Science Fiction', *Science Fiction Studies*, vol.10, March, pp. 35–48.

Spencer, Kathleen, L. (n.d.; pre-1985) 'Deconstructing *Tales of Nevèrÿon*: Delany, Derrida, and the "Modular Calculus, Parts I-IV"', typescript, Department of English, UCLA.

Spencer, Kathleen L. (1985) 'Trying the Reader's Patience' (review of Seth McEvoy, *Samuel R. Delany*), *Science Fiction Studies*, vol. 12, pp. 343–5.

Spencer, Kathleen L. (1987) 'Vintage Delany' (review of *Starboard Wine*), *Science Fiction Studies*, vol. 14, pp. 248–51.

Spinrad, Norman (1983) *Staying Alive: A Writer's Guide*, Norfolk, Virginia: Donning.

Stableford, Brian M. (1979) *A Clash of Symbols: The Triumph of James Blish*, San Bernardino, Calif.: Borgo Press.

Staicar, Tom (ed.) (1982) *Critical Encounters II. Writers and Themes in Science Fiction*, New York: Frederick Ungar.

Sterling, Bruce (ed.) (1986) *Mirrorshades. The Cyberpunk Anthology*, New York: Arbor House.

Stone, Robert (1966) *A Hall of Mirrors*, Boston: Houghton Mifflin.

Stone, Robert (1974) *Dog Soldiers*, Boston: Houghton Mifflin.

Stone, Robert (1981) *A Flag for Sunrise*, Boston: Houghton Mifflin.

Stone, Robert (1992) *Outerbridge Reach*, New York: Ticknor & Fields.

Sturgeon, Theodore (1986) *More than Human* [1953], London: Gollancz.

Sutton, Christine (1984) *The Particle Connection. The Discovery of the Missing Links of Nuclear Physics*, London: Hutchinson.

Suvin, Darko (1979) *Metamorphoses of Science Fiction: On the Poetics and History of a Literary Genre*, New Haven, Conn.: Yale University Press.

Suvin, Darko (1983) *Victorian Science Fiction in the UK: the Discourses of Knowledge and of Power*, Boston: G. K. Hall.

Swanwick, Michael (1988) *Vacuum Flowers* [1987], New York: Ace.

Swanwick, Michael (1992) *Stations of the Tide* [1991], New York: Avon.

Tallis, Raymond (1988) *Not Saussure. A Critique of Post-Saussurean Literary Theory*, London: Macmillan.

Tauber, Peter (1979) *The Last Best Hope*, San Diego, Calif.: Harcourt Brace Jovanovich.

Theroux, Paul (1986) *O-Zone*, New York: Putnam.

Thomas, D. M. (1981) *The White Hotel*, London: Gollancz.

Thurley, Geoffrey (1983) *Counter-Modernism in Current Critical Theory*, New York: St Martin's Press.

Todorov, Tzvetan (1975) *The Fantastic: A Structural Approach* [1970], Ithaca, NY: Cornell University Press.

Todorov, Tzvetan (1984) *Mikhail Bakhtin. The Dialogical Principle*, trans. Wlad Godzich, Minneapolis: University of Minnesota.

Tolley, Michael J. (1987). 'Chained to the Alien: Change and Delany', *Australian Science Fiction Review*, 2nd series, vol. 2, no. 3, May pp. 22–7.

Turner, George (1980) 'Delany: Victim of Great Applause', *SF Commentary*, no. 58, February, pp. 14–6.

Turner, George (1985) Letter in Leigh Edmonds and Valma Brown (eds) *The Notional*, no. 8, November, pp. 18–19.

Turner, George (1987) *The Sea and Summer*, London: Faber & Faber.

Turner, George (1988) 'The Real Science Fiction', *Australian Science Fiction Review*, 2nd series, vol. 3, no. 2, March pp. 17–25.

Van Vogt, A. E. (1951) *The Voyage of the Space Beagle*, London: Grayson & Grayson.

Van Vogt, A. E. (1984) *The World of Null-A* [1945], Wendover: John Goodchild.

Varley, John (1978a) *The Ophiuchi Hotline* [1977], New York: Dell.

Varley, John (1978b) *In the Hall of the Martian Kings* [US: *The Persistence of Vision*] London: Orbit.

Varley, John (1978c) 'The Persistence of Vision', *Fantasy & Science Fiction*, March, in Varley (1978b), pp. 263–316.

Varley, John (1979) *Titan*, New York: Berkley.

Varley, John (1980a) *Wizard*, New York: Berkley.

Varley, John (1980b) *The Barbie Murders*, New York: Berkley.

Varley, John (1984) *Demon*, New York: Berkley.

Varley, John (1986) *Blue Champagne*, New York: Berkley.

Varley, John (1992) *Steel Beach*, New York: Ace/Putnam.

Vinge, Vernor (1986) *Marooned in Real Time*, London: Pan.

Von Glahn, George A. (1978) 'A World of Difference: Samuel Delany's *The Einstein Intersection*, in Riley, *Critical Encounters*, above.

Walker, Jeanne Murray (1982) 'Reciprocity and Exchange in Samuel Delany's *Nova*', *Extrapolation*, vol. 23, no. 3, pp. 221–34.

Weedman, Jane (1978) 'Delany's *Babel-17*: Powers of Language', *Extrapolation*, vol. 19, no. 2, May, pp. 132–7.

Weedman, Jane Branham (1982) *Samuel Delany*, Washington: Starmont House.

Weiner, Andrew (1993) 'Sf – Not!', *New York Review of Science Fiction*, no. 57 (May), pp. 20–2.

White, Michael and John Gribbin (1992) *Stephen Hawking. A Life in Science*, London and New York: Viking.

Wilden, Anthony (1984) *System and Structure. Essays in Communication and Exchange* [1972], revised edn, London: Routledge & Kegan Paul.

Williams, Walter Jon (1992) *Aristoi*, New York: Tor.

Williamson, Jack (1980) *Three from the Legion*, New York: Pocket Books.

Wolfe, Gary K. (1979) *The Known and the Unknown*, Ohio: Kent State University Press.

Wolfe, Gary K. (1982) 'The Merits of Samuel R. Delany' [review of Douglas Barbour, *Worlds Out of Words*], *Science Fiction Studies*, vol. 9, pp. 98–9.

Womack, Jack (1988) *Ambient*, London: Unwin Hyman.

Wordsworth, William (1952) Preface to the *Lyrical Ballads* [1798], in W. J. Bate (ed.) *Criticism: the Major Texts*, New York: Harcourt, Brace & World.

Wymer, Thomas L., Alice Calderonello, Lowell P. Leland, Sara Jayne Steen and R. Michael Evers (1978) *Intersections. The Elements of Fiction in Science Fiction*, Ohio: Bowling Green State University Press.

Yoke, Carl (1979) *Roger Zelazny*, (Starmont Reader's Guide 2), West Linn, Oregon: Stormont House.

Zelazny, Roger (1968) *The Dream Master* [1966], London: Panther.

Zelazny, Roger (1980) *The Last Defender of Camelot*, New York: Pocket Books.

Zelazny, Roger (1983) *Eye of Cat*, New York: Pocket Books.

Zelazny, Roger (1984) *This Immortal* [1966], Wendover: John Goodchild.

Zindell, David (1989) *Neverness* [1988], London: Grafton.

INDEX